FRAMING HISTORY

A M E R I C A N   C U L T U R E

Cutting across traditional boundaries between the human and social sciences, volumes in the American Culture series study the multiplicity of cultural practices from theoretical, historical, and ethnographic perspectives by examining culture's production, circulation, and consumption.

Edited by Stanley Aronowitz, Nancy Fraser, and George Lipsitz

FRAMING HISTORY

The Rosenberg Story
and the
Cold War

Virginia Carmichael

AMERICAN CULTURE 6

University of Minnesota Press

Minneapolis and London

Published by the University of Minnesota Press
2037 University Avenue Southeast, Minneapolis, MN 55414
Printed in the United States of America on acid-free paper

Library of Congress Cataloging-in-Publication Data

Carmichael, Virginia.
    Framing history : the Rosenberg stories and the cold war / Virginia Carmichael.
        p.   cm. — (American culture ; 6)
    Includes bibliographical references and index.
    ISBN 0-8166-2041-5 (alk. paper). —
    ISBN 0-8166-2042-3 (pbk. : alk. paper)
        1. American fiction—20th century—History and criticism.
    2. Rosenberg, Julius, 1918–1953, in fiction, drama, poetry, etc.
    3. Rosenberg, Ethel, 1915–1953, in fiction, drama, poetry, etc.
    4. Literature and society—United States—History—20th century.
    5. Historical fiction, American—History and criticism. 6. Trials
    (Conspiracy) in literature. 7. Trials (Espionage) in literature.
    8. World politics in literature. 9. Communism in literature.
    10. Cold War in literature. I. Title. II. Series: American
    culture (Minneapolis, Minn.) ; 6.
    PS374.R67C37   1993
    813′.5409351—dc20   92-14752
                                                                CIP

Contents

Acknowledgments

This book is the outcome of my good fortune in discovering, participating in, and to some degree building a network of generous intellectuals. The book is truly a collaborative venture, built first on the shoulders of all those whose books and articles I read, especially Kenneth Burke, Robin Wagner-Pacifici, and James Grotstein; developed further from conversations, interviews, and arguments with people I encountered or sought out along the way; and finally constructed in the form presented here as the product of numerous critical readings by members of that extended network. The encouragement I received was no less important than the criticism. I hope the book is worthy of the goodwill directed toward it. And I hope it works to keep the argument about social justice and the seriousness of our uses of language viable among us all.

First, I thank my colleagues at Rice University, especially Ed Snow, Kit Wallingford, Bob Patten, Wes Morris, Walter Isle, and Elizabeth Long; Michele Farrell and Frank Lentricchia also made crucial contributions while at Rice to my writing and thinking. I am grateful to the circulation and reference staff of the Fondren Library at Rice for their unfailing help, especially Sarah Bentley, Charlotte Beaudet, Ola Moore, Tony Schwartz, and Virginia Martin. Jennifer Geran and Douglas Klopfenstein in the interlibrary loan department supplied me with, it seems, an entire library. Marianne Farr and her interlibrary loan staff at the University of Montana have provided me with the same excellent service.

From the University of Houston I appreciate the mentoring and tough criticism of Bill Simon, the interest and support of Steve and Lois Zamora and John McNamara, and the helpful readings of Tom Oldham and David Dow at the Law School. Lynn Randolph was uncompromising as usual, both in her criticism and in her unambivalent support. Barbara Harlow at the University of Texas at Austin had an uncanny way, in our occasional meetings, of asking a question or suggesting something to read that impelled my thinking into a new order of complexity. I also benefited from the readings of Susan Sage Heinzelman and Sanford Levinson at the UT Law School. Susan Hawkins at Oakland University in Rochester, Michigan; Jane Gallop, Kathleen Woodward, and Pat Mellencamp at the University of Wisconsin-Milwaukee; and my editors George Lipsitz at UC San Diego, Stanley Aronowitz at the CUNY Graduate Center, and Biodun Iginla at the University of Minnesota Press took the time to read the work in progress—several times in some cases—and to respond promptly, carefully, and honestly. I also value my discussions with Peter Hulme of the Sociology in Literature Program at the University of Essex.

After reading the manuscript, Andrew Ross, Vivian Gornick, and my mother, Virginia Walker, all encouraged me to free the book from academic limitations and write for an intelligent general audience. Other friends and colleagues who contributed to the book through ongoing conversation are my best reader, Bob Gilliland; my sister, Sara Beth Peacock; my friends and critics Martha Northington, Robin Brooks, Linda Walsh, Patti Birge Tyson, Pam Walker, Josephine Smith, Dolores Johnson, Jackie Schmeal, Elizabeth McBride, Joan Wicks, Amanda Spivey, and Marsha Recknagel; my conservative sparring partner John Kirkland; my New Orleans connection John Stocks; and my walking companion, Rosellen Brown. My primary and daily walking partner, Elvis, contributed by joyfully and wonderingly cavorting while I just thought.

The Rosenberg materials I needed were generously provided by Richard Corey, Rob Okun, and Robert Meeropol. E. L. Doctorow, Robert Coover, and Martha Rosler were kind in responding to my requests for information and materials. The production staff at the University of Minnesota Press, especially my copyeditor, Roberta Hughey, have remained committed to a sympathetic clarification of the book's argument.

Acknowledgments

My father, Ruel Walker, taught me to keep on working anyway. I thank my other friends, who know who they are, for remaining faithful when I was not. And finally, I thank my daughters, Shannon and Laurence Stewart, for doing their best all their lives to keep me honest.

Prologue
Motives of Narrative

*Every discourse has its own selfish and biased proprietor;
there are no words with meanings shared by all, no words
"belonging to no one." . . . When we seek to understand a
word, what matters is not the direct meaning the word gives to
objects and emotions—this is the false front of the word; what
matters is rather the actual and always self-interested use to
which this meaning is put and the way it is expressed by the
speaker, a use determined by the speaker's position and by the
concrete situation. Who speaks and under what conditions he
speaks: this is what determines the word's actual meaning. All
direct meanings and direct expressions are false, and this is
especially true of emotional meanings and expressions.*

M. M. Bakhtin, The Dialogic Imagination

The story of Julius and Ethel Rosenberg's conspiracy to commit
espionage—which led to their conviction and execution for treason in 1953—played a crucial explanatory and justifying role in
the formulation of the cold war. Accounts of their actions were
used to explain the Soviet test explosion of an atomic device in
1949 three to five years before expected by most U.S. scientific,
political, or military intelligence. The alleged Rosenberg trans-
mission of "the secret of the atomic bomb" to the Soviet Union
suddenly became both a complete and sufficient explanation of
Soviet emergence into a bipolar superpower atomic rivalry for
control of the postwar world and definitive proof that communist
subversion from within was as great a threat to the free world
as the bomb itself.

But at the same time that the Rosenberg story seemed to call for and support domestic and foreign policies and actions gathered under the rubric of the cold war, it also took on an ongoing critical cultural function still active in the 1990s. Most recently Don DeLillo used the Rosenbergs in his 1988 book, *Libra,* about the Kennedy assassination. Uses of their story also figure in Erica Jong's *Fear of Flying* (1974), John Updike's *Couples* (1968), Gore Vidal's *Myra Breckinridge* (1968), Howard Fast's *The Outsider* (1984), and Joyce Carol Oates's *You Must Remember This* (1988). The Rosenbergs serve as a thematic counterpart to the protagonist Esther Greenwood in Sylvia Plath's *Bell Jar* (1966), and they are the principal subject of a play and two major novels: Donald Freed's drama *Inquest* (1969), E. L. Doctorow's *Book of Daniel* (1971), and Robert Coover's *Public Burning* (1977). Since 1952 the Rosenbergs have been the occasion for and subject of musical compositions, poems, plays, sculpture, documentary and commercial films, public forums, newspaper and periodical articles, and visual and multimedia arts, as well as a number of historiographical books, articles, and biographies.

Despite this recurrent working of the Rosenberg story in the consciousnesses of some of our public, artistic, and academic intelligentsia, most people still consider the case closed: "Who needs another book about the Rosenbergs?" a *New York Times* book reviewer asked of Joseph Sharlitt's *Fatal Error* (1989), in which Sharlitt examines the legal and constitutional issues involved in the Supreme Court's responses to the Rosenbergs' attorneys' and "next friends'" last week of court appeals before the executions.[1] Or as an editor commented about a chapter of this book prepared for separate publication, "In light of the surfacing of the comments regarding the Rosenbergs [that is, their guilt] in Krushchev's memoirs . . . we would like to see you reframe . . . your material and argument with this new evidence in mind." In a sense this entire book is an attempt to engage seriously those two perhaps rhetorical questions.[2]

The Rosenberg story provides a particularly apt occasion for a consideration of the function of storytelling—of narrative—in history. It was a social drama, providing a starting point for an elaboration of many stories serving various and multiple functions. This social drama, while dismissed by many as finished business, is still unresolved. It partially fulfilled the function defined in Victor Turner's description of the dynamic operation of social drama as producing social reconciliation around crucial issues—in this case the question of a partisan struggle for control of the government and the definition of U.S. postwar domestic and foreign policy.[3] But it also produced the alternative and opposite outcome—social schism. It played a crucial symbolic role in the construction of a radically polarizing anticommunism, as well as in the postwar split of the domestic left. And the Rosenberg story's resistance to closure manifest in its repeated tellings in historiography, biography, literature, and the visual and performing arts suggests its ongoing cultural function as the occasion for acknowledging and coming to terms with an unresolved breach in the national narrative of moral purpose.

This ongoing activity might be considered an extension of Turner's category of potentiality he calls liminality, a moment in which "the possibility exists of standing aside not only from one's own social position but from all social positions and of formulating a potentially unlimited series of alternative social arrangements."[4] More probably, the repeated tellings suggest the reaction to a liminality prematurely foreclosed by the social and disciplinary forces of domestic ideological and political intimidation, information management, and an ensuing collective self-censorship. But in either case, the Rosenberg story continues to work or to be worked—in the arts, in the media, and in historiography—as an interrogation of a specific and costly period of politically motivated injustice practiced in the rationalized forms of U.S. procedural, criminal, and constitutional law. This interrogation also has the purpose and potential effect of interrupting and disturbing the official story's intended and ongoing subliminal and mythic function as the primary evidence of postwar international communism at work to destroy the United States from within—key evidence in support of the cold war rationale.

The Rosenberg story is a theoretically knowable but actually unknown historical story, which makes the political issues around the interactions of culture and history prominent and insistent in a consideration of any particular version of the Rosenberg story.[5] The reception of a particular version, including this one, is—or should be—inseparable from a consideration of the possible conditions and motives of its production. Short of a full release of FBI and related documents, or of an unexpected confession from someone with the debatable authority to know the real story, the elaboration of the historical version of the story has gone about as far as it can go.[6] That most people take absolutely for granted the Rosenbergs' guilt as atomic spies in some indeterminate magnitude of seriousness illustrates the thoroughness and endurability of the constitutive activities of our consciousness-making institutions and agencies.

The real Rosenberg story remains—to date—an undecidable one. The primary subjects did not and now cannot talk. And the informant of "unimpeachable reliability," who originally established in the mind of J. Edgar Hoover Julius Rosenberg's titular role in a still undiscovered atomic spy ring of enormous dimensions, "is not available under any circumstances."[7] Even after the litigated release of perhaps half of the related government documents under the Freedom of Information Act of 1974, no one knows the Rosenberg story. Its official public version, however, elaborated itself as discovered, known, and true, with quite real material effects.

A close and contextualized reading of any version of the Rosenberg story thus necessarily confronts the politics of writing and reading. The story can be considered as having a basic underlying narrative structure—mythic or historical, depending on one's critical positioning—with hundreds of textual variations.[8] But the Rosenberg story foregrounds the inevitability of assuming a political orientation—a point of view, that is—in the process of encountering, through telling or reading, any one version. This is a provocative detail, since critics of culture and ideology, in strong disagreement with those who would insist on the apolitical and universal values of literature, maintain that political positioning is oriented by and can be construed in the actual telling or reading of any story, even literature, including the limited group of basic narratives posited by folklorists.[9]

Accordingly, the Rosenberg story can be read either, in mythic terms, as a story of the betrayal of the patriarchal father (the nation–state, or perhaps civil society at large) by the children, in which case agency and guilt lie with the children, or as a story of the patriarchal father's allaying of family guilt, shame, and fear of retribution through the ritual of scapegoating sacrifice. Or the story, more complicated and nonmythic than either of these polarities, is exemplary of the impossibility of attempts to achieve full and coherent meaning. Or it is an unknowable story that should be read nevertheless as having shaped history and produced unambiguous material and cultural effects. That is, its unknowability did not stop its narratability as a highly motivated construction with real and lasting political effects.

These four rehearsals of the available structures for the story manifest four historically specific political and/or critical positions with respect to any of its versions: right, left, poststructuralist, and materialist.[10] The right and left versions differ markedly in their allocation and distribution of agency and responsibility, in their ordering of cause-effect relationships and attribution of guilt, as well as in their interpretation of the critical, moral, and political implications of the story for the relation of the individual to the nation-state. The poststructuralist and materialist versions are not necessarily mutually exclusive, although the arguments of a number of political theorists, literary critics, and historians would lead us to believe they are. Demonstrating language use as symbolic action that does work and has effect requires the use of multiple methodological strategies, while avoiding an absolute theoretical pluralism. Critical to this kind of reading is a tactical use of a rhetorical analysis that calls into question any facile assertions of identity between words and facts, or between facts and reality, while demonstrating the constitutive effects of words on facts and reality. Such a demonstration of the historical contingency and effects of language would necessarily, however, stop short of—or go further than—the limits of a radical and paralyzingly repetitive dissolution of meaning demonstrated by methodologically pure poststructuralist critics.[11]

In analyzing the narrative production of the Rosenberg story it will be necessary to construe—to narrate—a historical context for the story's official elaboration; to speculate on probable narrative motivations, intentions, and effects, grounding such speculations insofar as that is possible; to analyze the ways in which the rhetorical construction began to operate on its own, separate from sociopolitical data; to evaluate posited subjectivity as effective and strategic, as manipulated and imposed, or as self-defeating political positionality; and to critique essentialist assumptions and the polarized positions they entail in terms of the kinds of political and social work and exclusions they accomplish.[12] It will be necessary to consider formal qualities in relation to the issues being addressed, and to employ value-loaded terms, in order to use the various versions of the Rosenberg story as occasions for thinking through specific historical, social, and cultural issues. In all this, critiques of meaning and narrative constructions are at the service of a cultural analysis: an attempt to reveal or demonstrate the ways in which purposeful uses of language can both make history happen in particular ways and critique the ways in which history happens.[13]

David Riesman and Nathan Glazer said in 1955 that whereas the Sacco and Vanzetti case united the left, the Rosenberg case divided it.[14] The Rosenberg case was a symbolic watershed especially for those New York Jewish intellectuals who became ex-Communist cultural nationalists, dissociating themselves from socialist and even liberal programs of the left and right.[15] Those who aligned themselves with nationalist democratic capitalism, and who in justifiable outrage spurned Stalinism (and in doing so spurned socialism), found themselves rhetorically aligned with religious anti-Communists, racists, antiunionists, and business, military, and industrial interests. Those who continued to argue for international negotiations and for reformist or systemic changes in U.S. domestic economic and social policies found themselves rhetorically aligned with Democrats and liberals, labor, and eventually with socialists, Communists, and Stalinists, and thus subject to both job and social discrimination and to criminal prosecution, as well as to a self-censorship still operative in the 1990s.[16] Any more complicated positions between these two extremes lost their political bases as anticommunism reduced and polarized the culturally available political positions and became increasingly difficult to maintain and express. The division of a previously unified left manifested itself directly in the split response to the Rosenberg story as its official version unfolded. The nationalist and ex-Communist left, blinded by the Communist affiliations of the Rosenbergs, found it difficult to maintain a critical view of the juridical and extrajudicial operations of the system they espoused over and against communism.

In the writings of such ex-Communist liberal and left Jewish intellectuals, the analysis of the Rosenbergs, based on the media reports of the trial and the Rosenberg prison letters, was carried on in terms of Stalinized bourgeois kitsch, taste, and style, as well as in terms of the Rosenberg failures of heroism and masculinity. By not openly espousing their principles, the Rosenbergs "failed in the end to become martyrs or heroes, or even men."[17] This attack on the Rosenbergs was part of a larger activity of ex-Communist intellectual analysis of postwar politics and events in terms of high and low culture and the Stalinist "estrangement of cultural life from direct experience."[18] The effort was to make the strained artifice, polemics, and tone of the death house letters stand for the fundamental failures of communism. Rhetorical connections are there to be made, but a potentially political critique was thus aestheticized, moralized, and at the same time effectively displaced from the space of any domestic political-juridical realm. This kind of displacement was and continues to be one of the greatest costs of anticommunism and the cold war.[19]

A larger betrayal operative in the Rosenberg story, that between the government and its citizens, was at the time largely unknown, discounted, unacknowledged, or uncontested through fear. The major exception to general media acquiescence to and affirmation of the official government story was a well-researched series of investigative articles begun in August 1951 by William Reuben in the *National Guardian* after the death sentences had been issued. Immediately preceding—but not until then—and following the Rosenberg executions their story became the subject of revisionist historiography and mythologizing by the Communist left in the pages of both the *National Guardian* and the

Daily Worker, in a repetition of party-line Stalinist rhetoric so extreme as to counter the credibility and possible effects of Reuben's solid investigative journalism. According to this Communist party-produced version of the story, the Rosenbergs were innocent and heroic martyrs of U.S. fascism and its mockery of justice. A 1955 book that Reuben wrote from his articles was the first attempt at a more objective rehearsal of the historical context, ambiguities, anomalies, and irrationalities of the official story, beginning a still open series of reconsiderations and interpretations of a story of political misuse and corruption of contractual state power.

The 1986 publication of an updated version of Robert Meeropol and Michael Meeropol's 1975 *We Are Your Sons,* an exhibition of Rosenberg art, "Unknown Secrets: Art and the Rosenberg Era," appearing at major museums throughout the country from 1988 through 1991, and Joseph Sharlitt's 1989 book, *Fatal Error,* about the Supreme Court during the week of appeals before the Rosenberg executions all manifest a renewed interest in the Rosenberg story as a cautionary tale with implications for all constitutional democracies, especially for democracies in periods of disruptive and accelerated change, like the United States in the late twentieth century.

The historical conjuncture of the late 1980s–early 1990s produced, along with a nostalgic cultural return to the 1950s, a newly articulated nostalgia for the securities of cold war foreign policy despite the perceived end of that war.[20] Momentous worldwide political and economic changes opened up possibilities for new orders of economic, social, and international relationships, potentials welcomed, furthered, and exploited for political and economic gains by U.S. politicians and policymakers, by business, banking, military, and service interests, as well as by social issue, political interest, and humanitarian groups. But the potentials for a changing and healthier world order were at the same time threatened and resisted by a persistent return on the part of political, business, and military leaders to a repetition of the anachronistic cold war rhetoric and policies of the 1950s, utilizing polarized projections to support politically and economically motivated agendas for the maintenance of the domestic status quo, especially in terms of military installations, arms development and production, and defense spending and contracts—all at the cost of an increasingly critical collapse in the 1990s of domestic social systems and institutions.

Consider the political effects of George Bush's McCarthyite rhetorical strategies during the 1988 presidential campaign of repeatedly accusing his Democratic opponent of being "liberal," a "card-carrying member of the American Civil Liberties Union," and "soft" on (black) criminals. In foreign policy, members of the Bush administration repeatedly articulated a preference for cold war stability as the Soviet Union was withdrawing from its perceived role as major antagonist and allowing relatively blood-less democratic revolutions to take place in the Eastern bloc countries, while attempting still to hold itself together as a nation. As Deputy Secretary of State Lawrence Eagleburger and President Bush noted, "For all its risks and uncertainties, the cold war was characterized by a remarkably stable and predictable set of re-lations among the great powers"; and "[because of cold war stability] Europe has had peace for some 40 years now, and if you look at your textbooks, why you'll see that that's a long time in an area of the world that has been troubled by conflict, in an area of the world that has involved us in this century in two massive wars."[21] This unabashedly Eurocentric view of the world ignores the extent to which, during those same forty years of European peace, the cold war was played out as hot wars among the two superpowers on the emerging nationalist and conflictual governments, terrains, and populations of Third World countries: Korea, Guatemala, Iran, Hungary, Czechoslo-vakia, the Belgian Congo, Vietnam, Angola, Chile, and Nicaragua, among others. It is also an abstracted view of international pol-itics that overlooks entirely the internal domestic costs to each national participant in the cold war military buildup.

Bush's cautions in the early 1990s that military spending must not and would not decrease to the benefit of domestic social programs—despite revelations concerning the exhaustion and failure of the Soviet and Eastern bloc economies, and despite Soviet agreements to significant reductions of its armed forces and weapons—echo exactly in tone and diction similar cautions and reassurances following World War II when conservatives feared demilitarization while liberals and progressives argued for a return of resources to critical domestic needs.

There was also in late 1990 a déja vu reminder of Truman's cold war rubric in justification of the unilateral U.S. intervention in the Korean war in June 1950. Following the August 1990 invasion and conquest of Kuwait by Iraq, Bush and his military and diplomatic advisers struggled to provide a believable narrative rationale to secure congressional approval for and UN participation in a massive buildup of U.S. forces and state-of-the-art technology-fair matériel in the Middle East. It was instructive, however, that Bush and his secretary of state James A. Baker III both faltered on the old cold war arguments of containment in the interest of making the world safe for democracy, or of Eisenhower's domino theory that a threat to democracy anywhere was a threat to the United States. Restoring the Kuwaiti monarchy was hardly a move toward global democracy, nor did Kuwait's conquest by Iraq occur in a domino line leading directly to the United States. The threat that had to be contained, far from being that of international communism, was the expansionist ambitions of a Muslim military dictatorship armed and supported by both the United States and the Soviet Union. Both Bush and Baker realized that, as George Kennan had urged after World War II, it was more believable to argue in terms of our real interests—oil, economics, and balances of power—but their diction was still skewed toward universal moral principles and abstract doctrines of good and evil. Even when official rhetoric touched on material interests, they were only arguably identical with our interests as a nation.

The cold war mentality nevertheless has sufficed as a controlling ideology in foreign affairs for the past forty-five years; in its post–cold war exhausted stage it still continues functioning rhetorically and belatedly to inform and rationalize foreign politics and policies, as well as to provide more local rationales for specific social and economic relationships and practices, despite radical changes in actual historical conditions. The left invokes the Rosenberg case as a reminder of the use of such a totalizing explanatory narrative for the purposes of an ideologically enforced popular quiescence and adherence to one specific agenda in a time of intensified potentials for change. The Rosenberg story has been recalled, rehearsed, and retold again in the Reagan/Bush era perhaps in order to awaken dormant dissent from the conservative agenda and activism for political change in another period of potential liminality: the perceived end of the cold war.

It is difficult, therefore, to elaborate a history of the continual retellings of the Rosenberg story without feeling the attractions and implications of another story: the history of and potentials for resistance to official explanatory narratives; the story of analysis, critique, dissent, and opposition as cultural practice; and in particular a story of the achievements of and potentials for such practice in the United States in the second half of the twentieth century.

An examination of the Rosenberg stories also reveals particular responses to, instrumentalization of, fascinations with, and critiques of class, race, and the sex-gender system, specifically as they were implicated and instrumentalized or exploited in cold war social relations and practices of power. This is true for the official story as well as for the cultural representations of that story. And because the multimedia drama and fictional narratives, as well as much of the visual arts concerning the Rosenbergs, are postmodern in form and technique, the Rosenberg story provides the occasion for an analysis and evaluation of critical cultural practice and of the relations of class, race, and gender to power as represented in specific postmodern forms of articulation.[22]

Theorizing the functional relationship of culture to history is not within my ken.[23] Fredric Jameson says that for him "the problem of homologies (and the unsatisfactory nature of these parallels or analogies between levels)" is a constant theoretical concern. There are enormous and insurmountable difficulties in attempting a correlation between somewhat autonomous fields in all their heterogeneity and overdetermination. And yet it is imperative to critical cultural work to devise methods, albeit imperfect or theoretically problematic ones, for using one partially knowable object to comment on another partially knowable object, or for using the perceived interrelationship of both "to get a mental grasp of something else which one cannot represent or imagine."[24]

These problems certainly exist for and in this analysis of the Rosenberg stories, with the most immediate difficulty inhering in the desire to keep a textual communication open between literature, drama, historiography, and the visual arts—that is, to study the reciprocal relationships and intersections of different, relatively autonomous cultural fields as complementary, supplementary, complicating, contradictory, or all four within the total field of symbol making in any given period. The primary or first purpose of my analysis of the Rosenberg story is to explore the narrative constructions and political operations of language as deriving from, discontinuous with, and generative of historical circumstances—in this case, of the cold war. Without being able fully or scientifically either to theorize or to demonstrate these relationships, I suggest and argue for certain probable connections and implications. I then attempt provisionally to suggest the relationships between the ongoing Rosenberg stories—in fiction, drama, and the visual arts—and the operations of power and the possibilities for cultural criticism and dissent within the United States, using Jameson's comment that a given cultural phenomenon—postmodern fiction, for example—"is articulating something that is going on [in the material world]."[25]

What interests me, in short, is that the Rosenberg stories are "articulating something that is going on" in excess of any notion of the original or real story, whatever that may be construed to be. And that excess can be seen as variously motivated by specific and determined political interests—interests such as that of the conservative, Republican, and ultimately U.S. government stake in proving the communism-treason link; E. L. Doctorow's interest in a critique of the domestic left; Robert Coover's critical interrogation of cold war relationships among gender, class, myth, and power; Donald Freed's interest in fracturing the mythic (official) Rosenberg story; Martha Rosler's interest in exploring the irrationalities of cold war ideology and social practices; Peter Saul's interest in shocking the observer into an alien perception of reality; or my own interest in unpacking rhetorically and critically the motives for and construction of a specific history.

So my focus will be on the historical production and cultural uses of the Rosenbergs and the Rosenberg story with the understanding that scrutiny of my version of these stories will reveal its own excess.[26]

I know of no more illustrative example than the Rosenberg story of a rhetorical elaboration and production of events to serve political, institutional, and personal agendas, a construction that somehow, with indeterminate agency, manages to draw into its inscription the witting and unwitting contributions of the whole complex of juridical, political, military, scientific, religious, and telecommunications institutions. The story reads like a frame–up as described by John Dos Passos writing about the Sacco and Vanzetti case:

> The frameup is an unconscious (occasionally semiconscious) mechanism. An unconscious mechanism is a kink in the mind that makes people do something without knowing that they are doing it. It is the sub-rational act of a group, serving in this case, through a series of pointed unintentions, the ends of a governing class. . . . The frameup is a process that you can't help feeling, but like most unconscious processes it's very hard to trace step by step. Half the agents in such a process don't really know what they are doing. Hence the average moderately fairminded newspaper reader who never has had personal experience of a frameup in action is flabbergasted when you tell him that such and such a man who is being prosecuted for wife-beating is really being prosecuted because he knew the origin of certain bonds in a District Attorney's safe.[27]

Dos Passos's inability to trace the frame-up process "step by step" is perhaps in part a limitation of his and his nation's individualist view of human agency in history. For the frame-up process as a collective but not totally controlling historical enterprise that invariably works to the interests of dominant groups to the cost of other groups is just what some contemporary public and academic cultural critics claim to be demonstrating. Their readings of the world foreground the communications among texts in the same or different cultural fields. In this way they are able more or less persuasively to posit certain correspondences, chronologies, and found coherencies as linguistic evidence of governing but nonexplicit and nonprocedural political

arrangements that actually prevail in any historical period—
arrangements that acquire cultural and symbolic authority and
achieve material effects beyond any individualist concepts of intention or agency.[28]

Read in this way, the Rosenberg story thus serves as a participant in, key to, and commentary on the larger poetics of the
formation of cold war ideology. The effect of reading the official
Rosenberg story is an awareness of multiple and systemic agency
and authorship rather than of a single narrative voice or a sense
of conscious collusion among all or some of the contributing
authors. By the time of the executions the textually elaborated
official story had crystallized into the coherent form of a traditional novel or drama with distinct characters, a defined and
polarized conflictual plot, a strong and unambiguous linear cause-
and-effect development and narrative line, and a rising and falling
action bounded by a necessary beginning and the most definitive
ending available in history or fiction: death as retribution and
redemption. The U.S. cold war narrative, as it had developed by
1947, contained all the same elements, with three potential and
absolute endings posited: a free democratic and peaceful world
under U.S. protection and moral leadership, an enslaved Communist world controlled by the Soviet Union, or atomic holocaust
at the hands of the Soviet Union.

One might expect the Rosenberg story to have ended with
the narrative closure of the executions. But the FBI said at that
time that the "story" most definitely would not end with the
Rosenbergs' deaths, meaning that the larger story the government
wanted was still to be told: the story of the atomic spy ring, for
which Julius and Ethel stood as a part for the whole and at the
same time as intended elaborators of that whole—the spy ring
responsible for the theft of the secret of the atomic bomb. Yet,
in one of history's great ironies, it was the promised elaboration
of the larger story that did end with the Rosenberg deaths. No
U.S. citizen was subsequently indicted or convicted for any act
of atomic espionage. It was instead the Rosenberg story that took
on a life of its own, an ongoing elaboration that is still in process,
ungoverned by the plot development and formal closure of the

official story, and uninformed by the Atomic Spy Ring story the state had in mind.

It is indisputable that in 1950 an atom spy story served various individual, institutional, and political purposes, as well as a fairly large collective need. But given that story's strange history, it seems highly improbable that the official version of the Rosenberg story could have been produced in answer to those needs without sufficient audience development, including symbolic preparation and saturation of the public and institutional mind in terms of genre expectations and constructed linkages. It was these expectations and linkages, I argue, that allowed a particular version of the story to be received and a political show trial and execution to ensue. Yet, in a strong historical contradiction—especially in a period of aggressive worldwide propagation of the "American way of life"—the particular enactment of that drama of necessary punishment for extreme treason, I also argue, breached the constitutional covenant between the state and its people. This larger betrayal, made possible only by a high-level public acceptance as true of a story strongly marked by traces of motivated construction and imaged fictionality, continues, as we shall see, to work as a stimulating, provoking antagonism in the political and cultural imagination of the United States. My purpose in this study is to analyze and trace the politically motivated production of the official Rosenberg story and the historical and cultural critiques performed by its re-presentation in literature, drama, and the visual arts.

Part I
The Rosenberg Stories: History

[God] has made us the master organizers of the world to es-
tablish system where chaos reigns. . . . It is God's great purpose
made manifest in the instincts of the race whose present phase
is our personal profit, but whose far-off end is the redemption
of the world and the Christianization of mankind.

Senator Albert Beveridge, quoted in
Bailyn et al., The Great Republic

The sacrificial principle . . . is intrinsic to the idea of Order.
[Consider] the compulsions of Empire, as two mighty world or-
ders, each homicidally armed to the point of suicide, confront
each other. As with dominion always, each is much beset with
anxiety. And in keeping with the "curative" role of victimage,
each is apparently in acute need of blaming all its many trou-
bles on the other, wanting to feel certain that, if the other and
its tendencies were but eliminated, all governmental discord
(all the Disorder that goes with Order) would be eliminated.

Kenneth Burke, The Rhetoric of Religion

1

Cold War Frame Narrative

I want here to consider the symbolic emergence of what Kenneth Burke calls the justifying or "perfecting myth" for the material history of the cold war, to note "the role of symbolism as the motivating genius of secular enterprise." Burke perceives a double movement in history, from sociopolitical raw data to a justifying narrative, which then becomes the originator of a certain order and its rationale. Narrative then would both perform an ideological function, explaining and justifying the world, and play an active role, directing the production of that world.[1]

This understanding of narrative neither dismisses the potential of individual agency nor posits ideological narrative as an absolute saturation of human consciousness. The ongoing operations of national narrative are never entirely under or attributable to specific individual or group authorial control. But a critical awareness of the main line of any national narrative must always take into account the degree to which the story develops an acquiescent audience for the playing out of a specific history that immediately, or eventually and in retrospect, serves the interests of those managing the narrative and its dissemination at the expense of any notion of the public good.

I would argue then that the cold war narrative, among others—such as the U.S. version of the 1991 U.S.-Iraqi war—is a "relatively autonomous system of meaning production by which individuals are persuaded to live a distinctively imaginary relation to their real conditions of existence."[2] The more or less acquiescent subjects of national narratives are, in stable societies,

3

sometimes known as good citizens; but even in a constitutional democracy, the values and substance of good citizenship vary with time and changing dominant interests, as evidenced by the cold war construction of the category "un-American" for people who had until recently been American.[3] An understanding of ideological narrative as managing the subject's experience of historical reality complements Burke's analysis of the extent to which the symbolic process—culture—orders history itself. And the cold war "perfecting myth" worked in both of these senses to articulate and produce a specific working relationship between individuals and their state and its policies—a relationship that ensured individuals' voluntary acquiescence to, support for, and daily investment in a specific history not of their choosing. Daniel Isaacson, Doctorow's narrator in *The Book of Daniel,* notices this same phenomenon:

> No matter what is laid down there will be people to put their lives on it. Soldiers will instantly appear, fall into rank, and be ready to die for it. And scientists who are happy to direct their research toward it. And keen-witted academics who in all rationality develop the truth of it. And poets who find their voice in proclaiming the personal feeling of it. And in every house in the land the muscles of the face will arrange in smug knowledge of it. And people will go on and make their living from it. And the religious will pray for a just end to it, in terms satisfactory to it.[4]

The developing postwar policies and programs, as well as their narrative rationale, appeared to be the studied and rational product of a political process of transition from New Deal democratic and internationalist liberalism to a more nationalist conservatism in a time of circumstances perceived as urgently threatening to national security and economic well-being. But the emergence and articulation of a cover story for a specific configuration of postwar policy were also the result of an opportunistic political struggle—financed by business and waged through the popular electoral process—for control of government and thus of the national agenda. The power elites—conservative Republicans and Democrats and business, industry, and military interests—were its underwriters; President Truman, conservative political, military, and business leaders, J. Edgar Hoover, and the House Un-American Activities Committee (HUAC) were its leading actors; and the mainstream media were its promoters.

The production of the cold war narrative both set the stage for and to some degree required, in time, the production of the Rosenberg story. That story, the frame-up of the Rosenbergs, is a narrative embedded in a frame narrative that is also, in the Dos Passos definition, a frame-up: the cold war.[5] Throughout this elaboration of the symbolic production of that frame narrative, I will also be indicating the use of that narrative and its symbolic strategies for framing dissent from that same narrative. I intend the ambiguity here with framing in the visual arts as the construction of a containing border. A crucial word—and form—for the FBI, HUAC, the Department of Justice, and the media during this period was *list,* whose roots mean border and boundary. The drawing of a frame around all voices to the left of center and labeling them left spelled with a capital "C" was a formalist symbolic enterprise at the service of the implementation of the cold war agenda.[6]

Meaning Making

The use of language is a purposeful meaning-seeking and -making endeavor involving certain fundamental operations that have their analogues in our understanding of both individual psychic and collective political processes. In the rubric of linguistics, the basic operation is one of the utilization of differences and similarities to establish one meaning to the exclusion of its opposite and many other middle-ground meanings; in the psychological rubric it is one of splitting and projection, a primary process that is both the means of knowing and a defensive way of not knowing; at the political level, the operation is one of national ideological and institutional definitions, enclosures, and exclusions based on motivated and more or less projective understandings of self and other, or "us" and "them."[7]

As the level of syntactic and perceptual/cognitive complexity increases, other operations and phenomena come into play, operations that as constitutive mechanisms are more performative than assertive or descriptive: the naturalizing of arbitrary relationships, through repetition and saturation, into received wisdom, common sense, or the way things are; the establishment of cause-effect relationships and semantic and political similarities and differences through constructed rhetorical linkages; the transformation of meaning through incremental or discontinuous but repetitive shifts among categories and codes; the drive toward a narrative or mythic coherence that masks gaps, irrationalities, and contradictions; and the establishment of widespread and subconscious generic expectations with their specific outcome or closures.

Just as the struggle for dominance among postwar political interests was apparently the way things happen in a constitutional and representative democracy, these linguistic and semantic operations are apparently no more than the ways in which meanings happen. But in both cases, the results are not innocent; they are driven by perceptions of interest and are corrupt to the extent that individualist and group practices of power and greed skew semantic and political definitions and practices against the good of specific groups, or of the polity as a whole.

What happens, then, when the inevitable inclusions and exclusions and drives to coherence in meaning making coincide with a period of rapidly changing socioeconomic relationships, widespread popular insecurities and anxieties, a nation-state's emerging will to global power, and threats to the survival instincts of an economically and politically empowered business-military alliance? What happens when both the individual citizens and their institutional leaders have a historically high intolerance for ambiguity, uncertainty, and process and require, for the alleviation of anxieties and the exercise of power, coherent and unambiguous definitions and explanatory narratives that claim a universal moral authority?[8]

What happens is a tyranny of meaning that approaches the dimensions of myth.[9] Explanatory narrative for specific and local phenomena and actions develops in the sudden emergence of a

6

compelling and comprehensive metaphor or cluster of metaphors with its own "jumble of plot," and then through the elaboration of that plot and its official, public repetition over time.[10] Such a narrative provides an abstract, idealistic, and totalizing national rationale for the inconsistent, conflicting, deceitful, and corrupt policies and actions of an entire era—policies and actions carried out for the purpose of order–making dominion for an order of a specific material nature. An explanatory narrative that achieves the status of perfecting myth serves to reconcile discrepancies and irrationalities while appearing to obviate public or official scrutiny of actual circumstances. Such a narrative becomes effectively monolithic and saturating, demonizing its opposite and canceling or absorbing all mediatory and intermediate terms and kinds of activity.[11]

There is an inbuilt contradiction—one overtly displayed and exploited by what are identified as postmodern strategies of interrogation—in my narration of what is purported to be a discovery and un-narrating of the cold war frame narrative.[12] It becomes necessary to narrate in order to un-narrate, and in so doing I face the very dilemma that I criticize here for its potential for purposeful deceit and political exclusions and oppressions. Any coherent and persuasive argument I make for the arbitrary and motivated construction of the cold war narrative is *formally* indistinguishable from the work of cold war mythographers: a gathering of selected sociopolitical data into a coherent story, speculating on and positing a beginning and ending, cause-effect relationships, and possible motivations. Despite the inevitability of these kinds of narrative reductions and distortions, my intention is to keep the story as open to the documented incoherencies and uncertainties of the period as possible, remembering the multiple and differing voices as well as those not yet hearable or not yet expressed, and resisting the reductions, exclusions, and order-making extremes of both right "consensus" and left "revisionist" cold war historiography.

It is practically impossible to demonstrate the cold war perfecting myth taking hold of the public consciousness, as it is impossible to demonstrate the cultural and historical effects of literature or of the visual and performing arts. Despite the pervasive use of popular polls to discover what we think, there is no effective theory of reading or reception and no scientific means for determining how words and events determine the ways in which people think. What I can do is demonstrate—albeit selectively and partially—a complexity of circumstances, ideas, and interests that would seem to work against the clear emergence of the cold war narrative with its specific history. I can then, in the form of a chronology with an arbitrary but purposeful beginning, indicate specific textual moments in the temporal course of political events when the cold war narrative began to emerge metaphorically in terms of an "iron curtain," "rotten apples," "dominoes," "containment," and a "cold war," generating a specific plot and evolving toward more and more coherent form. Such a chronology, despite its selectivity, eliminates to some degree the problem of the construction of a linear narrative positing coherent cause-and-effect relationships from a plethora of infinitely implicated and implicating material and cultural sociopolitical data. In the interest of keeping open my story of the cold war story, I begin with a gross anatomy of the material circumstances, dominant clusters of ideas, and vested interests at play in the immediate postwar period.

Circumstances

The immediate postwar period was informed and structured by certain material and cultural givens, circumstances inherited by the U.S. postwar polity, but not necessarily or completely of its people's or leaders' choosing or agency.[13]

> A disrupted U.S. domestic postwar social and economic order in a period of accelerated change.

> Emergent U.S. first-power global status in an atomic era.

> A threatening great-power antagonist whose national ambitions were expansionist, whose articulated ideology was that of worldwide communist revolution, and whose armies occupied Central and Eastern Europe.

> National postwar prosperity dependent on ongoing military expenditures, reconversion to increased consumer-goods productivity, and expanding international markets.

A liberal democratic administration, heir of the New Deal, opposed by a Republican party out of power since 1932.

An increasingly mass-culture society inaugurated by electronic technology and communications.

Concepts

From these material circumstances derived a number of compelling concepts demanding political consensus as to their interpretation as well as to their enactment. A close reading of the various expressions of these dominant concepts in public and private papers from a linguistic, psychoanalytic, or political perspective reveals them as actively containing their opposites and at the same time evoking clusters of mediating ideas and terms— all of which made the complex work of their interpretation a charged and deadly serious political contest.

Change. The idea of *change*—as possibility or threat—was perhaps the summary idea for all others; indeed it is the motivating idea and problem of human history. The last years of the war and the immediate postwar period (1944–50) were a period of accelerated change for the United States, a necessary opportunity for rethinking and rearticulating national interests and those interests in relation to the larger world. This was a period of liminality rather than of transition, because the war had been the occasion for a major discontinuity in the exercise of global power: the exhaustion of British imperial energies and capacities, and the sudden emergence of the relatively young United States as the richest and most powerful nation in the world.[14] The exigencies of the depression followed by those of the war had also radically disrupted socioeconomic relationships in the United States in terms of class, race, and gender.

These vertical and horizontal disruptions opened up domestic society to potentially new formations challenging to the status quo of a country at that time governed by a wartime continuation of the New Deal business-government partnership, with the participation of the military and the defense industry as a third partner by the end of the war. These new formations included proportionate representation in public bodies for all citizens, labor-management partnerships equal to the contribution of each, civil rights—including voting rights, the right to a fair trial, the right to work, and equal pay—and for women, all of the above, plus day care, family assistance, and equal division of labor.[15]

Such ideas for change evoked and provoked into play strong centripetal counterconcepts and forces in the institutionalized operations of daily life gathered under the rubric of tradition as the semantic opposite of change. These ideas included corporate paternalism; a policy of separate-but-equal institutions for African Americans; states' rights; a postwar regendered family-centered separation of public and private life; and the continuation of the business–government partnership that had, with the stimulus of war, brought the United States unprecedented economic prosperity.

Global power. The historically isolationist United States had emerged from the war with first-power status, and the idea of global power was both seductive and terrifying. It contained notions of total responsibility, megalomania, and grandiosity, the threat of loss of position and control or of anarchy or destruction by the other(s), as well as intermediate and seemingly less predictable and manageable possibilities for ongoing negotiations of multijurisdictional pragmatic relationships among differing national autonomies.

Atomic warfare. This was not just one idea among others, as only some of the scientists—most eloquently Niels Bohr—and a few statesmen recognized: after Alamogordo the idea of global atomic war, while always a historical possibility, was no longer a possibility that, if realized, would remain *within* history. Nor apparently has its opposite, peace, ever been a real historical possibility. The bomb thus had no practical use as an instrument of diplomacy, a fact most diplomats, military leaders, and policy advisers were remarkably slow to understand. The United States had financed and directed the secret development of the atomic bomb as a strategic military weapon, and its use contributed to the sense of absolute power that prevailed for a brief period after September 1945.

By the end of that year a quite specific and contradictory cluster of ideas and fears was forming in the institutional, collective, and individual minds of the nation: Hiroshima and Nagasaki evoked not only notions of ultimate power or total powerlessness and of politically necessary first strikes or guilt, anxiety, fears of retribution, and generalized paranoia, but also mediating concepts of scientific and technological cooperation, international negotiation, and global arms control. Crucial to the development of the cold war, as well as of the Rosenberg story, were the ways in which the cluster of ideas around that of atomic warfare was manipulated and imaginatively displaced, through mobilization of fears and anxieties, into ideas of ownership, secrecy, and defensive aggression.

National security. The idea of national security was certainly not new, but with the development and use of electronic technology and atomic weapons it had become a qualitatively different idea. Even more than the other ideas, that of national security was actively driven by its opposites: breach, espionage, betrayal, treason, aggression, take-over, overthrow, revolution. Clearly these ideas contained both an external (foreign) and an internal (domestic) dimension—another aspect essential to the symbolic fashioning of the cold war rationale and to the implementation of its program. The national security state operating under the demands of the cold war allowed and seemed to require an arrogation of power by the executive and a practice of executive privilege and governmental secrecy, subterfuge, and deceit so extensive as to override and eventually corrupt the democratic principles and integrity of government that national security was in part intended to protect.[15]

National prosperity. And finally, but certainly not least in consideration, was national prosperity. Its opposite, economic depression, had been a terrifying material reality for the United States and the western world in the Great Depression. And herein lay a real contradiction: business and industrial interests that were attempting to promote growth in international markets, with foreigners as necessary consumers for an expanding U.S. economy, feared an intensification of certain New Deal policies as

11

much as they feared depression. That is, they wanted a continuation, in the name of economic growth, of basically the same
relationships of production that had led to the depression, while
preserving selected New Deal and wartime tax credits and forms
of government spending that favored supply-side reinvestment
and growth.

The linguistic opposition prosperity/depression also elided
crucial distinctions in favor of gross national indexes. The real
postwar prosperity, as statistically described, occluded the actual
disparities that existed within the macrodimension of national
economic well-being.[16] The opposition, because it also continued
to be thought and preached only in the context of capitalism,
also masked another relevant critical opposition, capitalist accumulation (partially through the federal government's socializing
subsidies for capital through tax expenditures) and its functional
and performative opposite, socialist distribution.

The assimilation in the United States of all arguments for a
recognition and institutionalization of the more democratic wartime sociopolitical and economic changes to the idea of communism was made possible by a cold war semantic polarization
of terms. Tradition was aligned against change, nationalist global
power against internationalist approaches, atomic superiority
against cooperation, the national security state against the securing of a democratic economic and social order, and capital
and labor against labor, farmers, minorities, and women.[17]

Interests

The dominant, dissenting, and emergent voices engaged in the
immediate postwar struggle to determine the national agenda
had the potential to "make their own history in circumstances
not of their choosing."[18] I identify these circumstances for the
purposes of this argument as the material phenomena and the
clusters of predominant ideas emanating from those phenomena
outlined in the preceding section. The various interested groups
did not necessarily fall into mutually exclusive categories, nor
did the disposition of the prevalent ideas among them strictly
follow at first any previously determined divisions of political

ideology or party politics, although certain affiliations and alignments suggested themselves immediately.

There was a promising confusion of boundaries, positions,
theories, and possibilities in the moment of liminality during
which the struggle took place, as policymakers and politicians
sought to come to terms with new realities. More alternatives to
what we now know as the history of the cold war were envisioned, voiced, and even attempted than is commonly recognized
by the largely naturalized cold war mentality operative in U.S.
policies and affairs during the latter half of the twentieth century.[19] Some of these voices were intelligent, informed, and eloquent; some were simply powerful and prejudiced, with neither
eloquence nor adequate information; some were relatively powerless and inarticulate but for a moment of potential political
presence enhanced by emergent postwar socioeconomic relationships. Some merged into coalitions as mutual interests were
articulated, and some were exploited as their usefulness became
apparent. This scenario is formally nothing more than the political process of a representative democracy, misleadingly and
ideologically represented in the United States, however, as political pluralism.[20] So how did it produce the virtual extinction
of the expression of all interests to the left of center? How did
it institute an ideology of moral purpose protected by secrecy
and fear that promoted and maintained not only a certain economic and political order but also a self-induced moratorium on
critical thinking and dissent?

Business and industry, fearing a slowdown of the full mo-
mentum generated by wartime productivity and lamenting the
loss of Axis and Central European resources and industries destroyed during the war or held within the Soviet sphere of influence, were determined to maintain and expand their position
as government's managing partner—a position held with only
minor interruptions since the time of Alexander Hamilton.[21]

For the representatives of business interests, the cold war
possibilities read like an investment prospectus in an infinitely
expanding world economy. In 1947, as the cold war was emerging as national explanatory narrative, business already understood and asserted it as the economic boon it would indeed

become. Headlines in *Business Week* that year read "New Democracy, New Business. U. S. Drive to Stop Communism Abroad Means Heavy Outlays for Bases, Relief and Reconstruction. But in Return American Business is Bound to Get New Markets Abroad." By 1950, when the cold war was functioning and its returns were beginning to be abundantly apparent, *U.S. News and World Report* said, "Government planners figure they have found the magic formula for almost endless [economic] good times. . . . Cold War is the catalyst. Cold War is an automatic pump–primer. Turn the spigot and the public clamors for more arms spending. Turn another, the clamor ceases. . . . Cold War demands, if fully exploited, are almost limitless."[22]

The military ended the war in a position of political strength and peak mobilization, having primed for the anticipated invasion of Japan. But this global distribution of military and thus strategic political and diplomatic strength was canceled by the widespread expectations of and demands for demobilization and disarmament after the Japanese surrender. The ensuing presidential and congressional orders for immediate and rapid demobilization were popular, idealistic, and naïve, if not irresponsible. They were an abdication of the country's new preeminent world position in a disrupted world order before the major powers had completed negotiating crucial and complicated territorial and political arrangements concerning Europe, Asia, and colonies worldwide.[23]

The military was, however, in the historically unique position of having directed the development and use of the atomic bomb. For many members of the military and of the government the atomic bomb continued—despite scientists' insistence to the contrary—to be construed as a nationally owned, secret offensive weapon and a deployable means of guaranteeing U.S. security and first-power status. These assumptions concerning the atomic bomb—contested by a few top-level policy advisers, notably Henry L. Stimson—misconstrued the practical uses to which the atomic bomb could be put and underestimated the continuing need for flexible and limited local military operations with conventional weapons, ground forces, an air force, and a navy. This misconstrual led to John Foster Dulles's concept of "massive retaliation," with its buildup of an atomic weapons arsenal disproportionate to any conceivable real world needs.[24]

Conservatives, represented—but not exclusively—by the Republican party, were determined to regain control of national foreign and domestic policy from liberal New Dealers; they held power locally but were weak nationally. In analyzing Republican postwar strategies it is important to acknowledge a distinction between the extent to which the right found itself increasingly solidified by a perceived conflation of Stalinist/Russian national security needs for protected borders as territorial ambitions with the world-revolutionary ideology of the Soviet-dominated Communist party, and the degree to which the right interpreted these two conditions and exploited them as one in order to unify conservatives and eliminate all other voices in its drive for dominance. The cold war as totalizing myth depended on such a conflation of Soviet national interest with international communism; as enduring totalizing myth for forty-five years it has depended on a largely successful naturalization of that conflation and a sustained ignorance of the real and at one time acknowledged material distinctions between the two.[25]

The FBI had as its head from 1924 a genius of bureaucratic administration and a master of the legal and illegal manipulation of government officials as well as of the uses and dissemination of secrets and public information and misinformation. Obsessed with contamination phobias, J. Edgar Hoover's personal ambition was to be the agent of national purification from the "enemy within." He began his lifelong mission during the 1920s Red Scare, led the FBI through its successful campaign against the flamboyant gangsters of the 1930s, identified Nazi agents during World War II, and "discovered" the "thousands" of communists, radicals, and liberals working to destroy the United States from within during and following World War II. Hoover was gratified to find his own prejudices and paranoias against the left increasingly supported by the power elites and eventually by millions of U.S. citizens.[26]

The House Un-American Activities Committee (HUAC) was organized in 1938 to investigate foreign "isms" in a context of prewar anxieties about Nazi, Communist, and other foreign subversion. J. Edgar Hoover, by interpreting a presidential directive from Roosevelt broadly—and unconstitutionally—had by 1945 already compiled several thousand files on people allegedly engaged, or "likely" to engage, in various forms of foreign espionage.[27]

When HUAC was formed, it began a competitive and collaborative venture with the FBI, with Hoover secretly providing information that emerged from the committee as lists, subpoenas, and public extrajudicial interrogations. HUAC, with the assistance of Senator Joseph McCarthy, constructed anticommunism as a police-state operation that worked to intimidate the left into self-imposed silence and thus unwitting complicity with the developing cold war narrative and agenda. Despite McCarthy's censure by the Senate in 1954, HUAC was still supported in 1970 by an $800,000 appropriation, the product of a perceived ongoing political necessity for bipartisan support for the elimination of "un-American" behavior.[28] In all of the committee's activities the mainstream and conservative media were uncritical and supporting partners, until Edward R. Murrow's and Fred Friendly's CBS exposure of McCarthy on "See It Now" in 1954.

The print media, whose interests since the turn of the century had become increasingly identified with those of business, and which were operating more and more under monopoly ownership, were increasingly supported by advertising and motivated by profit.[29] In 1945, utilizing national network news sources and chain journalism reproduction and distribution processes, the press still worked primarily as it had during the war to represent and reproduce national unity in terms of dominant interests. There had been an effectively consistent strain of anticommunist consensus journalism since the 1920s in the major chains and urban dailies.[30] With the press willing to accept and report FBI and HUAC news releases from "informed sources" as factual, the apparatus for the construction of anticommunism as a necessary national political safeguard in the interests of a prevailing cold war agenda was in place.[31]

The Democratic administration, made up of New Dealers, other liberals, and conservative Democrats, demonstrated the greatest degree of confusion and openness, an openness that was exploited as the potential vulnerability it can be in high-stake political battles. With a presidential administrative and advisory organization inadequate to the complexity of the demands upon the executive of a newly global power, and with dispersed and compartmentalized information sources, Truman insisted on taking what he—and the public—regarded as simple decisive actions in the most charged policy matters, increasing his administration's vulnerability to criticism and manipulation.[32] During his presidency Truman, as the national and Democratic party leader, achieved popular success in using the liberal rhetoric of his Fair Deal while effectively acting in accord with white male business interests.

Policy advisers addressed the potentials and responsibilities of the country's postwar global status from positions articulated variously by moralism, idealism, humanitarianism, pragmatism, national interests, or opportunism and realpolitik. A perusal of policy papers reveals the changing complexities over time of attempts to "know" and explain the Soviet Union, its motivations, ambitions, and capabilities. Private communications tended toward the realistic end of the spectrum but often reflected subtextual assumptions of the relative material entitlement and superior purchase on objectivity on the part of the United States and its leaders in reading and interpreting the world. Public communications and declaratory policy statements, continuing in the successful tradition of the disinterested and moral global mission publicly articulated for the United States by both Wilson and Roosevelt, tended rhetorically to occlude the language of national and special interests—those of the United States, the Soviet Union, or any other nation—in favor of idealistic claims for U.S. responsibilities and capabilities. These public representations, consciously used to ensure public support for specific policies and actions, also had the effect of representing diplomacy as a primarily moral forum for political negotiations.[33]

Atomic scientists, some of whom had opposed use of the atomic bomb, began active information campaigns as soon as the secrecy constraint was removed in 1945 in an urgent effort to accomplish the grounding of postwar policy in an understanding

17

of a world changed utterly by the realities and possibilities of atomic energy. Nobel Prize–winning physicist James Franck in a memorandum to Secretary of Commerce Henry Wallace, April 21, 1945, asked, "How is it possible that the statesmen are not informed that the aspect of the world and its future is entirely changed by the knowledge that atomic energy can be tapped, and how is it possible that the men who know these facts are prevented from informing the statesmen about the situation?"[34] The discounting and containment of scientists' attempts to inform policy advisers of the nature of atomic energy constituted another crucial step in the elaboration of the cold war as well as of the official Rosenberg story.

Liberals in the 1940s were too diverse in their outlooks to be defined effectively by that label, although *liberal* in the United States had developed a meaning relatively specific to New Deal political history. In the postwar era *liberal* referred to all formulators and supporters of New Deal policies, as well as to anyone who argued the necessity for state correction or management of a misnamed and imaginary free market economy.[35] Following the war, many who considered themselves as left were more accurately liberal in their reformist rather than systemic critique of U.S. capitalism, and in their reliance on a national narrative of democratic individualism accompanied by blindness to historically operative categories of exclusion and disempowerment. Confusingly, however, ex-Communist intellectuals also accused the remaining members of the Communist left of being "liberals." Excluding those Communists who remained loyal to Stalinism, and those who subscribed to various versions of Marxism or socialism, postwar liberals comprised a diverse group of reformists who saw themselves as representing the Lockean ethic of individual liberties in a contractual democratic government, but who stopped short of any kind of systemic critique of the confounding of that ethic by the oligarchic, individualist, and masculist form of capitalism that prevailed in the U.S. political economy.[36] Crucial to the elaboration of the national agenda was a strategic shifting of liberal allegiances to the right under the multiform pressures and demands of a constructed anticommunism.

Labor, reaching across the entire political spectrum, had been shaped by the depression, the New Deal, and strong left leadership, including members of the U.S. Communist party, into the beginning of a horizontal organization with primary concern for social and workplace issues. As an organized group with articulated concerns it emerged from the war as a strong and active political presence, eager to consolidate its gains during the war as a full partner in planning and productivity while working voluntarily under wartime no-strike agreements and wage controls. In the postwar inflation, without a release of the artificial wage structure labor faced a decline in the real value of wages as profits rapidly rose. Also, jobs at all levels were threatened by reconversion and eleven million returning soldiers. Seeking compensation commensurate with its contribution to wartime and postwar profitability, a stabilizing of its position in the forms of participatory management and bargaining agreements, and improvements in workplace conditions, labor began the period of its greatest activism in U.S. history to date.[37]

The left was in disarray after the end of the wartime Popular Front coalition of Communist, left, and liberal organizations, depleted by disillusionment with Stalinist communism as well as with socialism on the part of those who confused socialist theory with the despotic form of state socialism practiced by Stalin. At the end of the war the U.S. Communist party (CPUSA) was the largest left organization, followed by the socialists, who had been steadily losing their political base since Roosevelt's Democratic administration had enacted reformist versions of various socialist programs as components of the New Deal. There were the Socialist Workers party; the Workers party; the New York–based American Labor party;[38] several hundred organizations labeled by the attorney general as Communist-front organizations— including the National Farmers Union, the National Lawyers Guild, and the Peace Information Center—innumerable smaller left sectarian groups; and the youth groups attached to many of these left organizations.

Although the U.S. left was described by the right as a simmering mass movement threatening to domestic stability, its numbers in 1945 were smaller than imagined or represented.[39] But even more surprising to the average newspaper reader in 1945 would have been the actual nature of left political activity, fragmented and deprived of a national economic or political base except for that which existed through labor organizations and civil rights groups such as the Urban League, the National Association for the Advancement of Colored People (NAACP), the Congress of Racial Equality (CORE), and voter registration teams. That these groups were (and still are) taken for granted as left, subversive, and even Communist-inspired or -directed in a constitutional democracy is one of the deeper contradictions of the nation's society and history.

With the exception of U.S. Communist party leader William Z. Foster's insistence on the Stalinist hard line for the CPUSA, left groups had almost entirely abandoned notions of apocalyptic revolutionary change and come to embrace a gradualist politics that they advocated through speeches, education, and publications, a rhetorical activity that Daniel Bell mocked for its moralism and idealism as "mimetic combat in the plains of destiny."[40] The left was represented by one member of Congress in 1945: Vito Marcantonio of New York, head of the American Labor party.

The CPUSA by the end of the war had reached the acme of its power as a Popular Front political force working actively in labor unions (especially the Congress of Industrial Organizations [CIO]) and left organizations, as well as in the Democratic party. After the end of its wartime open participation in left and liberal political, social, and cultural activities, it returned to a more rigorous and covert internationalist Stalinist politics through local organizations, attempting to generate political energy and ideas through membership in non-Communist and Communist-front organizations.

However, by mid–1945 many members of the party were redefining their allegiances and withdrawing from Communist affiliations.[41] This was in large part a result of the discipline and purges enforced when Foster replaced the Popular Front American party leader Earl Browder in 1945 under a Moscow directive to return the party to a rigid adherence to Soviet ideological interpretations and foreign policy. Browder's termination and Foster's regime effectively foreclosed any possibility for a continuation of open Communist political participation in the formulation of a domestic agenda, rendering the party vulnerable to and even complicit in the political and juridical construction of anticommunism.[42]

In its refusal of open political participation and its failure to challenge postwar anticommunist political strategies publicly on First Amendment or direct ideological grounds, the party played into the hands of conservative interests.[43] The profound and costly irony of anticommunism was that "it developed in the absence of any real internal Communist menace; for by 1950 Communism in America had lost whatever influence it once possessed."[44]

But while communism (as a Soviet-directed ideology of and program for worldwide anticapitalist revolutionary practice) had lost whatever influence it once possessed in the United States, its opposite, domestic anticommunism, was by 1950 approaching a high point in its staged public and private policy career as promoter and protector of the conservative national agenda. In the interest of warding off the threat of international communism perceived and publicized as working from without and boring from within, anticommunism was shaping U.S. domestic and international affairs, intersecting and dividing public and private realms, thwarting the work of groups attempting to secure fundamental economic and civil rights, shutting down dissenting forms of critical thinking and acting, and justifying illegal U.S. intervention in the affairs of other countries.[45]

Artists, writers, filmmakers, educators, and intellectuals emerged from the wartime period of national unity quietism and from the preceding era of 1930s and 1940s social criticism and activism into a postatomic, post-Holocaust, rapidly polarizing world. Many of these men and women had been committed socialists or Marxists; many had at one time, especially during the Popular Front, been members of the Communist party. But the familiar liberal and objective or realistic forms of artistic and intellectual apprehension and critique suddenly seemed pitifully inadequate to postwar reality, as did the utopian theories of Marxism and socialism. In an extended moment of postwar rethinking and hesitation on the part of critical artists and intellectuals, an emergent cultural right, which had been reductively and powerfully defining itself and contemporary culture in terms of modernism and formalism, was positioned for dominance.[46]

Women and ethnic and racial minorities had been increasingly tolerated as working—but not management, administrative, or policy-making—equals during the war because of industrial and military needs for replacement workers for the twelve million men and women in the armed services during the war. They found themselves at the end of the war not only without real political and economic gains, but also threatened by a substantial loss of wartime gains as they were fired in favor of returning soldiers, relegating them to unemployment and, in the case of the women, a forced return to their traditionally proper domain, the home.

As early as 1900, *farmers,* still a significant proportion of the population (35.7 percent), had already been relegated in terms of economic position and power to the status of a special interest group.[47] The Knights of Labor had rejected the opportunity for a farm-labor alliance in 1890, and farmer participation in political power and reform or left politics had come to an end with the New Deal and the rise of the CIO, which had articulated itself against rural interests.[48] World War II brought a new level of agricultural prosperity, followed by the protections of parity and the stimulus of the cold war economy. This prosperity for a while ensured the allegiance of the farmers to the cold war economic program, while deferring a consideration of the costs of the increasing corporate industrialization of agriculture after 1945—a consideration still being deferred in the 1990s.

The people of the United States, with their varying and multiform allegiances to the preceding groups, were almost all giving voice to relief, elation, pride, and diffuse fears and anxieties, as well as, most crucially, a virtually untested and abstract faith in the rectitude and justice of the American way of life and the deserved authority of the U.S. government and its institutions.

In addition to these interests, there were four groups that—had they not been emergent and lacking in the critical mass necessary to be heard or taken seriously, or culturally disciplined to acquiescent roles—held the potentiality for complicating, mitigating, and keeping open to changing circumstances the national postwar narrative. These were women, minorities, scientists, and farmers.

Women workers and union members; women's civic, business, and professional organizations; women's reading and reform groups; and women members of the Women's Advisory Committee to the War Manpower Commission in the Department of Labor had all been active during the war. But as a self-conscious political force women had not yet assimilated the ways in which the achievement of suffrage in the 1920s was still only a formal victory, or the ways in which their massive entry into the job market during the war was only a beginning and temporary step in a long struggle for equality.[49] Also, a linkage between Communist conspiracy and women's reform groups had been established in the public mind during the 1920s by representations of women committed to social reform as part of a "spider web" conspiracy directed by Moscow to subvert the family and traditional American values.[50]

There were isolated feminist voices, but as a collective critical speaking mass, women were not protagonists in the argument in the postwar period. This silence was largely due to the force of a national social narrative for women that worked to define subjects who would voluntarily live "an imaginary relationship . . . to their real conditions of existence."[51] The Women's Advisory Committee in 1942 had not raised questions of wages and hours for the vastly increased number of women workers in order that the committee might "quietly go about its business, without offending propriety or tradition . . . [insisting that] it embraced larger objectives than special privilege." The committee did advocate family assistance programs and child-care facilities to support women workers, but only for the duration of the war, since women were only temporarily abandoning their private domestic and moral sphere for patriotic purposes. The 1952 report by the Women's Bureau on the work of the advisory committee during the war insisted that the self-limiting nature of the recommendations for improved conditions for women "should set at rest

the alarm of those who wince at the memory of objectives as-
cribed to the early feminists as seeking to usurp the traditional
masculine role or seeking special privileges which have no justification."[52] This is affirmative culture at its best. Members of the
social body ascribe to an ideational "good, true, and beautiful"
that is unrelated to and requires a blindness to actual conditions
of life in order to achieve a culturally defined and politically motivated happiness.[53]

Minorities were in the position of having achieved higher
socioeconomic value through wartime needs for their labor and
a new degree of collective self-awareness as reflected in increasingly active civil rights organizations. But their white male and
female audience was determinedly resistant to the political implications of the necessary emergence of minorities to a more
equal and visible military and socioeconomic presence. Demo-
bilized black soldiers and blacks displaced by returning white
workers found themselves back in the patterns and practices of
segregation and discrimination. They faced a sharp upsurge in
local, systematic efforts—including sanctioned threats, blatant illegalities, terrorism, burnings, bombings, shotgun murders, and
lynchings—to deprive them of the political and social rights implied by their use as equals during the war.

National and local civil rights organizations did ground-break-
ing work in establishing larger collective self-awareness and effective patterns of protest and resistance. A. Philip Randolph,
who as leader of the Brotherhood of Sleeping Car Porters had
conceived and established the March on Washington Movement
in 1941 to call for fair employment practices in all defense industries, mobilized college students all over the country in 1947
for a black antidraft movement that forced Truman to desegregate
the armed forces. The Urban League and NAACP fought restrictive
housing covenants and urban renewal; CORE organized sit-ins
and boycotts; and local communities attempted voter registration
drives despite threats and violence.

In 1946 Truman created a Committee on Civil Rights, which
recommended a permanent Commission on Civil Rights and legislation against lynching and voting discrimination, but the program expired without legislative action. Without legislative or

judicial backing, the crucial equation articulated by the committee between inequality and segregation had no power to challenge existing structures of racism. So much for white masculist, liberal reform: minorities had still ahead of them the task of their own constitutional self-empowerment and the achievement of an active role in establishing national political and social agendas.[54]

The scientists' commodification and cancellation as challenging and mediatory voices I discuss more fully in chapter 2 in an analysis of the production of secrecy, a key motivating and enabling term for the official Rosenberg story. The scientists had been virtually eliminated as effective voices in policy deliberations by 1949 when the Soviet Union exploded its first atomic test bomb. The eloquence and informed intelligence of their appeals for international cooperation and negotiations, as well as those of informed policy advisers like George Kennan and Henry Stimson, were overridden by the military and political proponents of secrecy and protective ownership as the only adequate response to the possession by the United States of atomic bomb technology. The ensuing competitive strategies of secrecy, deterrence, massive retaliation, and mutual assured destruction (MAD) had their origins in this competitive ownership model. Thus the official adoption of a capitalist, national security state model for arms production and control as the alternative, even for a few crucial years, to international cooperation and negotiations labeled as Communist-inspired became a long-term and not-yet-finished domestic disaster for all competing countries.

Farmers, lacking the means and numbers for organized political power proportionate to their socioeconomic function, and despite increasing marginalization by processing, marketing, banking, and other business operations, were beginning in 1945 to turn to conservatives for the protection of their interests. This alliance has its own contradictions, as well as potentials for long-term diminishing returns, but in the postwar period it meant the absence of any postwar program for food production and distribution that might oppose the costly and counterproductive dominant ideas of maximum national output—overproduction—

and ever-expanding markets. The theoretically rational operations of a national capitalist and protectionist production system
for a global market—even with the attempted corrections of a
regulated market—have proven to be an especially irrational formula for food production and distribution, domestically as well
as internationally.

Official blindness to the presence of these groups, and deaf-
ness to their voices, even within left organizations left the way
clear for traditional white masculist methods of decision and consensus making. Postwar policy was formulated almost entirely
without the complications and ethical or political imperatives of
feminist perspectives, minority nationalist and internationalist
class and ethnic sympathies, scientific global and collaborative
perspectives, or the anticapitalist (but not nostalgic) logic required for the maintenance and protection of perishable or de-
pletable resources. The ideological adversaries that remained
were a configuration of business and industry, the military, Republicans, the FBI, and HUAC facing the Democratic administration and party membership, liberals, the organized left, labor,
socialists, and Communists. The print media and radio had for
some time thrown in their lots with their owners, abandoning
entirely a practice by some journalists in the 1920s and 1930s of
investigative and polemical critical journalism. But many Democratic and Republican policymakers and advisers, politicians, artists, intellectuals, and educators—interested and informed people
without rigid affiliations to already articulated right or left positions—were in a still mediatory position in the brief struggle for
the nation's postwar agenda.

There was also the unmeasurable, unmanageable, and unpredictable voice of the people, those hypothesized unorganized
masses with intermittently activated self- and political awareness.
There is always a latent potentiality for an effective intervention
and mediation by the people, as evidenced in the civil rights,
student, antiwar, feminist, consumer, and environmental movements of the 1960s, 1970s, 1980s, and 1990s, and most recently
in the democratic national liberation uprisings in Eastern and
Central Europe and the Soviet Union. More often, however, the
people play a political role by and large unwittingly; they act as

an ideal audience for the dominant national narrative and work by themselves, producing and reproducing specific relationships without realizing it.[55] Nevertheless, in the immediate postwar re-working of domestic socioeconomic relationships, the people possessed a volatile coalition potential like that of unbonded chemicals, unpredictably valuable or threatening to right and left.

With public politics as the stage upon which the argument and its resolution in cold war ideology took place, it is possible to see how conservative interests seized and rhetorically organized—metaphorized, polarized, and dramatized—the historical circum-stances and their clusters of ideas in order to protect and promote a program that would guard and foster specific economic and po-litical interests against the perceived Soviet threat to free enter-prise and national economic expansion. It is also possible to see, in retrospect, that the conservative cold war narrative—whatever else it was intended to accomplish—made possible precisely what Eisenhower warned against, too late, in his farewell address: the unprecedented development, expansion, and hegemony of U.S. business and military interests worldwide. The basic elements of the cold war perfecting myth were effectively in place by 1947; its costly narrative fulfillment in global material history will reach into the twenty-first century.

Chronology

(Asterisk denotes events primarily or significantly linguistic in nature.)

1917   *United States enters WWI with Wilsonian goals of saving the world for democracy and instituting per-manent global peace.

Bolsheviks revolt in Soviet Union.

Wilson-Brandeis efforts to prevent U.S. economic and political consolidation as a business oligarchy.[56]

U.S. Espionage Act passed.

1918   U.S. Sedition Act passed.

United States participates in Western powers' anti-Bolshevik invasion of Russia.

U.S. antilabor Red Scare and Palmer Raids.

1919   *At Third International Comintern Stalin declares: "the Third International is the International of open mass action of revolutionary realization. Socialist criticism has sufficiently stigmatized the bourgeois world order. The aim of the International Communist Party is to overthrow it and raise in its place the structure of the socialist order."[57]

1924   J. Edgar Hoover is named Director of FBI.

1930–40s *U.S. New Deal is called Communist by opponents.

1933   United States recognizes Soviet Union.

Moscow directs Communist party Popular Front political and cultural alliances worldwide.

1936–38 Stalin eliminates 6 million officials and intellectuals through institutionalization, imprisonment, work camps, and murder.

1938   Congress establishes U.S. House Un-American Activities Committee to identify internal Nazi and Communist subversives.

1939   *Nazi-Soviet Non-Aggression Pact signed.

Germany invades Poland.

Soviet Union participates in partition of Poland, annexes Latvia, Lithuania, and Estonia, and invades Finland.

1940   U.S. Alien Registration Act (Smith Act) passed.

1941   Germany invades Russia.

Soviet Union joins Allies and U.S. Lend-Lease program.

Japan attacks U.S. fleet in Pearl Harbor; United States declares war.

1942–45 *U.S. government, media, and entertainment industries disseminate pro-Soviet propaganda.

1943   *At Tehran Conference Stalin, Churchill, and Roosevelt disagree over postwar "spheres of influence" or
"universal democracy" as governing concept for occupied territories.

1944   After two-year delay, Allies open second (western)
front to relieve Russia from German occupation and
siege.[58]

Moscow-exiled Polish government is installed in
Poland despite Allied insistence on democracy.

Stalin and Churchill, with Roosevelt's accord, agree
informally on areas and percentages for Soviet and
Western spheres of influence in postwar Europe and
Asia.

1945   Soviet Union requests $6 billion from United States
for reconstruction after war devastation.[59]

At Yalta Conference Soviet Union is granted effective control over Poland, but Stalin, Churchill, and
Truman fail to resolve differences over national interests in or moral universalism toward occupied
territories.

Roosevelt dies; Truman becomes president with limited knowledge of Roosevelt's international objectives and understandings.

*U.S. domestic policy debate continues and intensi-
fies over national or global nature of Soviet
objectives.

Germany surrenders unconditionally; Red Army oc-
cupies Eastern half of Germany and Berlin, as well
as all East European capitals except Athens and
Belgrade.

Truman signs executive order halting Lend-Lease aid
to the Soviet Union.

At Potsdam Conference Stalin, Churchill, and Truman set German reparations by zone and Polish
border at the Niesse, agree on U.S. hegemony in

Italy and Japan, and sign contradictory accord on treaties with the "recognized democratic governments" of Rumania, Bulgaria, and Hungary.

At time of Potsdam Conference first U.S. atomic test explosion is conducted at Alamogordo.[60]

United States explodes atomic bombs over Hiroshima and Nagasaki; Japan surrenders unconditionally.

At Foreign Ministers' Conference to establish protocols for implementation of Potsdam agreements, United States refuses to recognize Balkan countries.

Truman warns against interference by any non-American power in affairs of the nations of North, Central, and South America.

United States claims islands in Pacific for national security and exclusive responsibility for Japan.

State Department claims to have lost $6 billion loan request from Soviet Union and defers indefinitely any consideration of Soviet reconstruction aid.[61]

At Moscow Three Power Conference, Soviet Union agrees to include non-Communists in Rumanian and Bulgarian cabinets, endorses plan for U.N. Atomic Energy Commission, agrees to U.S. troops in China and Korean reunification plan.[62]

*Secretary of State James Byrnes is accused of appeasement for treating Soviet Union as an equal with legitimate national interests.

Canadian prime minister informs Truman of possibility of Soviet atomic espionage network in the United Kingdom, Canada, and the United States.

Eberstadt Report proposes permanent institutional coordination of all U.S. political, military, and economic resources to protect national security.

*Truman's Navy Day speech insists on principles of righteousness in foreign policy and claims U.S. possession of the atomic bomb as a "sacred trust."

1946   *Saying "I'm tired of babying the Soviets," Truman declares intention of facing Russia with an "iron fist and strong language," a decision he later regards as "the point of departure of our [postwar foreign] policy."[63]

U.S. policy advisers and scientists urge open communications with Soviet Union to avoid arms war.[64]

Stalin's speech cites capitalist contradictions as cause of WWII and announces Five Year Plan for national reconstruction as Soviet priority.

Report by Joint Intelligence Committee describes national security, rather than world revolution, as ultimate Soviet goal.

*George Kennan's Long Telegram diagnoses the Russian national personality as that of an "unruly and unreasonable individual," incapable of "objective analysis" of the world, "impervious to logic of reason," "highly sensitive to logic of force," and bent on destroying "our traditional way of life." Kennan recommends realistic diplomacy, public education, and development of domestic strength and integrity to avoid "hysterical anti-sovietism."[65]

*Churchill delivers "iron curtain" speech in Missouri, claiming God as U.S.-U.K. protector.[66]

*Justice William O. Douglas calls Stalin's February speech and Stalin calls Churchill's iron curtain speech declarations of war.

First postwar crisis, Soviet Union failure to withdraw troops from Northern Iran by March deadline, ends when troops begin moving out as Soviets negotiate oil concessions with Iranian government.

At Paris Council of Foreign Ministers Soviet Union argues for reparations from Germany, while United States argues for demilitarization and, finally, division of Germany.

McMahon-Douglas Atomic Energy Act passed.

*Soviet Union delivers note to Turkey calling for joint control of Dardanelle Straits, per Churchill-Stalin agreements in 1944 and at Yalta and Potsdam. Stalin cites Western control of Suez, Gibraltar, and Panama as comparable national interests. Truman and Acheson interpret Soviet note as beginning of Soviet move through Middle East to India and China.

State Department ends consideration of reconstruction aid or credit to Russia and withdraws $50 million credit to Czechoslovakia for purchase of U.S. surplus materials.

Secretary of War Robert Patterson proposes government funding of long-term basic research and a systematic effort to integrate industry and academe with defense by awarding grant and contract funds sufficient to "maintain a minimum [defense] production potential."[67]

*Clark Clifford memorandum to Truman summarizes complete agreement among top officials (except for Henry Wallace) on global aggressive nature of Soviet aims and capabilities as outlined in Kennan's 1946 telegram. In response the United States "must conduct a global policy and not expect to advance our interests by treating each question on its apparent merits as it arises," according to State Department.[68]

Union activism and strikes spread throughout major U.S. industries.

Truman proposes draft labor bill.

Truman replaces Roosevelt cabinet with conservatives.

*Republican party adopts "Republicanism vs. Communism" as slogan for congressional campaigns.[69]

*U.S. National Association of Manufacturers allocates $6 million for anticommunist publicity.

*U.S. Chamber of Commerce produces and distributes anticommunist publications with FBI assistance.

First Republican congressional victory in 16 years includes election of Richard Nixon and Joseph McCarthy.

Air Force and Army intelligence assess limited Soviet air and ground strength as offering minimal threat to U.S. security.

1947   Western powers sign peace treaties with Italy, Rumania, Bulgaria, Hungary, and Finland in final post-war effort toward a negotiated peace among the Great Powers.

*Secretary of State Byrnes's resignation is accepted; General George C. Marshall takes his place. State Department briefing paper to Marshall on Soviet intentions misquotes Lenin as having called for "one step back, two steps forward" and recommends global U.S. policy based on visible military strength.[70]

U.S. antilabor Taft-Hartley act passed.

Britain notifies the United States of its withdrawal of support for Greece as a client state.

*Dean Acheson tells congressional leaders that Soviet breakthrough in Greece will open three continents to Soviet penetration: "Like apples in a barrel infected by the corruption of one rotten one, the corruption of Greece would infect Iran and all to the East."[71]

*Truman presents Truman Doctrine to Congress in order to secure aid for Greek military government: "I believe that it must be the policy of the United States to support free peoples who are resisting attempted subjugation by armed minorities or by outside pressures."[72]

Cominform is established at Warsaw Conference.

*Bernard Baruch coins "cold war" in a speech and characterizes Truman Doctrine as "a declaration of ideological or religious war."[73]

*Truman issues Executive Order 9835, the Loyalty Oath order.

In Harvard commencement address secretary of state announces Marshall plan for economic aid to war-devastated countries.

U.S. National Security Act passed establishing the Central Intelligence Agency and the National Security Council.

*Article by Mr. "X" (George Kennan) on containment appears in *Foreign Affairs*.[74]

*Walter Lippmann analyzes unrealistic nature of a global, universalist containment policy.[75]

*HUAC hearings begin to identify Communist sympathizers among artists and intellectuals.

Business Week headline reads "New Democracy, New Business. U.S. Drive to Stop Communism Abroad Means Heavy Outlays for Bases, Relief and Reconstruction. But in Return American Business is Bound to Get New Markets Abroad."[76]

Cold War Perfecting Myth

Official closure on the debate over Soviet objectives had been accomplished with the unanimous policy recommendations summarized for Truman in the Clifford memorandum in the September before the 1946 congressional campaigns. What became the public narrative of national purpose was announced as the Truman Doctrine in March 1947 and entitled the cold war—"a religious war"—a few months later by Bernard Baruch. Thus, before the events occurred that are sometimes remembered as the initiating events of the cold war—the Soviet coup in Cze-choslovakia, the Berlin blockade, the Chinese Communist victory led by Mao Zedong, the Soviet atomic test explosion, or the invasion of South Korea by North Korea—the narrative itself was in place.

I argue, from a chronological consideration of events from 1917 to 1947, that the cause-effect sequence for the development of this narrative is neither clear nor direct. In fact, a chronology indicates moments in which language precedes and exceeds ma-terial events, serving in turn as an interpretive framework for those events. When language use manifests this priority in the interpretation of history in the making, a historical analysis of cause and effect must give way to a cultural analysis that depends on a rhetorical analysis of motives—what Kenneth Burke analyzes as the motives of grammar and rhetoric. This kind of analysis, while speculative rather than scientific, is neither mystical nor intuitive. Language gives us away, at least to a close reading that respects the material operations, power, and implications of lan-guage in history.

The chronology above reveals the extent to which material events and intellectual arguments and analyses were both se-lected and selectively ignored from 1945 to 1947 in favor of the development of the interpretive narrative culminating in the Tru-man Doctrine. This development, even as outlined in the chro-nology, leaves itself linguistically open to charges of a rather radical process of denial, splitting, and projection on the part of the United States. The assumptions undergirding the Manichaean myth of apocalyptic struggle between forces of good and evil, evoking the two-sided response in the United States of the cold war in foreign affairs and of anticommunism in domestic affairs, reveal themselves in the language used in the construction of this myth over time:

1. The Soviet Union was developmentally inferior, with the cognitive capabilities of a two-year-old, incapable of objectivity or reason, and responsive only to force.

2. The Soviet Union was dominated by a monolithic mastermind mentality bent on global omnipotence,

with the political and material capability to realize such an ambition.

3. Whether the Soviet Union acted constructively or destructively in its national and international activities, its objective, global domination, was pure and constant.

4. The United States was inherently objective, rational, and moral and furthermore was divinely appointed to fulfill a sacred trust in history to uphold righteousness and justice.

5. Therefore, the United States must subordinate all its interests and those of its people to the implementation of a global mastermind mentality in response to the Soviet Union's global mastermind mentality.

This narrative served simultaneously the multiple functions of means, end, moral rationale, and self-fulfilling prophecy to and for a specific political and economic postwar agenda that achieved its material fulfillment in what we now know as the cold war: the national security state, with foreign policy priority over domestic;[77] massive military development and build-up; overt and covert nondemocratic political, economic, military, and cultural intervention in and manipulation of the affairs of other nations; and the most effective and enduring dispersal and silencing of dissent in a (legally) totally enfranchised and constitutional democracy in history—all in the name of a universal moral imperative for global democracy, freedom, and peace.

But because one of the arguments critical of the formulation of cold war policy maintains that the United States was unable to deal in real power concepts, how can we imagine an alternative postwar narrative and its historical fulfillment—one that might more accurately have reflected U.S. material interests? George Kennan, who first instituted and then objected to the totalizing claims and moral universalism of the developing cold war narrative, argued in a 1948 secret State Department memorandum the importance of policy and practice based instead on realistic local assessments of other national interests, and expressed in realistic self-interested power concepts:

We have about 50% of the world's wealth, but only 6.3% of its population. In this situation we cannot fail to be the object of envy and resentment. Our real task in the coming period is to devise a pattern of relationships which will permit us to maintain this position of disparity without positive detriment to our national security. To do so, we will have to dispense with all sentimentality and daydreaming and our attention will have to be concentrated everywhere on our immediate national objectives. We need not deceive ourselves that we can afford today the luxury of altruism and world-benefaction. We should cease to talk about vague and unreal objectives such as human rights, the raising of living standards and democratization. The day is not far off when we are going to have to deal in straight power concepts. The less we are then hampered by idealistic slogans the better.[78]

Kennan's forthright analysis contains and expresses the central contradiction which made it necessary in the first place for the government to resort to a mythic and moral narrative resolution in the pursuit of its policies: the masculist-capitalist assumption that the long-term interests of the United States could and would best be served by policy directed toward the global maintenance of its "position of [economic] disparity." His analysis also effects an unexamined privileging of foreign over domestic policy and reveals a blindness to what were quite real material domestic needs. These included the protection of civil rights as expressed in specific practices such as voting and fair employment;[79] the raising of living standards for the third of the population still poor in the world's richest nation; and democratization of the world's model for democracy, the racist and sexist U.S. political economy—all of which, measured against actual daily U.S. sociopolitical and economic life or invoked as universal imperatives for the world, Kennan cynically but accurately recognized as "idealistic slogans." The cold war perfecting myth that prevailed over Kennan's advice thus morally and abstractly transcended the real contradiction in the polity that the material interests of those empowered to articulate "national interests" were consistent with neither democracy, freedom, nor peace.

Anticommunism and the End of Dissent

The splitting off and projecting of all ideas of political, social, and economic abuse onto an evil other made possible a national myth of moral purpose and an increasingly subsuming priority of foreign over domestic policy. It also provided the most effective means of silencing the expression and analysis of domestic needs and the criticism of and dissent from existing and developing policy ever practiced in a constitutional democracy: anticommunism. Such a massive projection of all that was undesirable or evil in civil society onto the Soviet Union established a Manichaean structure of difference and exclusion that could be manipulated linguistically to absorb all internal political opposition—legally, illegally, and through the production of self-censorship through fear. The major task for conservatives in their drive to achieve control of national policy was to identify with the demonized other all groups or individuals dissenting from their program. The task in retrospect was relatively simple.

The Republicans formulated anticommunism as the primary political strategy in their successful initiative for the recovery of national power in the elections of 1946. The theme for the congressional elections that year was "Republicanism versus Communism," an asymmetrical moralizing and polarizing slogan whose value conservative groups were quick to realize and utilize. The successes of the 1946 election established anticommunism, in various permutations, as a permanent conservative strategy for acquiring and securing political power for the rest of the century.

The history of the postwar reformulation and instrumentalization of anticommunism as a highly effective conservative political weapon is primarily that of a rhetorical operation staged at the public, party politics level. This operation could not have flourished as it did without the supporting development of a national security state and its judiciary; but the national security state and its judiciary could not have developed without a supporting anticommunism. The linguistic operation necessary to unify all groups sympathetic to or willing to forgo criticism of the conservative agenda, and to silence all others, was that of linking—asserting similarity or identity between nonidentical groups and individuals. The construction of a potentially infinite series of linked terms depended upon an initial and crucial identification of domestic communism with treason.

Richard Nixon's 1948 dramatically staged and televised display of the "pumpkin papers" he had secured as evidence in the Communist espionage case against Alger Hiss prepared a popular audience for the widespread official use of the Communist-treason connection.[80] Hiss's conviction after a second trial in 1950, though only for perjury for having denied knowing the self-confessed Soviet espionage agent Whittaker Chambers, seemed to affirm the connection: Communists were potential traitors serving the interests of a hostile and aggressive world antagonist.

The extension of the primary link between communism and treason to equate treason with dissent was accomplished by an incremental and mutual interplay of rhetoric and events. The linkage of dissent with treason was questionably but legally established by government witness Louis Budenz and Judge Harold Medina in the trial and conviction of eleven Communist party leaders in 1949 for "intent to overthrow the government," despite his testimony against the Communist party members' having referred only to their statements of belief, not to incitements to action.[81] This linkage made possible an inferred tautology, a circularity of the terms *Communist-treason-dissent* that established, in a sleight of words in the form of a false syllogism, an identity between dissent and communism: if all Communists are traitors, and traitors are also dissenters, then all dissenters are Communists.[82]

But long before the communist—treason—dissent connection had been juridically established, Republicans and other conservatives, Hoover and the FBI Crime Records Division, HUAC, and the media were making it real in daily language use in speeches, popular articles, press releases, newspaper articles, and public hearings. Political and business leaders began a practice of programmatic serialization by incremental translations and shifts from one order of terms to another, rhetorically changing discontinuities and non sequiturs into continuities and tautologies.[83] By positing arbitrary connections as a logical and natural series, it was possible eventually to assert identity between communism and any groups dissenting from or likely to dissent from the conservative agenda: labor; the organized left; radicals; liberals; Democrats; Jews; non-native-born citizens; aliens; proponents of and organizations devoted to civil rights and women's rights; social reformers and activists of any kind; and artists, intellectuals, and educators.

These identifications produced political and social ostracism, loss of employment, and ruined careers, but they also worked to fragment organized and unorganized groups from within. Defensive behaviors of self-imposed censorship and of leadership and membership purges rendered such organizations even more vulnerable to manipulation and control. Each one of the silenced groups has its own history in the face of mounting anticommunism, but it is revealing to analyze these political histories from a rhetorical point of view. In this way it is possible to see words being used to impose arbitrary and polarized values upon a range of complex and socially situated beliefs and behaviors with the result that individuals and entire groups become silent and withdraw from the argument—without legal coercion—in order to dissociate themselves from those pejorative and politically dangerous words.[84]

The first to succumb to anticommunism were those dissenting voices with the greatest organized power and also the greatest political vulnerability: the Democratic administration and labor, followed closely by liberals, the left, former Communists and the CPUSA, and artists, educators, and intellectuals.

The Democratic administration and liberals. The Truman administration came out of the war facing the enormous responsibility of articulating domestic and foreign policy. The Republicans rearticulated this charge almost immediately into a challenge over the control of domestic political power, a task requiring a different expenditure of energies from those of policy-making and implementing. In this case the Democratic position quickly and perhaps unnecessarily became defensive. Despite Truman's liberal rhetoric, by February of 1946 he had replaced Roosevelt's cabinet with conservatives, except for Secretary of Commerce Henry Wallace, for whose resignation he asked in

September of that year when Wallace remained critical of developing foreign policy.

The conservative and Republican strategy increasingly subjected the administration to a squeeze play between the left and the right, thus keeping it off balance and pushing it into contradictory positions and actions that were ultimately self-destructive. Business organizations like the Chamber of Commerce played a major anticommunist role in the successful 1946 "Republicanism versus Communism" congressional campaign. In September 1946, just before the midterm elections, the Chamber distributed 683,000 copies of its *Communist Infiltration in the United States,* written with the assistance of the FBI, and in January 1947 a revised report called *Communists within the Government* appeared, followed by *Communists within Labor.*[85] In December 1946 the National Association of Manufacturers allocated $6 million for anticommunist advertisements and continued to spend several million dollars a year to reinforce the idea that labor's program was Moscow directed.[86]

The Republican victory of 1946 included the elections of Nixon and McCarthy to the House and the Senate, and the campaign worked effectively to establish the syllogism of liberals as red. By 1947 liberal anticommunists, New Dealers, and labor anticommunists had reformed themselves into the anticommunist Americans for Democratic Action, in support of Truman's foreign policy. Michael Rogin suggests that Democrats and liberals had a weakened will to resist the onslaught of anticommunism. They were having to adjust to the loss of the Popular Front, the New Deal, and the wartime Soviet alliance by developing new attitudes and policies. But at the same time the old Popular Front forms of thought made them feel vaguely guilty of accusations by anticommunists, and thus both vulnerable to and eager to avoid attack.[87]

Truman's response to Republican charges of softness toward communism was rapid, in preparation for the 1948 presidential campaign. He set up in November 1946 the Commission on Employee Loyalty to suggest bipartisan ways of dealing with the alleged Communists in government. This resulted in the March 1947 Executive Order 9835, instituting the Federal Employee

Loyalty Program and creating a board with unchecked powers to investigate employees for loyalty. Loyalty was the first of several crucial secondary and supporting key terms in the elaboration of anticommunism. It was a concept, like patriotism, without content and impossible to define, discoverable only through disclaimers regarding arbitrarily defined breaches. Under Executive Order 9835 loyalty could only be enacted through written denial under oath of affiliation with organizations suspected of being on the left and thus vulnerable to Communist infiltration.

The concept of loyalty generated the production of the list. The Loyalty Order empowered Attorney General Tom Clark to use the list as a rhetorical and practical method for linking left organizations to communism and treason and thus for containing dissent through prosecution. These powers were extended by the McCarran Internal Security Act in 1950, a successful repetition of the unsuccessful 1948 Mundt-Nixon bill requiring registration of all Communist party members *as well as members of all listed organizations.* With the introduction of this extra-legal list, Hoover's long-term accumulation of secret files on people and organizations likely to commit espionage came into play, *likely* being a linking word itself, rhetorically and subjectively establishing identity between two nonidentical entities.

Lists were crucial to McCarthy's method of publicly linking and implicating individual names in shifting and unreliable quantities with little respect for facts or human beings. Over four million federal employees were eventually checked for loyalty, resulting in the loss of jobs by 378 people, with no evidence in any instance of any form of espionage. The accomplishment of the Loyalty Order was not to be found in these numbers; it lay in the production of an empty discriminatory concept, "Loyalty." By 1950 there were loyalty oath ordinances in thirty-three states as well as in innumerable local communities, the effects of which were to create a pervasive atmosphere of fear inhibiting the articulation and exchange of critical thought among the citizenry at large.[88]

By 1946 Truman had irrevocably cast his lot with conservative anticommunists in an attempt to maintain his position. In the

1948 presidential campaign he effectively displaced any remaining taint of liberalism/communism onto Henry Wallace and his third-party Progressives, while moving rhetorically to the left himself in favor of labor gains, civil rights, and a Vinson peace mission to Moscow. This move proved to be solely a rhetorical strategy. Following the election Truman's administration became instead increasingly probusiness, hostile to labor and civil rights, and aggressive in cold war foreign policy. In the 1952 presidential election, Truman's government was replaced by business conservatives under Eisenhower.

Labor and the activist left. Within labor organizations the pressures were great to consolidate their wartime gains and to transform expanded formal and instrumental relationships into positions of real authority and political power commensurate with their function in the postwar economy. They required leadership and programs that focused on domestic workplace and social issues, and once the fixed wages of wartime were lifted, they needed to negotiate new contracts with management providing for worker participation in the postwar national prosperity.

Three factors undermined the political strength derived from their actual role in national productivity. One was the tenacity of a vertical and corporatist mentality among labor leaders. Postwar corporate policies of liberal paternalism undercut wartime and postwar organizational efforts toward a more horizontal transcorporate collective awareness and activism. Another was organized labor's postwar return to and intensification of exclusionary practices toward female and minority workers. These bad-faith practices, producing internal distrust and hostilities, further fractured labor's position. Finally, labor was also caught in the same squeeze play as the Democratic administration, between conservative business and industrial interests and what was being elaborated as the left and Communist threat to domestic security. The conservative purpose was to win labor's uncritical partnership with business and government for the cold war, meaning for military production, expansion into foreign markets, and the Marshall Plan for reconstruction aid to Western Europe—all of which meant a focus away from labor's real issues in favor of a continuing "sacrifice for unity" rhetoric of the war years.

The year 1946 was the year of confrontation. After bargaining failed, railroad, mine, maritime, automobile, electrical, and steel workers scheduled and began strikes in what was to become the greatest period of assertion to date of demands based on labor's actual and crucial socioeconomic position in the United States. Truman responded with a draft labor bill in May 1946, authorizing government seizure of vital industries and the imprisonment of striking union leaders, and he established fact-finding committees to take over bargaining when such action was deemed necessary by the government. The media had established the link between labor's requirements, strikes, and communism in hyperbolic headlines during the Red Scare of the 1920s. Now that rhetorical connection was again established in mainstream publications. The rhetorical linking of the left with communism mitigated the effects of the few remaining leadership voices encouraging labor to hold to its own purposes.

The Communist party under William Z. Foster's hard-line leadership was in effect complicit with the conservative antilabor program, for in maintaining allegiance to Moscow, it offered neither practical, political support to workers—the people it was theoretically designed to serve—nor a realistic alternative to a conservative partnership between business and labor. Labor thus began, with the help of its own major leaders and despite important and local exceptions, to reorganize itself for a collaboration with business and industry in the form of corporate paternalism. It jettisoned workplace and management-sharing issues in favor of wage packages, removed Communists from boards and positions of leadership, voted anticommunist and antisocialist resolutions, and gave discretion over local funds and bargaining positions to central authorities.

Truman's actions and the 1947 passage of the Taft-Hartley Act, to which labor failed to mount effective opposition, promoted a relatively rapid collapse of the autonomy of labor despite its quantifiable position of bargaining strength with management. Taft-Hartley eliminated closed shops, allowed presidential use of injunctions, and banned sympathy strikes, mass picketing, and secondary boycotts, undercutting and fracturing labor solidarity entirely. It also made unions responsible for damages by wildcat strikers, forcing unions to police their own workers. Section 9-H required that all union officers sign annual affidavits disavowing Communist party membership or beliefs. With the confusion of Communist and prolabor beliefs operative by 1947, 9-H produced a degree of self-censorship that deprived the remaining independent and dissenting voices of any effective political base.

Labor leadership cooperated with Taft-Hartley requirements and restrictions, using cold war production needs for labor-management unity as the rationale for its actions. Business had found a way to have the economic benefits and controls of a war without a war, by rhetorical construction. Walter Reuther erased the Communist-associated left from the United Auto Workers (UAW) board by 1947, and CIO president Philip Murray had Secretary of State George Marshall—the articulator of the Marshall Plan for European reconstruction aid—as the keynote speaker for the annual convention that same year. By the 1948 convention the CIO was actively silencing and eliminating effective left membership; Reuther demanded of delegates attending that convention, in the same specious rhetoric as that of the "Republicanism versus Communism" slogan, "Are you going to be loyal to the CIO or loyal to the Communist Party?"[89]

By 1950 eleven major unions had significantly reduced active left membership, and all workers had been successfully deprived, by legislation, executive actions, and the defection of their own leaders, of an opportunity to construct a working partnership with management, in a relationship that reflected labor's actual contributions to productivity rather than hegemonic power relationships based on paternalistic exploitation of workers by management. By 1953 overall union membership was below five million, and when the CIO merged with the American Federation of Labor (AFL) in 1955 national union membership was still declining in relative terms; in the early 1990s it was down to 10 percent of the private work force.[90]

The Communist party. The Communist party played an unwitting role in the eradication of dissent from the unions. The unions provided the party with a power base, its only chance for effective participation in the U.S. political process. But under William Z. Foster's leadership the party had maintained a rigid stance since the spring of 1945: opposition to the cold war and the Marshall Plan, and no deviation from the Stalinist internationalist line. Foster's intransigence isolated it from all forms of practical domestic politics and made the party a relatively easy victim of domestic anticommunist silencing tactics. Foster began his own internal purges for "white chauvinism" in 1948 and took the leadership underground after the conviction of eleven party leaders in 1949, thus eliminating the CPUSA from the domestic scene.

Artists, educators, and intellectuals. HUAC began its Hollywood hearings in 1947, the first move of an extended national assault against artists, educators, and intellectuals. Many of these people were willing to face psychological and economic hardships for themselves and their families in order to maintain the principle and substance of their intellectual freedom. On the other hand, the extent to which many artists and intellectuals converted to patriotic ex- and anticommunism, not only through fear, evasion, or even threatened loss of a job, but also through a high-principled conviction based on bitter disillusionment with Stalinism, requires a complex historical imagination to comprehend.

As a political forum for their intellectual and cultural work after 1950 many ex-Communist intellectuals chose the American Committee for Cultural Freedom and its parent organization, the Congress for Cultural Freedom—a non-grass-roots organization of artists and intellectuals that later was found to have been initiated and funded by the CIA. The shift, especially by New York Jewish intellectuals, from radical left critical work to pro-American affirmations of extreme cold war rhetoric and policies was a product of the conjuncture of the Holocaust and Stalinism with U.S. government and media terrorism against the left, especially the non-native-born left.

These ex-Communists chose to align themselves actively and eloquently with "our country and our culture" as a defensive move not unlike that of many Democrats, liberals, and union members.[91] They engaged in anticommunist rhetorical attacks against former colleagues, while retaining the appearance if not the reality of doing critical work. Their attempts to continue their work as artists and intellectuals in the service of their country were compromised by a defensive allegiance that blinded them to the official oppressions and abuses that were occurring in "our country." By defining totalitarianism and communism as dialectical elaborations of liberalism, they made a putatively logical connection reinforcing the same rhetorical connections being established by conservative anticommunists, thus playing into the hands of the larger betrayal by a constitutional government of its own people.[92]

Some, like Irving Howe and Lewis Coser, cofounders of the journal *Dissent,* managed eventually to maintain a more critical distance from compromising alignments, thus keeping open a space for ongoing argument.[93] There were other men and women called before HUAC or loyalty boards who spoke truthfully and went to jail for refusing to implicate their associates; many lost their jobs over loyalty issues. Others, wittingly or unwittingly, depoliticized their beliefs and practices through a formalistically interpreted abstract expressionism in the visual arts, New Criticism in literature, phenomenology and existentialism in philosophy, and a claim to rigorous objectivity in the social and natural sciences. This voluntary withdrawal of intellectual work from the public and political realms enabled an increasing business, industrial, military, and academic commodification of education, critical work, the arts, and theoretical science during the second half of the twentieth century.[94]

A conservative constellation of anticommunist or depoliticized interests and voices was positioned for control of government by the time McCarthy inaugurated his career on February 9, 1950, in a talk to the Republican Women's Club in Wheeling, West Virginia: "I hold here in my hand a list" of 205, or 57, or 81— the exact number varied in reports—names of State Department employees "who have been named as members of the Communist Party *and* members of a spy ring" [italics mine].[95] The fundamental political work of organizing the right, excluding or silencing the left, and quashing dissent under the sign of anticommunism had been accomplished by 1950, when 99 percent of people in the United States did not worry about Communists.[96]

Was the production of anticommunism so complete that the people stopped worrying? More probably, commonsense understanding of the populist nature of anticommunism notwithstanding, a pervasive fear of Communists among the people was neither existent nor necessary for a manipulated anticommunism to succeed, at the political leadership level and in electoral politics, in securing conservative control of the construction and implementation of the cold war agenda.

For forty-five years this agenda remained the dominant program for U.S. policy under cover of its humanitarian perfecting myth, regardless of its inadequacy and costs to domestic needs, regardless of the historical conditions of multiple autonomies and local nationalist and often democratic revolutionary movements, and regardless of the disparity between the explanatory rhetoric and the motivations and effects of U.S. actions and interventions in the world. As Freud said about splitting and projection, the cold war has indeed been an extremely costly means of avoiding conflict, cruelly oblivious to past realities as well as blind to present and future possibilities.[97]

2

Embedded Story

Ownership, Secrecy, and Spies

One of the keystones of cold war policy, especially from 1945 to 1949, was the premise that the United States owned the atomic bomb and the secret of its production. This belief made possible an absoluteness that prevailed in the diction and decisions of policymakers during those years. Whether the premise presumed an absoluteness of political power or an absoluteness of military force, it supported reckless talk about possible courses of action for the United States in protecting and pursuing its interests. This premise was also the basis for the death sentences given the Rosenbergs by the trial judge in 1951, as well as for Eisenhower's denial of clemency in 1953.

Ownership is a concept not limited to capitalist nations when it concerns military and industrial technology and production. Ownership of the atomic bomb, however, which involved complicated questions of ownership of collaboratively and internationally generated epistemology and technology, was a concept difficult to maintain in theory as well as in practice. It was maintained, however, in terms of secrecy and monopoly before the Soviet test explosion in 1949, and thereafter in terms of quantitative and qualitative superiority.

The concept was a natural if illogical one—especially in the months immediately following the devastation of Hiroshima and Nagasaki—to the country that had financed and directed the development of the atomic bomb. During the next few years, despite all knowledgeable arguments to the contrary, monopoly ownership and secrecy were represented and used as the political and military keys to U.S. success in the cold war struggle for world dominance in the name of freedom. The country would own and manage this particular piece of epistemology and technology, this time responsibly, in the name of world peace, while preventing the aggressive and demonized other, intent on the conquest of the world, from acquiring it. This public rhetoric of peace masked the diary entries, memoranda, and policy papers that dealt with expected war in terms of preemptive atomic strikes against the Soviet Union.[1]

Ownership and Secrecy

The production of the concepts of ownership and secrecy regarding the bomb has a specific history. After Pearl Harbor, when Roosevelt and his advisers decided to provide the resources for the secret development under military control of a usable atomic bomb, the president did so at the urging of refugee scientists and engineers from Germany and Eastern Europe. These scientists feared a German first use of such a weapon, the basic physics of which had been discovered and published in 1939 by Niels Bohr and Enrico Fermi as part of open, collaborative, international work in atomic physics. Russian scientists had participated in this collaborative effort. In significant numbers Manhattan Project scientists gradually and radically changed their thinking about the military use of atomic energy as they came closer to the realization of their concerted work. During the war and in the immediate postwar period the voices of some of these scientists were among the most urgent and eloquent in the argument over postwar policies.

But placing the scientists under military control and the constraints of absolute secrecy had unforeseen results that militated against their ability to engage persuasively in policy matters. They were effectively commodified by this action, as producers with little say about the conditions or uses of their production. Not only was free and open discussion among the scientists themselves curtailed, but the military and security lines of command cut the scientists off from any kind of exchange with politicians, policymakers, the media, and the public. This secrecy constraint also meant that the politicians and policymakers were deprived of the benefits of open inquiry and critique from informed people outside their policy-making field as crucial decisions were being made.

Most of the scientists recognized the threat to scientific enterprise and the danger to world affairs accomplished by this compartmentalization of their work, but the bomb had been developed at their behest and kept secret in the interests of national security, against which there was no effective argument. So scientists' ability to intervene concerning the uses of their own work—of which only they recognized the full potential—was badly constrained just when the most urgent reasons existed for them to be heard. By the end of the war, when some of the secrecy constraints were lifted and many scientists began to lobby actively for arms control negotiations and international scientific and technological cooperation, their commodification had already succeeded in transforming them—in the minds of politicians and of the public—into political innocents with strictly instrumental and limited value.

They were heard, though—some of them even before the bomb had been developed and tested. Niels Bohr was the foremost among scientists at that time to perceive the institution and practice of science as a "profoundly political force in the world," and among the first to see the full political implications of atomic weapons. Without invitation he actively lobbied Roosevelt and Churchill and other statesmen to persuade them of the radical ways atomic energy would transform world politics. As Robert Oppenheimer explained it, "[Bohr] was clear that one could not have an effective control of . . . atomic energy . . . without a very open world. . . . The very fact that knowledge is itself the basis for civilization points directly to openness as the way to overcome the present crisis."[2] Bohr argued at every opportunity that the atomic bomb was the ultimate occasion for the development of an open world, a recommendation that translated specifically into informing the Russians of the work in progress and involving them in negotiations on postwar arms control. In retrospect he wrote, in 1950, "It appeared to me that the very necessity of a concerted effort to forestall such ominous threats to civilization would offer quite unique opportunities to bridge international divergencies."[3]

Bohr began his urgent diplomatic missions before the bomb had been developed, and he was joined by seven scientists working on the atomic project at the University of Chicago who served on the Metallurgical Laboratory's Committee on Social and Political Implications of Atomic Energy. They issued on June 11, 1945, what became known as the Franck Report in which they emphasized that atomic weapons could not possibly remain a monopoly for more than a few years and urged action toward a postwar international agreement on the control of such weapons. They anticipated that Russia and other nations would have the bomb within a few years, "even if we should make every attempt to conceal [our steps]." After they and other policymakers of like mind had failed to deter Truman from using the bomb on Japan, urging instead a demonstration explosion, they took their appeal to the public. As Selig Hecht of Columbia University said, "If there was one great secret we gave it away in July 1945." The chief assistant to Major Leslie Groves, head of the Manhattan Project, had spoken for all of them when he said after observing the Alamogordo test explosion:

> All seemed to feel that they had been present at the birth of a new age—The Age of Atomic Energy—and felt their profound responsibility to help in guiding into right channels the tremendous forces which had been unlocked for the first time in history.[4]

As this cross section of concerns indicates, the scientists' imperative was one of responsibility, both to the real issues of atomic energy development and to the global community. The critical issue upon which their argument turned was that of secrecy, the key term for the production of the Rosenberg story as well as for the development of the national security state with all its economies and apparatuses of information production. Secrecy—the thing that the scientists agreed did not exist—became the justifying term for the inauguration of a newly systematized deprivation by the federal government of individual rights in the interests of national security. It is particularly revealing to read the documents, letters, and speeches prepared and delivered by the scientists in every available forum following the war; they show the complex realities that had to be masked, obfuscated, and denied rhetorically in order to produce an irrational, tyrannical, and far-reaching concept of secrecy.

The scientists were not alone in their assessment of secrecy as an inadequate and even dangerous concept for explaining policy. In a September 1945 memorandum to the president, Secretary of War Henry L. Stimson, probably the most knowledgeable nonscientist in the administration, noted that without a cooperative agreement with the Russians a secret arms race "of a rather desperate character" would develop; that the Soviet Union would be able to produce bombs on its own; and that our refusal to negotiate would lead to relations between the two countries becoming perhaps "irretrievably embittered." He advised that we agree to pool our knowledge, stop the production of atomic weapons, and "encourage the development of atomic power for peaceful and humanitarian purposes."[5]

In a column that reflected his agreement with Hanson Baldwin of the *New York Times,* Walter Lippmann wrote on October 2, 1945, in the *New York Herald Tribune:*

> If the secret cannot be kept, it is unnecessary to argue whether it ought to be kept. Moreover, it would be in the highest degree dangerous to suppose we were keeping the secret if in fact we were not. For that could only give us, as it has already given many, a false sense of security and a false sense of our own power. . . . How then can we best protect mankind against the terrible possibility of this new scientific knowledge? In the last analysis, only by making the knowledge so universal that it would be impossible for any government to perfect in secret some new devilish application of it. . . . The object of our policy cannot be to keep the secret. That cannot be done. To those who contend that we should guard this secret, we must, I believe, reply that on the contrary the safest course is to guard against its being a secret anywhere.[6]

In December 1945 scientists at Oak Ridge delivered this statement:

> Let no one mistake us; we do not want to give the bomb away.
> Rather we want to take it out of the control of any one
> nation—including our own.[7]

As late as 1949, even after the 1948 Republican congressional victory and after the first Soviet test explosion, Congress's Joint Committee on Atomic Energy acknowledged the fallacy of the secrecy and ownership illusions:

> Actually, the basic knowledge underlying the explosive release
> of atomic energy—and it would fill a library—never has been
> the property of one nation. On the contrary, nuclear physicists
> throughout the world (including those who live behind the iron
> curtain) were thoroughly familiar with the theoretical advances
> which paved the way for practical development of an atomic
> bomb. . . . The Soviet Union, for its part, possesses some of the
> world's most gifted scientists . . . men whose abilities and whose
> understanding of the fundamental physics behind the bomb
> only the unrealistic were prone to underestimate.[8]

An International News Service dispatch datelined Washington, D.C., in December 1949 reported:

> The Atomic Energy Commission Friday bared secret documen-
> tary proof that Russia has known the scientific secrets of the
> Atom-bomb manufacture since 1940, the year the United States
> began attempts to develop the missile.[9]

Truman in his first public statement about the bomb had said that the United States, Great Britain, and Canada "do not intend to reveal the secret."[10] There is documentation that the Truman administration had established the secrecy and ownership policy as a primary operating principle for national security and foreign affairs as early as September 1945.[11] But for the next five years a real discussion appeared to be under way: scientists and journalists published articles, sat on advisory commissions, visited members of Congress and other policymakers, and spoke before civic groups and at colleges and universities. Joined by some policy advisers and government officials, they were successful in the bitter and crucial struggle to secure civilian control of atomic energy development.[12] They continued to speak on behalf of negotiations and open inquiry until the Soviet test explosion in 1949 delivered such a wound to national self-esteem that "responsibility" in the political mind took on the value of stringent security, an opposite value from that of open communications advocated by the scientists.

The immediate response to the Soviet bomb test—chauvinistic, proprietary, and outraged—was a demand to find the spies who had stolen the bomb. The public and policy-making mind had been well prepared, by the monopoly ownership concept, for the narrative of a domestic atomic spy ring. As the scientist Edward U. Condon, the director of the Bureau of Standards, had predicted in 1946:

> It is sinister indeed how one evil step leads to another. Having created an air of suspicion and mistrust, there will be persons among us who think other nations can know nothing except what is learned by espionage. So, when other countries make atom bombs, these persons will cry "treason" at our scientists, for they will find it inconceivable that another country could make a bomb in any other way except by aid from Americans.[15]

The Atomic Spy Ring

The other major component in developing ideal readers for the official Rosenberg story was the rhetorical production of the concept of the Soviet atomic spy ring.[14] Soviet intelligence was of course operative in the United States before, during, and after the war and continues today, as does U.S. intelligence worldwide. But the rhetorical dimensions of the alleged domestic Soviet atomic spy ring, according to any available documents in either country, seem to have far outreached the actual dimensions of Soviet atomic intelligence work.

Soviet intelligence had been directed by Stalin in 1942 to find out the state of weapons development in the United States—especially that of the atomic bomb—and from that time Soviet agents tracked Manhattan Project developments. Even then, Stalin did not place priority on Soviet atomic bomb development, necessarily halted when the Germans invaded Russia, until the two bombs were exploded over Hiroshima and Nagasaki in 1945, when he instructed the director of the Soviet atomic project, physicist Igor Kurchatov: "Provide the bomb—it will remove a great danger to us."[15]

In February 1946 Canadian newspapers reported the sensational story of a Canadian spy ring involved in trading atomic energy secrets. Eventually twenty-six people were named and arrested, six of whom were finally convicted for self-confessed and undocumented acts of minor espionage not having to do with atomic energy.[16] The Canadian prime minister told Parliament five weeks after the story broke, "This espionage business has not arisen out of the atomic bomb in any way or secrecy in connection with it."[17]

In March the British physicist Allan Nunn May, a former member of the Canadian Research Council, confessed when questioned by British Intelligence to having given atomic energy (not atomic bomb) information to a foreign individual on principle, believing that "it was necessary to convey general information on atomic energy and make sure it was taken seriously."[18] It was assumed that May was part of the so-called Canadian atomic spy ring, but no evidence for that has appeared. May had not worked on the atomic bomb, and no scientists—U.S., British, or Canadian—considered it possible that he knew enough to reveal any information about its development. He was sentenced to ten years in prison and served six.

True to its practice of reporting charges and allegations as fact, the U.S. media picked up the Canadian story when it first broke at its most sensational "informed source" stage of narrative and continued to base articles on those claims, ignoring the Canadians' subsequent failure to produce evidence or convictions. The report throughout the United States of this Canadian spy ring, despite neither supporting testimony nor indictments, inaugurated the public narrative of a Soviet atomic espionage network operating in Canada, the United States, and Britain and began the process of a public and strategic linking of the domestic left and Communist party membership with espionage. The day after the story appeared in Canadian papers, a United Press dispatch picked up by newspapers across the United States read:

Rep. John Rankin, Democrat of Mississippi, said tonight that a "Communist spy ring had been uncovered in Canada that extends throughout the U.S. and is working through various

Communist front organizations." Mr. Rankin, a member of the House Committee on Un-American Activities, said the Committee was "on the trail" of the Communist spies.[19]

In the same month, *Time* ran an editorial stating:

> It took no imagination to visualize what kind of a Soviet network was operating in much larger nations, like the U.S. and Britain. One source, in Washington, said that the FBI could crack down at any moment on 1,500 irresponsible secret-peddlers in the U.S. Such a crack-down was probably not far away.[20]

Such a crackdown was quite far away. It has yet to occur. But the notion of a Soviet atomic spy ring became a transcendent concept requiring and generating its own historical narrative fulfillment, while also serving the interests of those whose well-being depended on the promulgation of the cold war. It served the Republicans and HUAC in their battle against Truman, it served Hoover's personal ambitions and paranoias, it served the members of the military who were actively lobbying for war preparations, and it served business and industrial interests whose investments were based on arms escalation.[21] Because the media also served these interests, it was to the media's benefit to keep reporting the story as it was released by the informed sources that represented them, only rarely with any degree of critical awareness. Cyrus Sulzberger reported in the *New York Times* on March 21, 1946:

> The momentum of pro-Soviet feeling worked up during the war to support the Grand Alliance had continued too heavily after the armistice. This made it difficult for the Administration to carry out the stiffer diplomatic policy required now. For this reason . . . a campaign was worked up to obtain a better psychological balance of public opinion to permit the Government to adopt a harder line.

Because of Hoover's rigid and blanket association of Communist party membership with espionage and sabotage, the FBI maintained files on thousands of people discovered to be members of the party and of affiliated organizations. Some FBI files were the product of U.S. intelligence—espionage—and of specific allegations of espionage by former party members. The

HUAC testimony of Whittaker Chambers in 1939 and that of Louis Budenz and Elizabeth Bentley in 1945 greatly exceeded the information developed by Canadian, British, and U.S. intelligence work. But a federal grand jury especially impaneled in 1947 to investigate the hundreds of spies named by Budenz and Bentley disbanded a year later with no indictments. The testimony of Bentley, Budenz, and Chambers may have led Hoover to believe that a gigantic espionage network was operative in the United States following the war, but no such network was then or has been since discovered, and no documents supporting the claim have ever been released, for national security reasons.[22]

In 1956 Attorney General Herbert Brownell at the FBI's suggestion had the Justice Department look into bringing all alleged members of the atomic spy ring before a grand jury where they might be forced to testify under immunity. After investigation of FBI documents, the department concluded that "additional information sufficient to warrant further prosecutive proceedings has not been developed. Investigation of all logical leads has, so far, failed to produce any appreciable results."[23] In 1957 the entire project was abandoned. But in 1946 the idea of an extensive Soviet atomic spy ring operating throughout the United States was active.

By the time of the test explosion of Russia's first atomic bomb in August 1949 the stage was set for the Rosenberg story to develop in the way that it did. The imaginative narrative of U.S. ownership of the secret of the atomic bomb had been rudely interrupted on August 29, 1949, not by the realities of international epistemological and technological development, but by secrecy's counternarrative, red atomic spies. A thoroughly contextualized reading of the ensuing Rosenberg story, with special attention to its managing images, themes, and tones as well as to the metanarrative commentary of FBI documents and relevant historiographies, suggests that the controlling narrative shift for the story was not from the raw data to a coherent story, but the other way around: an organizing principle was imposed on the available data to generate its own supporting narrative. This principle was the complex cold war anticommunist national security state, with all its political, social, and economic determinations.

By 1949 a considerable social complex had begun to make its living from the narrative, economic, and political enactments of this overdetermined and polarizing concept of the national security state: business and industry (the military-industrial complex, the exporting manufacturers, and the media, among others), government agencies and political groups (the internal and external surveillance apparatuses, special congressional committees, Republicans, and other conservative and liberal politicians), and institutions (the legal system to some extent, public education, the Atomic Energy Commission).[24]

In order to dramatize the ways in which ownership and secrecy came into force as organizing principles for the official Rosenberg story, it is worth reviewing some of the high-level and contradictory responses to the first Soviet atomic bomb test. Walter and Miriam Schneir compiled a number of these responses for their Rosenberg history, *Invitation to an Inquest.* Truman's announcement on September 23 of the Soviet test explosion contained this realistic assessment that contradicts his own administration's chosen policy of bomb ownership and secrecy:

> Ever since atomic energy was first released by man, the eventual development of this new force by other nations was to be expected. This probability has always been taken into account by us. Nearly four years ago I pointed out that "scientific opinion appears to be practically unanimous that the essential theoretical knowledge upon which the discovery is based is already widely known. There is also substantial agreement that foreign research can come abreast of our present theoretical knowledge in time."

General Eisenhower agreed with Truman:

> The news we have been given by the President merely confirms scientific predictions. I see no reason why a development that was anticipated years ago should cause any revolutionary change in our thinking or in our actions.

The *New York Times* concurred:

> There is no valid reason for surprise at this development. . . . Only those Americans who failed to pay attention to what was said of the atomic bomb by the men who knew most about

it—namely, the men who made it—could ever have believed that we possessed a permanent and exclusive monopoly of this destructive weapon.

But Senator Karl Mundt's press release stated:

> It now appears that earlier and prevailing laxity in safeguarding this country against Communist espionage has permitted what were once the secrets of our atomic bomb to fall into the hands of America's only potential enemy.[25]

And Representative Richard Nixon of HUAC stated for the media that Russia's atomic know-how was "hastened" by the Truman administration's failure to act against red spies in the United States:

> If the President says the American people are entitled to know all the facts—I feel the American people are also entitled to know the facts about the espionage ring which was responsible for turning over information on the atom bomb to agents of the Russian government.[26]

Hoover's response was to set into operation the FBI machinery to "find the thieves."[27]

The Official Story

Hoover's program for the identification of the unknown spies began in Manhattan and reached to Los Alamos and California. The search for the Unknown Subject, the person responsible for stealing the secret of the atomic bomb, began with the atomic scientists.[28] Among those investigated were Hans Bethe, Richard Feynman, Edward Teller, Victor Weisskopf, Philip Morrison, and George Kistiakowski, some of whom were Nobel Prize recipients for physics and scientific policy advisers to Truman and later to Eisenhower. Several hundred suspects were identified from the wartime Los Alamos project. No espionage activities were found. A concurrent and overlapping investigation began when British Manhattan Project physicist Klaus Fuchs confessed in England in February 1950 to having given the Soviet Union information on the atomic bomb project through a U.S. courier. When the FBI identified a suspect for this role who confessed to being Fuchs's courier, it had the beginning of what would eventually become the official story, the story that would end with the Rosenbergs' deaths.

Early Drafts

The case is a necessary by-product of the atomic age. Let us hope that it will serve to supply the democracies of the world with some significant lessons.
        —*Chief Prosecutor Irving Saypol,* U.S. v. Rosenberg

Choosing a historical or chronological starting point for the story is already a positioned interpretive act, but in keeping with the genre of literary history, I will begin with the first "writing" of the Rosenberg story unfolded in time to a public audience: a list of events in chronological order. The most neutral and apparently transparent form of the story, this chronology is derived from the print media, whose sources were at first news releases from the FBI and the Department of Justice and then observable events. It occludes the ways in which Hoover's press release of Julius Rosenberg's arrest rearranged Julius's words in order to make them appear to be a confession to aiding the Soviet Union, as it occludes all other official and media distortions of the story as it developed. (These distortions are detailed later in this account.) An analysis of the media's role is not my purpose here, although I trust I have argued persuasively that the media uncritically accepted "informed source" news releases as facts, to the despair and detriment of thousands of people.

The media's "neutral" account then necessarily occludes the arbitrary linkages, gaps, contradictions, and denials, as well as the naturalized assumptions, underpinning the chronology.[29] These phenomena have been gradually revealed through historical research, especially as a result of the release of 200,000 FBI documents following legal proceedings by the Rosenberg sons and historian Allen Weinstein against the government under the 1974 Freedom of Information Act. The contradictions, constructed linkages, and purposeful occlusions did not go wholly unnoticed in the period surrounding the trial, appeals, and executions; still, the coherence of the government story in the

larger context of the developing cold war, as well as the interactions of the main actors in the trial (a factor impossible to
account for by reading the trial record), worked successfully to
convince a twelve-person jury that the Rosenbergs were guilty
of conspiracy to commit espionage. The rest, as far as evidence
can be found, is a story of the limitations of legal formalism and
of the excesses to which politics and ideology carried both that
formalism and juridical and moral concepts of justice.

The chronology inscribes within it what Hayden White con-
siders to be the fundamental narrative conflict: it "presupposes
the existence of a legal system against which or on behalf of which
the agents of the narrative account militate."[30] It raises questions
of agency, authority, and legality, as well as of origins, motivations,
selections, articulations, endings, and interpretations.

Chronology

August 6 and 9, 1945: The United States dropped first a
fission and then a fusion bomb, Thin Man and Fat Boy,
on Hiroshima and Nagasaki, with an immediate death toll
of 152,034.

February 15 and 16, 1946: A Canadian spy ring and the
existence of an atomic spy ring in the United States were
announced; Alan Nunn May confessed to having delivered atomic energy information to the Soviet Union.

August 1949: The Communist People's Republic was declared in China.

September 23, 1949: Truman announced that the Soviet
Union had tested its first atomic bomb. J. Edgar Hoover
announced to his staff, "The bomb has been stolen. Find
the thieves."[31]

February 3, 1950: Dr. Klaus Fuchs, German-born British
nuclear physicist who had worked on the atomic bomb
project at Los Alamos as part of the British participation,
voluntarily confessed to having given atomic bomb information to the Soviet Union.

March 1, 1950: Fuchs was tried and sentenced to four-
teen years in prison.

May 23, 1950: The FBI arrested Harry Gold, a Philadelphia chemist, on the basis of his voluntary confession that he had been a courier between Fuchs and a Russian vice-consul.

June 15, 1950: The FBI arrested David Greenglass, formerly a machinist at Los Alamos, for having been an accomplice of Gold in 1945.

June 25, 1950: The Korean War began with North Korea's invasion of South Korea.

July 17, 1950: Julius Rosenberg, David Greenglass's brother-in-law, was arrested for conspiracy to commit espionage with Greenglass and Gold in 1944–45.

August 11, 1950: Julius's wife, Ethel, was arrested on the same charges as her husband.

December 9, 1950: Gold was sentenced to thirty years in prison.

March 6–29, 1951: The trial of the Rosenbergs and another named accomplice, Morton Sobell, was held in Foley Square Courthouse in New York City. The main prosecution witnesses called by the chief prosecutor, Irving Saypol, and his assistant, Roy Cohn, were David and Ruth Greenglass and Harry Gold. Verdict: guilty.

April 5, 1951: Ethel and Julius Rosenberg were sentenced to death by electrocution by Judge Irving R. Kaufman.

April 6, 1951: David Greenglass was sentenced to fifteen years.

February 25, 1952: The Rosenberg-Sobell conviction was affirmed by the U.S. Court of Appeals for the Second Circuit.

February 25, 1952–June 19, 1953: Twenty-three motions and appeals for new trial, reduction of sentence, stay of execution, and presidential clemency were made on the basis of perjury; unfair trial; cruel, excessive, inapplicable, and unprecedented sentencing; newly discovered evidence; subornation of perjury by the prosecution;

application of incorrect law; and justice, mercy, or both. All appeals were denied.

June 19, 1953: Julius and Ethel Rosenberg were electrocuted.

June 20, 1953: Justice Hugo Black's majority opinion was published, noting that the Supreme Court "had never reviewed the record of this trial and therefore never affirmed the fairness of this trial."

A less neutral beginning version of the story is a summary of the government charge, which institutes an unfolding narration of the chronological events. The charge posits a provisional causality and agency for events past and to come. Formally it is still not a story; it is narrated, but it has no closure, explains nothing, and leaves several crucial relationships—legal, narrative, and motivational—unresolved. The charge is a step in the process of elaborating the coherent narrative it ultimately will become. It assumes a legally structured and bounded nation-state and claims a severe threat to and breach of the state's integrity by individual agency, but its incompleteness militates against its narrative authority to constitute and enforce an ending.

Government Charge Summary

In 1944 Julius Rosenberg and his wife, Ethel, persuaded her brother, David Greenglass, and his wife, Ruth, to enter a conspiracy to commit espionage by transmitting atomic secrets to the Soviet Union. The Greenglasses delivered such secrets to the Rosenbergs in 1945. From 1946 to 1949 Julius Rosenberg told his brother-in-law of other espionage he and his spy ring had committed.

Included in the spy ring were two former college classmates of Julius Rosenberg, Max Elitcher and Morton Sobell. Since their part in the conspiracy was not connected to atomic espionage, neither was known as a coconspirator to the Greenglasses.

In 1945 Julius Rosenberg arranged by unknown means with the New York Soviet vice-consul, Anatoli Yakovlev, to send a courier to the Greenglasses in Albuquerque,

New Mexico, to pick up atomic information. Yakovlev sent Harry Gold for this purpose, the latter a self-styled "American partner" of Dr. Klaus Fuchs.

In 1950 after Fuchs, the German-born British atomic scientist, was arrested in England, and after the FBI had subsequently arrested Gold in Philadelphia, the latter implicated David Greenglass. Upon Greenglass's arrest he confessed and implicated his sister and his brother-in-law, as well as his own wife, Ruth.

The Rosenbergs were subsequently arrested, but in the meantime the FBI had obtained from Max Elitcher a confession implicating both Julius Rosenberg and Morton Sobell. The latter, known to be on a trip to Mexico with his family, was arrested in Texas after the Mexican authorities had deported him. The Soviet official, Yakovlev, could not be apprehended because he and his family had returned to the Soviet Union in 1946.[32]

These two versions, a chronology and a synthesis of the government charge, leave us knowing a sequence of events, documented or asserted, as well as aware of much that is not being said. Building on extended interrogations of the principals (Harry Gold, Ruth and David Greenglass) and on the testimony of an ex-Communist government witness and of a Rosenberg associate open to a perjury charge for having falsified his loyalty oath, the FBI was able to develop a fuller and more coherent narrative, an activity that from the beginning was a coordinated and collaborative effort based on the founding assumption of an extensive domestic atomic spy ring.

For example, Klaus Fuchs described his U.S. courier and the approximate dates of their meetings to the FBI agents allowed by the British government to interview him, but when certain clues led to the arrest of a Philadelphia chemist, Harry Gold, and he confessed to being Fuchs's courier, Fuchs altered his statement to fit Gold's.[33] When David Greenglass, who confessed to having given Gold information about the atomic bomb, told a story that did not match Gold's, the FBI interviewed them together in order to coordinate their stories. When the government needed a conviction for Ethel, for whom there was no incriminating evidence,

David and his wife, Ruth, recalled Ethel's participation in the conspiracy, an involvement that they had both repeatedly denied during the previous nine months. Ten days before the trial they remembered that she had typed all the papers passed to the Soviet agents.[34]

It is important to acknowledge that, for better or for worse, this is exactly how the U.S. justice system works to prepare adversarial litigation: through professional questioning of witnesses and informers in order to construct a story that will prevail. What needs to be considered in this case are not so much the systematic procedures of the adversarial process—the legal profession itself produces persuasive critiques of this system—but the various interests served by the production of this particular story, a narrative with a coherence and authority that the Rosenbergs' defense could not mitigate, and against which the Rosenbergs were unable to prevail.

The causes for the failure of the defense are of course multiple and complex and reach into the unknowable, in terms both of the Rosenbergs' own private story and of the evidentiary basis for the government story, documents that allegedly supported Hoover's and the Justice Department's assertions of the existence of a large atomic spy ring headed by Julius Rosenberg. Any such evidence was unavailable to the Rosenberg defense and remains not "available under any circumstances" forty years later and many years after the passage of the Freedom of Information Act in 1974.[35] Hoover's belief in the extensive atomic spy ring was the immediate and primary motivation for the production of the official story, a motive for narrative that I will discuss at length later in this chapter.

Whatever the internal coherence of the government story, the causes for its persuasiveness to the jury and the judges who ruled on it can also be located *outside* the explicit arguments and constructed data of the trial. The diction and imagery of the prosecution and the trial judge, as well as of the appellate judges, link their bases for argument and rationales for judgment not only to testimony, statutory law, rules of procedure and evidence, or precedent, but also to the historical context and frame narrative of the cold war. As a scholar and critic of legal theory and practice concludes:

> The persuasiveness of a story is not the product merely of the arguments it explicitly presents, but of the relationship between those arguments, and other, more tacit, arguments—tantamount to already in place beliefs—that are not so much being urged as they are being traded on. It is this second, recessed, tier of arguments—of beliefs so much a part of the background that they are partly determinative of what will be heard as an argument—that does much of the work of fashioning a persuasive story.[36]

That is, the persuasive story is always an embedded narrative. The purpose of the preceding chapter was to articulate a frame narrative sufficient to the purposes of this analysis of the official Rosenberg story.[37]

Before the narrative motivations, strategies, and anomalies of the official story are laid out, it should be noted that the causes for the inadequacy of the Rosenbergs' own story also rested to some extent in the defendants' more immediate surround, in economic, legal, and political conditions. The Rosenbergs had none of the financial, professional, institutional, legal, political, or media resources available to the prosecution. They were limited financially, politically, and ethnically in their choice of an attorney, as well as in the size of their defense staff; the media were not interested in their story or in their attorney's story; their attorney had limited (effectively, no) ability to call witnesses, while the prosecution had the power to call any officials or scientists conceivably helpful to its case; the prosecution had the full institutional authority and expertise of the FBI and the Justice Department, in consultation with the Atomic Energy Commission (AEC), at its disposal; and finally the judge, in highly irregular ex parte communications with representatives of these institutions, was manipulated into a position of ideological certainty that made him a partisan and active agent in constructing the official story.[38]

In a cruel irony, the Rosenbergs were hampered by their trust and that of their attorney in the forms and practices of U.S. constitutional law and jurisprudence. They had been members of the Communist party and insisted on testing, first, their belief that the Fifth Amendment would work to protect their constitutional rights against self-incrimination concerning a membership that was legal, and, second, their expectation that the Fourteenth

Amendment, assuring each citizen of due process before the law, would ensure a fair trial or recourse to one through the appellate procedure. But in a maneuver later declared unconstitutional, the prosecution rhetorically converted this Fifth Amendment pleading into a sign of guilt, especially where Ethel was concerned.[39] Due process was arguably violated at the trial court and Supreme Court levels in a number of problematic and illegal ways.

In an oral history of his legal career, a former Frankfurter clerk and federal trade commissioner, Philip Elman, comments on the situation regarding the Supreme Court:

> The whole thing was an absolute shambles, a disaster for the Court—as well as the Rosenbergs, of course. Frankfurter wrote a little dissent in which he was writing really to me and to other friends of his, former law clerks, whose whole faith in the Supreme Court had been shaken. We knew the Supreme Court was one institution that worked the way it was supposed to work, where people got a fair shake, where equal justice under law was more than a slogan. And here the whole thing was falling down and we were shattered. This was our court, The Supreme Court of the United States, for which we had feelings of admiration and closeness. And Frankfurter wrote for us: "This isn't the end, errors are inevitably made but you go on, you don't lose faith in the processes of law."[40]

The Rosenbergs' full story, for reasons that are unknowable, never became fully articulated, while the parts they told—containing serious gaps and silences—were inadequate to their defense. And too rarely did they or their attorneys challenge profoundly questionable assertions and equally dubious dramatic strategies of the prosecution or of the trial judge.

Before analyzing specific rhetorical operations in the construction of the official story, I will conclude this introduction to that story with the sentencing speech of the trial judge, Irving Kaufman. The sentencing took place April 5, 1951. At that time, British Los Alamos atomic physicist Klaus Fuchs was serving a fourteen-year prison sentence—the maximum allowed under the British Official Secrets Act—for transmitting to the Soviet Union on four occasions from 1944 to 1946 documents covering Manhattan Project atomic bomb developments. This period included the crucial development of the gaseous diffusion process for U-235 separation, the development of the plutonium bomb design with its implosion lens, and the Alamogordo test explosion of the first atomic bomb. FBI counterintelligence agents had in the summer of 1949 decoded one of the transmitted Fuchs documents and alerted the British government to Fuchs's activities, to which he confessed.

Judge Kaufman thus had to ignore Fuchs's much-publicized documentary and testimonial evidence in order to credit the Rosenbergs with "putting into the hands of the Russians the A-bomb." His statement is in many ways a handbook of cold war mentality, manifesting in diction, tone, and hyperbolic, Manichaean, and apocalyptic imagery the background assumptions supporting the particular closure he narrated for the official Rosenberg story. It points to the ownership theory of the bomb, which supported U.S. notions of absolute competitive superiority; it assumes a complete projection of aggressive energies onto and demonizing of another nation-state; it manifests the show-trial motivations and dimensions of the government case, especially on the part of Judge Kaufman himself; and it reveals the massive displacement of international concern with atomic warfare onto concern with the alleged actions of the Rosenbergs, actions that become through semantic level shifting tantamount to their actually using the bomb to destroy lives, an effect that to date only the U.S. government has achieved.[11]

Sentence

The issue of punishment in this case is presented in a unique framework of history. It is so difficult to make people realize that this country is engaged in a life and death struggle with a completely different system. This struggle is not only manifested externally between these two forces but this case indicates quite clearly that it also involves the employment by the enemy of secret as well as overt outspoken forces among our own people. All of our democratic institutions are, therefore, directly involved in this great conflict. I believe that never at any time in our history were we ever confronted to the same degree that we are today with such a challenge to our very existence. The atom bomb was unknown when the espionage statute was drafted. I emphasize this because we must realize that we are dealing with a missile of destruction which can wipe out millions of Americans.

The competitive advantage held by the United States in super-weapons has put a premium on the services of a new school of spies—the homegrown variety that places allegiance to a foreign power before loyalty to the United States. The punishment to be meted out in this case must therefore serve the maximum interest for the preservation of our society against these traitors in our midst.

[While the defendants prefer our justice system], they made a choice of devoting themselves to the Russian ideology of denial of God, denial of the sanctity of the individual and aggression against free men everywhere instead of serving the cause of liberty and freedom.

I consider your crime worse than murder. . . . I believe your conduct in putting into the hands of the Russians the A-bomb years before our best scientists predicted Russia would perfect the bomb has already caused, in my opinion, the Communist aggression in Korea, with the resultant casualties exceeding 50,000 and who knows but that millions more of innocent people may pay the price of your treason. Indeed, by your betrayal you undoubtedly have altered the course of history to the disadvantage of our country. . . . We have evidence of your treachery all around us every day. . . . [You] passed what [you] knew was this nation's most deadly and closely guarded secret weapon to Soviet agents.

The evidence indicated quite clearly that Julius Rosenberg was the prime mover in this conspiracy. However, let no mistake be made about the role which his wife, Ethel Rosenberg, played. . . . Instead of deterring him from pursuing his ignoble cause, she encouraged and assisted the cause. She was a mature woman—almost three years older than her husband and almost seven years older than her younger brother. She was a full-fledged partner in this crime.

Indeed the defendants Julius and Ethel Rosenberg placed their devotion to their cause above their own personal safety and were conscious that they were sacrificing their own children. . . . Love for their cause dominated their lives—it was even greater than love for their children.

It is not in my power, Julius and Ethel Rosenberg, to forgive you. Only the Lord can find mercy for what you have done. . . . You are hereby sentenced to the punishment of death, and it is ordered . . . you shall be executed according to law.[42]

Plotting

The official Rosenberg story had the potential for serving two primary functions in addition to providing general support for the cold war polarization favored by the vested interests. The story could aid the military in its efforts to secure congressional approval of Truman's 1950 mandate for the development of the hydrogen bomb, and it could provide dramatic support for military-industrial attempts to institute a permanent arms race based on a superiority, first-strike, and retaliatory model.[43] But more significantly for the course the story eventually took, the government believed that a conviction and harsh sentence might force the elaboration of another frame story—the story Hoover, the FBI, and HUAC had been working on overtly since 1946, and indirectly since 1944: the narrative of the atomic spy ring. As the prosecution argued in its summation at the end of the trial:

> The identity of some of the other traitors who sold their country down the river along with Rosenberg and Sobell remains undisclosed. We know that such people exist because of Rosenberg's boasting to Greenglass of the extent of his espionage activities. . . . We know of these other henchmen of Rosenberg. . . . We don't know all the details, because the only living people who can supply the details are the defendants.[44]

Later, in a hearing for reduction of sentence before the trial judge, the prosecution made the point again:

> I submit that on the evidence which has been introduced to the Court, and on other material which I personally know of, that the Rosenbergs are the centers or were the centers of a real widespread network of spies, and if I am correct, the Rosenbergs have ample information which, if they wanted to cooperate, could lead to the detection of any number of people who, in my opinion, are today doing everything that they can to obtain additional information for the Soviet Union.[45]

The cold war frame narrative as elaborated by 1947 set up and required its own embedded narrative explanation of "premature" Soviet possession of the atomic bomb. The Rosenberg story, while appearing to satisfy that need, thus also pointed to its own status as an embedded narrative within a frame not yet elaborated: the story of the atomic spy ring. So before the official Rosenberg story had been cast and constructed, its frame story existed in concept as a widespread network of Soviet spies without verifiable names or identifiable acts of espionage. For reasons of political strategies, personal ambitions, and obsessions, which can be tracked in political histories and biographies as well as in media reports of the time, this larger narrative of the extended spy ring also had to be produced. The means for producing that story would be a stiff sentence—ultimately a death sentence—for the Rosenbergs in order to make them talk.

Ruth Greenglass said the FBI agents told her in her first interview, on June 16, 1950, just after her husband's arrest, that "this thing is bigger than you understand, perhaps the biggest thing the F.B.I. has done in this country. . . . It meant [the agents'] reputations, their jobs." The Greenglasses' attorney, John Rogge, ten days later visited Irving Saypol, the chief prosecutor in the case, to plea-bargain for the Greenglasses, saying "that perhaps the information he could furnish might be used to prosecute those more responsible for espionage activities than his clients."[46] At the same time the Justice Department communicated to the FBI that there was not sufficient evidence to convict Julius Rosenberg: "We have only Greenglass's statement, which he probably will repudiate."[47] When FBI agents arrested Julius Rosenberg on July 17, they also described the arrest in terms of its potential for generating the spy story:

> The indications are definite that he possesses the identity of a number of other individuals who have been engaged in Soviet espionage. . . . New York should consider every possible means to bring pressure on Rosenberg to make him talk, including . . . a careful study of the involvement of Ethel Rosenberg in order that charges can be placed against her, if possible.[48]

Hoover, reading this report, added a marginal comment, "Yes, by all means," and then wrote to Attorney General J. Howard McGrath that "proceedings against [Julius Rosenberg's wife]

[handwritten margin note: why Ethel implicated]

might serve as a lever" to make Julius name his espionage part-
ners.[49] But Ethel's arrest a month after her husband's, without
evidence of illegal activities on her part and without grand jury
action, and the threat to prosecute her as a coconspirator failed
to produce the desired revelations from Julius.

On February 8, 1950, eight months after David Greenglass's
arrest, six weeks before the Rosenberg trial began, before Ethel
had been implicated by the Greenglasses as a coconspirator, and
before Harry Gold had remembered that his code greeting to
David had been "I come from Julius," an unusual meeting took
place. At this meeting with members of the Justice Department,
Congress's Joint Committee on Atomic Energy, and the Atomic
Energy Commission, Myles Lane from the Justice Department,
the assistant prosecutor in the Rosenberg case, solicited approval
for prosecution plans to prove that Greenglass had access to vital
atomic secrets, plans that might require courtroom use of classified information. As Lane explained:

> The only thing that will break this man Rosenberg is the pros-
> pect of a death penalty or getting the chair, plus if we can con-
> vict his wife, too, and give her a stiff sentence of 25 or 30
> years, that combination may serve to make this fellow disgorge
> and give us the information on those other individuals. I can't
> guarantee that. . . . [But] it is about the only thing you can use
> as a lever on these people. . . . the case is not too strong against
> Mrs. Rosenberg. But for the purpose of acting as a deterrent, I
> think it is very important that she be convicted too, and given
> a strong sentence.[50]

The agreement to seek a death penalty for Julius to force him
to provide the frame for his own alleged espionage activities
established the plotting requirements for the government case:
the information David Greenglass allegedly gave to Gold and
Rosenberg had to be shown to be "vital secrets"; Julius had to
be linked to Gold and to Gold's Russian agent; and Ethel had
to be implicated as a knowing participant in the espionage activities. In short, the government would make a case for treason
within the legal framework of a conspiracy charge—a charge for
which the death penalty was unprecedented in the nation's
history.

Casting

Judge Jerome Frank of the Second Circuit Court of Appeals noted in his opinion denying the defense motion for a retrial that when reviewing a trial by jury the higher court was not allowed to consider the credibility of witnesses or the reliability of their testimony. Since my study concerns itself with the motives and effects of narrative in the Rosenberg case, the imaginative capacities of the key witnesses implicating the Rosenbergs— Harry Gold, David Greenglass, and Elizabeth Bentley—are worth noting.

Harry Gold had developed a complicated game for one person using playing cards to simulate baseball games, seasons, play-offs, and series, cumulatively producing a complete history with full statistics.[51] His representation of himself was an extension of this kind of make-believe populating and furnishing of the world. Apparently he had always lived an elaborate fantasy life, a concoction that he conflated with real aspects of his relationship with his mother, about whom he felt guilty; he even blamed himself for her death. He modeled much of this fantasy on the lives and environments of people he actually knew. Gold had an especially dramatic invitation to continue such fiction making when he was asked to testify by the prosecution in a conspiracy trial. The government was soliciting the uncorroborated and detailed accounts of any conversations he might have had with anyone at any time concerning the passing of information on the atomic bomb to the Soviet Union.

For sixteen years Gold had led his employer and associates to believe that he was married to a woman named Sarah O'Ken whom he had met, he said, while courting another girl with one blue eye and one brown eye who had spurned Gold for a rival named Frank whose uncle manufactured peanut-chew candy; Sarah's previous boyfriend had been Nigger Nate, an underworld pimp. Gold and Sarah, he said, had two children, twins named David and Essie, one of whom had had polio. When he and Sarah separated, Gold said, he traveled on weekends to watch his children playing in the park, since he could not bear the pain of visiting them. His brother, Joe, he said had been killed during the war.[52]

In the 1950 industrial espionage trial of Gold's employer Abraham Brothman, before the Rosenberg trial took place, Gold on cross-examination explained the extent of his lying and said, "It is a wonder steam didn't come out of my ears at times." On cross-examination in the 1955 perjury trial of Benjamin Smilg, an engineer from whom Gold had attempted to acquire information, Gold testified, "First I created this wife whom I did not have. Then there had to be children to go along with the wife, and they had to grow old, so I had to keep building one on top of the other." And his brother Joe was alive and lived with Gold and their father. In an autobiographical statement prepared for his defense attorney in the Rosenberg trial he wrote, "I definitely did spend a great deal of time in the very enjoyable pastime of imagining Harry Gold . . . always of course in a stern and self-sacrificing role." His attorney in the Brothman trial said in Gold's defense, in words that can only be read as radically and ironically true in light of what is now known about Gold, "I say to your Honor, after forty years of association with men . . . that Harry Gold is the most extraordinarily selfless person I have ever met in my life."[53]

Gold claimed that he had for many years given his Soviet agents fictitious names of recruits and accounts of information he was receiving; after his arrest, during interrogation for the Rosenberg trial, he also gave the FBI names of espionage suspects who were revealed upon investigation to be nonexistent. He was willing to make significant fictitious assertions under oath. In the 1955 Smilg trial he admitted under cross-examination that his testimony before a grand jury in 1947 regarding elaborate conversations with the Soviet agent Jacob Golos was entirely false; he did not even know Jacob Golos.[54] It is obvious that in the murky area of conspiracy and espionage—especially where there is no documented crime or activity—the labeling of a statement as true or false by Gold has no orienting frame of reference. Such claims were eventually revealed as meaningless and without value.

I have noted that Gold took details for his fantasy life from the conversations of his associates. His explanation of his ability to lead a double life likewise mimics the diction, phrases, and rationale of Klaus Fuchs's explanation for his own acts of espionage. Fuchs had said in a statement made public that his mind operated by a sort of "controlled schizophrenia" by which he kept his life in "two separate compartments"; Gold said he used one track of his mind for Soviet work and then just turned the switch to another track for his own work. There is no publicly known evidence that connects him with Fuchs, but he told his attorney after his confession and arrest, "I am absolutely fascinated by a person with ability. . . . And therefore I was fascinated by—or rather, attracted to—Klaus. . . . [We] were somewhat kindred souls . . . we were as good friends as it is possible for two men to be."[55]

Gold received deep satisfaction from his alleged association with Fuchs, as well as from the crucial roles he played in the Brothman and Rosenberg trials, evidenced by the perverse pride reflected in the statement he delivered at his sentencing hearing, at which he was given thirty years in prison:

> Your Honor, I feel that an explanation is due to the people of the United States . . . all of whom I have besmirched by my crime. . . . and a horrible and heinous one it is. . . . For in the end, a far more terrible weapon than any Atomic Bomb was created, namely, Harry Gold, Soviet courier, a name . . . now an anathema to all decent people.[56]

Nevertheless, Gold's career and fame as ex-Soviet courier and valuable government witness were short-lived. When he was called from prison in 1956 to testify before a congressional committee about Soviet espionage, his obvious blurring of boundaries between fiction and fact rendered his testimony useless. An Associated Press report called it "fiction rivaling."[57]

David Greenglass, while not nearly so imaginative as Gold, had his own proclivities to fantasy and "selflessness." His wife, Ruth, told his attorney that her husband had a "tendency to hysteria," that he had one time run through the house nude yelling of "elephants" and "lead pants," and that since he was ten years old "he would say things were so even if they were not." Greenglass himself said to his attorneys the morning after his arrest that he had allowed the FBI investigators to shape and supplement his confession.[58]

Greenglass attorney John Rogge said in an interview after Greenglass's release from prison in 1960 that Ruth was "the more stable" of the two, and that David could be "easily led." A Justice Department attorney who spoke with Greenglass in prison during the department's last and abortive attempts in 1957 to identify and bring to justice a spy ring said that Greenglass had begun their conversation by saying he was the smartest man the attorney would ever meet, and that his work at Los Alamos was crucial to the development of the atomic bomb. This attorney left the interview feeling that David was a man with "no conscience at all," and that if he were a judge, he would not take his testimony too seriously.[59]

Elizabeth Bentley, represented by the prosecution as offering crucial corroboration for the Gold and Greenglass testimony, had never met Julius and knew nothing of the alleged conspiracy. She was an ex-Communist and self-confessed Soviet spy who was frequently used as a government witness to establish, by assertion, the link between the Communist party and espionage. Her naming of eighty people as Soviet spies had failed to produce any indictments after a year-long grand jury investigation in 1947. She also was unable to substantiate the reality of the dramatic life she described for herself as a high-level agent for Soviet espionage, who frequently, she claimed, "gave orders to Earl Browder . . . [the head of the American Communist party until 1945] from Moscow to him, and he had to accept them."[60] Despite the failure of her testimony to produce indictments, it had inaugurated her career as a professional witness and writer; Bentley received a book contract, as well as commissions for articles, to write about her life as a Soviet spy. And her story to FBI agents in November 1945 was largely responsible for reinforcing Hoover's belief in a widespread espionage network operating in the United States and within the government, a belief he promulgated for the rest of his powerful and productive career as a public servant in charge of discovering un-American thought and activity. In this quest he consistently found support among the media: after the grand jury had been unable to indict anyone Bentley named, a 1948 New York *World-Telegram* story headlined "Red Ring Bared By Blond Queen" reported the widespread espionage Bentley had described. By then even HUAC was acknowledging internally that there was neither material evidence for any of her allegations nor substantive corroborating testimony.[61]

Because of the failure of the Rosenbergs' attorneys to cross-examine Gold or Bentley, the jury was not privy to the fantasy element of these key witnesses' lives and experiences, much of which was discoverable at the time of the trial. Those who have no doubts about the Rosenbergs' guilt and the correctness of the trial and punishment attribute this failure to the defense's fear of the additionally damaging testimony that might result from such questioning. But it is difficult to imagine that, given the resources to research Bentley's and Gold's records, including their previous, inconsistent, and contrived trial testimony, the defense would not have wanted to make the jury aware of its incriminating gaps, inconsistencies, contradictions, and outright fabrications. Whatever the reasons, the absence of interference and interruptions allowed the government witnesses to recount a single narrative that was persuasive and credible for its internal coherence, lock-step sequence, and mutually reinforcing repetitions.

Rehearsals

The apparent chain-reaction linking of Fuchs to Gold to Greenglass to Julius to Ethel Rosenberg was the most persuasive element of the government story, the one that Eisenhower cited in his memoirs, *The White House Years,* to explain his denial of clemency to the Rosenbergs: "Klaus Fuchs . . . implicated Gold, who in turn named Greenglass."[62]

This impressive lock-step agreement of the protagonists' stories, however, was not evident in their original versions. As I have noted, Fuchs was not able to identify Gold as his U.S. courier until after Gold had confessed. During the three days in May 1950 following Gold's arrest, cables crossed between London and Philadelphia as FBI agents used Gold's and Fuchs's statements to refresh each other's memory. After Gold had confessed, he was induced to incorporate into his story some details from Fuchs's May 22 statement that had not appeared in his original statement, such as Fuchs's having told him in June 1945 of the first scheduled test explosion of the atomic bomb, the July 16 test at Alamogordo. On May 23, portions of Gold's statement were cabled to London for incorporation into Fuchs's statement. The cable, signed "Hoover," urged the agents in London to "reconcile discrepancies in statements of Fuchs and Gold."[63]

Of the testimony by the three principal prosecution witnesses, Gold's shows the greatest discrepancies between his original statement and the courtroom narrative. This narrative was the cumulative product of some four hundred hours of FBI interrogation, as well as of the time Gold spent with government attorneys preparing for the trial and in joint sessions with David Greenglass.[64] Ten days after his first confession, Gold remembered that he had met with a soldier in Albuquerque after meeting with Fuchs in June 1945.

Gold was not able to remember at that time any of the links to Julius he would testify to in the courtroom, even though by then he was a cooperating government witness. Crucial to the government story in the trial some ten months later were not documents but Gold's recollection of a torn Jell-O box used to establish his link to Julius, as well as his greeting to Greenglass, "I come from Julius." But Gold's early statements do not mention a torn Jell-O box, the soldier's name, or registering at the Hilton hotel. He said that he did not know the soldier's name, had used the greeting, "Benny from New York sent me,"and had spent the night in the hall of a rooming house.[65]

This testimony from Gold took place about three weeks before David Greenglass was arrested as the Unknown Subject, the person responsible for giving away "the secret of the atomic bomb," the person Gold would refer to later as his "extra added attraction." The FBI presented Gold with a list of names, including that of Hank Greenberg the baseball star and Manny Wolf, the name of a restaurant where Gold had dined. The first ten names were alphabetized by first and last names: Arnold Blume, Charles Drusher, Ezra Finkelstein, and so on. None of the names except Greenglass's is known from the FBI files to have been that of a suspect in an investigation. Gold preferred Max Schwartz but thought Greenglass might be a possibility. He first agreed that the address 209 High Street "was not at all impossible" and later, after viewing "dozens of reels of motion pictures" of Albuquerque streets and houses, "finally succeeded in picking out the correct house."[66]

Before Gold had been able to recall anything about a Hilton hotel, to establish that indeed he was in Albuquerque on the day he said, a Hilton hotel registration card was produced. Gold was unable to recall the Hilton registration until his trial testimony, which allowed the introduction of the card at the trial, after which this crucial piece of evidence was returned to the hotel and destroyed four months later, even though appeals were pending in the case. The Schneirs believe that card to have been a forgery because of irregularities in form, procedures, and handwriting; their account, as well as the irregular destruction of the card following the trial, casts serious doubt on FBI practices.[67]

After Gold had identified Greenglass as the man who gave him information in Albuquerque, Greenglass was questioned in an all-night session in which he confessed and implicated his wife as the instigator of his activities. He mentioned a torn card given him by Ruth that he had used to identify the courier and summarized the information he had given that courier in 1945. He at first insisted that he did not know who was directing his wife's recruitment of him, but for his typed statement asserted that it was his brother-in-law Julius.[68] He later reported in confidential conversations with his attorneys that the FBI had given him the framework of the story he narrated, and documents indicate that his statement was dictated by FBI agents and signed by Greenglass. All the agents' logs of this first interview have been destroyed, but Greenglass also told his attorneys that the technical information he had given Gold "may not be at all" what he had described to the FBI, and that while he did not recall two visits in one day from Gold, he had "allowed" the second visit to be included in his statement. In this same conversation with his attorneys he indicated that he had tried, unsuccessfully, to keep Julius out of the picture and wanted to contact him as soon as possible.[69]

After Greenglass's arrest and confession, and just before Julius's arrest on July 17, David's wife, Ruth, decided to cooperate with the government by giving evidence against Julius. The Greenglasses' attorney and the prosecution agreed that Ruth would testify in return for immunity from prosecution, as her husband's testimony could not be used against her, and that David would also cooperate, with the expectation that he would receive a light sentence.[70] The FBI agents then began the careful process of "reconciling discrepancies" between Gold's and David Greenglass's statements, and of developing Ruth's and David's stories to establish coherence, especially in their implication of Julius and Ethel.[71]

Gold was finally able to recall both the torn card and that he had been given it by his Soviet agent. Because the Greenglasses had attributed the torn card to Julius, Gold's testimony established the only link between Julius and the Soviet agent. Gold was also able to remember that Ruth had said in Albuquerque in 1945 that she had talked with a "Julius" by phone about a subsequent meeting between Gold and David Greenglass. David's and Ruth's signed statements on July 17, prior to Julius's arrest, had not agreed; on July 19 David met with agents to make the narratives congruent, which was accomplished by David's adopting Ruth's version. He was also able at later meetings to remember the dates and purposes of other espionage contacts he had made that coincided with the requirements of the FBI's Unknown Subject profile.[72]

In December 1950 FBI agents met with Gold and David Greenglass together in order to have their "concerted effort in recalling" their June 1945 meeting. The agency report reads:

> Concerning the reported salutation "Greetings from Ben," Greenglass says that he has no recollection of such a statement made by Gold. . . . Greenglass proposed that possibly Gold had said "greetings from Julius"; which would of course make sense to Greenglass. Gold's spontaneous comment to this was that possibly Greenglass was right . . . [but Gold] is not at all clear on this point.[73]

In a report in February 1951, a month before the trial and nine months after Gold's questioning began, the agent stated:

> Subsequent to these interviews with Greenglass and Gold, the latter averred that after considerable reflection he is quite certain that on the occasion of the first meeting he had with Greenglass he brought greetings from Julius, and that such was done under the direction of Yakovlev [the Soviet agent].[74]

Greenglass subsequently agreed. In a report by Myles Lane on February 12, Greenglass was said to be "under the impression that when Harry Gold came to Albuquerque to see him in June 1945, Harry Gold said that Julius sent him."[75]

This final reconciliation, as the prosecutor would note in his summation, "forged the necessary link in the chain" of evidence to connect the Rosenbergs to the Soviet Union and to espionage.[76] The documents and the personalities of the leading characters allow the inference that this vital link may have been nothing more than a narrative construction. As Gold wrote in a pretrial statement:

> The manner in which all of the pieces of the giant jig-saw puzzle, of which I was a part, are falling ever so gloriously into place—to reveal the whole picture—has added a tremendous zest and sense of achievement to my life.[77]

Dramatic Strategies

In terms of courtroom strategy the prosecution had another significant advantage over the defense counsel in addition to its superior resources: its sense of the rhetorical and the dramatic. Julius and Ethel's defense team consisted of Emanuel Bloch, an attorney whose experience was in personal injury and civil liberties cases and who at first had thought Julius was just another routine Fifth Amendment case; his father, Alexander Bloch, whose primary legal experience had been as an attorney for the furriers union; and their assistant, Gloria Agrin, a recent law school graduate. None of these three had any scientific background, knowledge, or information, especially concerning the development of the atomic bomb, an undertaking that remained to a large extent under the category of classified information. The prosecution consisted of Irving Saypol—heralded as "the nation's number one legal hunter of top Communists" because of his successful prosecution of Alger Hiss and the eleven Smith

Act defendants—and assistant prosecutors Roy Cohn and James Kilsheimer.[78]

Cohn's place in the annals of unscrupulous legal manipulators is now secure, and at least one of the Rosenberg historians holds him as among those most responsible for the production of the Rosenberg case.[79] Not only was Cohn's dramatic style suited to public interrogation and prosecution, but apparently his skills in the manipulation and rehearsal of narratives for courtroom use exceeded the broadest constructions of legally sanctioned methods for the development of testimony. According to Harvey Matusow, an ex-Communist professional government witness like Elizabeth Bentley, he and Cohn "developed" testimony frequently, both knowing that it was false. At times testimony was formulated by Cohn and memorized by Matusow for the trial.[80] Cohn was in charge of preparing David Greenglass and Gold for the trial and in charge of David Greenglass's courtroom examination; and Manny Bloch had Ruth Greenglass demonstrate for the jury on cross-examination her remarkable ability to repeat verbatim long, complicated paragraphs of testimony.

The prosecution team was in dramatic control of the trial from the beginning, with its version of the Rosenberg story amply heralded by pretrial publicity. During the trial several strategies worked powerfully to reinforce the prosecution's representation of the Rosenbergs as those persons responsible for the theft of the atomic bomb, and as the hubs of a widespread domestic espionage network. These strategies were rhetorical, and they bordered on deceit or deliberate misleading of the defense and of the jury. Although two such instances were cited as potential reversible errors by the Second Circuit Court of Appeals, they were errors to which that court was, with no defense objections recorded during the trial, powerless to respond.[81] But in February 1953, the Second Circuit Court stayed the March 9 execution until a petition for certiorari could be filed with the Supreme Court concerning one of those errors, the prosecution's prejudicial use of the media during the trial.[82]

The prosecution's rhetorical and dramatic strategies included the anticommunist ploy of the list; a crucial exploitation of an ambiguous pronoun antecedent; a manipulation of the media to further implicate the defendants; a double-bind attack on Ethel Rosenberg's recourse to the Fifth Amendment; and the construction of imagery and arbitrary connections and translations of terms to build a concept of treason and a picture of an extended atomic spy ring masterminded by Julius and Ethel Rosenberg.

The Bomb Itself

As I have noted, only because the prosecution successfully represented the sketches allegedly delivered by David Greenglass as conveying "the secret of the atomic bomb" were the Rosenbergs tried and sentenced to death, in effect for treason. In his pretrial meeting with members of the AEC and the Joint Committee on Atomic Energy, Myles Lane secured approval to represent as "vital secrets" the information Greenglass said he had conveyed to Gold, although no original documents existed. Lane felt that this claim would produce stiff sentences for Julius and Ethel as a strategy to force Julius, as he put it, to "disgorge" the real spy ring. Saypol's opening argument set this strategy up:

> We will prove that the Rosenbergs devised and put into operation, with the aid of Soviet . . . agents in this country, an elaborate scheme which enabled them to steal through David Greenglass this one weapon, that might well hold the key to the survival of this nation and means the peace of the world, the atomic bomb.[83]

The cold war assumptions of secrecy and ownership and a contradictory Manichaean moral dichotomy are implicit background beliefs apparent in the diction and tone of this one sentence of Saypol's statement: an elaborate atomic spy ring has stolen the secret weapon that, in the sole possession of the United States, could have been the key to world peace, but that, in the hands of the Soviet Union, is now a potential weapon for world destruction. Opening statements always beg questions, but the questions Saypol begs all fit neatly into the prepared mental ground of cold war ideology that members of the jury and the press as well as the judge by then shared to some degree. This prior contextual preparation had the effect of decreasing the prosecution's burden of proof. And, in a circular movement, the

Rosenbergs' convictions then had the effect of supporting and reifying the context that made their conviction possible.

The prosecution's pretrial strategy had been to present the defense and the jury with a list of the 120 witnesses it intended to call, including the military and scientific directors of the Manhattan Project, General Leslie Groves and J. Robert Oppenheimer, as well as Harold Urey and George B. Kistiakowski. The prosecution also received permission from the judge for AEC representatives, including Dr. James Beckerley, director of the AEC Classification Office, to sit at the prosecution table during the trial.

Neither General Groves nor any of the scientists was called to testify; indications are that none of them was ever contacted to appear in court or to evaluate the information Greenglass allegedly had given to Gold and Rosenberg.[84] Only twenty-three witnesses were called by the prosecution, five of whom gave testimony implicating the Rosenbergs. Only two people were called to testify to the significance of the information in the sketches Greenglass had drawn for the jury to illustrate what he claimed to have given Gold and Rosenberg in 1945: Walter S. Koski, a chemical engineer at Los Alamos for whom Greenglass did machine work on implosion lens models, and John Derry, an electrical engineer, who testified that one of Greenglass's sketches referred to the type of bomb dropped at Nagasaki.

The AEC representatives were in the courtroom theoretically to protect against exposure of classified information in testimony; the effect of their presence was to lend powerful credence to the notion that the Greenglass sketches were in fact what was repeatedly referred to by the prosecution and Greenglass himself as "the atomic bomb." There were aspects of Greenglass's information that the AEC preferred not be brought out in the trial, but most of it was declassified for the trial and then reclassified to discourage open conversation among working nuclear scientists. For the jury's benefit, the chief prosecutor entered into the record a statement to the effect that "the Atomic Energy Committee has declassified this information under the Atomic Energy Act and has made the ruling as authorized by Congress that subsequent to the trial it is to be reclassified."[85]

But the atomic bomb it was not. Nor, according to some of the senior scientists who worked on the development of the bomb, was John Derry, who acknowledged his lack of technical background in nuclear physics or in engineering related to nuclear physics, in a position to evaluate the importance of Greenglass's sketch. The names of well-known senior scientists on the prosecution's witness list established for the defense and the judge, however, the seriousness and authenticity of the Greenglass information. The list was so overpowering that it may have worked successfully to deter the defense from calling its own rebuttal witnesses. The scientists who responded to Emanuel Bloch's post-trial request for evaluation of the sketches that Greenglass prepared for the trial, and that Bloch of course did not see until the trial, said that while the sketches contained no real technical information, they might have supported in a general way Fuchs's technical report that was delivered to the Soviet Union.

All of these elements conspired to convince the defense attorneys that in fact Greenglass had given away the secret of the bomb. Greenglass testified repeatedly that his sketch was the result of knowledge accumulated over months of work at Los Alamos and was "the atom bomb itself," and the prosecution reiterated his assertion with the effect of a litany: "the bomb itself," "the sketch of the bomb itself." The defense neither objected to any of the repetitions nor called expert witnesses to challenge the assertions.

The strongest such assertion, that of John Derry, actually depended on a pronoun antecedent ambiguity. He was referring to the sketch that Greenglass had characterized as "the bomb itself" when he said that it "related to the atomic weapon being developed in 1945." Then he was asked:

Q. Does the information that has been read to you, together with the sketch concern a type of atomic bomb which was actually used by the United States of America?

A. *It does. It is the bomb* we dropped at Nagasaki, similar to it. [italics mine][86]

It does and it is: there is an enormous slippage between these two "its," and their antecedent is not necessarily identical. Unless

Derry himself was seriously deluded about the significance of the sketch, the antecedent of the second "it" is the bomb that the sketch concerns: so his statement extended by antecedents reads, "Yes, the sketch concerns a bomb that we used; the bomb that the sketch concerns is the bomb we dropped at Nagasaki, similar to it." But in the rhetorical context established for the jury by Greenglass and the prosecution, it is likely that the jury heard the syntactic echo in Derry's second clause as also a semantic echo. That is, both clauses were heard as having the same antecedent, Greenglass's sketch. Then the semantic inference is that "it," the sketch, is, just as Greenglass had said, "the bomb itself."

It is impossible to say what any of the senior scientists would have testified, had they been called by the prosecution or the defense. Given the Communist leanings of which many scientists were suspected in 1950 because of their arguments in favor of negotiation with the Soviet Union on arms control and against the development of the hydrogen bomb, it is understandable that they were not called. The only scientists to speak out actively in defense of the Rosenbergs were Albert Einstein and Harold Urey, the latter being one of the named but not called witnesses for the prosecution. They both wrote letters—Einstein to the president, and Urey to many people—some of which were published in the *New York Times,* arguing the injustice of the trial and the dishonesty of the media in reporting it.

Subsequently the Greenglass sketches and information have been much reviewed, and scientists have been forthcoming with their opinions. They have called Greenglass's sketches a "caricature," "confused and imprecise," lacking any crucial data and details; one nuclear physicist has pointed out that "the atomic bomb itself" "is an industry, not a recipe."[87] He and another atomic scientist said, "It is not possible in any technologically useful way to condense the results of a two-billion-dollar development effort into a diagram, drawn by a high school graduate machinist on a single piece of paper." Dr. James Beckerley, the AEC Director of Classification who sat at the prosecution table during the trial, said in a speech before a group of industrialists in New York in 1954 that the atom bomb and the hydrogen bomb were not stolen from us by spies, and that such bombs are "not matters that can be stolen and transmitted in the form of information."[88]

In April 1954 General Leslie Groves, head of the Manhattan Project, testified at the AEC's special Personnel Security Board hearing on J. Robert Oppenheimer, who opposed the government's plans to develop the hydrogen bomb. Some of Groves's testimony was deleted from the hearing transcript on the grounds that his statement "was irrelevant and was unfortunate in that it could be used by the Communists for propaganda if the testimony was ever released to the press," a rationale similar to that of several Supreme Court justices regarding their deliberations and opinions in the final days of appeals before the executions. In the portion of his testimony later deleted from the record, Groves had conceded:

> I think the data that went out in the case of the Rosenbergs was of minor value. I would never say that publicly. Again, that is something, while it is not secret, I think should be kept very quiet because irrespective of the value of that in the over–all picture, the Rosenbergs deserved to hang and I would not like to say anything that would make people say General Groves thinks that they didn't do much damage after all.[89]

Trial by Newspaper

On July 18, 1950, the day after Julius Rosenberg's arrest, the newspaper headlines represented him as a self-confessed member of the Klaus Fuchs spy ring; details of his alleged espionage were reported as facts rather than as the vague government charges they were at that time. Many papers printed what were apparently direct quotations from Julius, as in this excerpt from the *New York Times*: "The FBI investigation revealed, Mr. Hoover said, that Rosenberg made himself available to Soviet espionage agents 'so he could do the work he was fated for' and 'so he might do something to help Russia.'" The apparent facts and quotations are all from Hoover's press release following Julius's arrest, not from Julius's own comments. These news reports represented as facts attested to by Julius himself, all of the allegations that would be at issue in the Rosenberg trial, and that the Rosenbergs consistently denied; the reports also appeared to be explaining

Julius's motivation for espionage in his own words. If the reports were to be believed, the only role left to Julius was that of government witness; he had already been tried and convicted in the newspapers.

Since Ethel's arrest was construed by the government as necessary both to make Julius talk and to disallow Ethel's testifying in behalf of her husband, there had to be a crime; with a conspiracy charge this was easy. Ethel Rosenberg was arrested and charged on August 11, 1950, with assisting her husband in recruiting her brother to obtain for the Soviet Union information concerning the atomic bomb. The grand jury until then had had no interest in Ethel; they intended to bring charges against Ruth Greenglass as the self-confessed person most implicated in atomic espionage for the Soviet Union. Myles Lane convinced the grand jury that charges against Ruth would keep the government from being able to make its case—that is, charges against the person who confessed to the espionage would prevent them from being able to prosecute those who did not. Ruth's pretrial testimony became the only evidence the government could develop against Julius in several crucial connections, and as it turned out, the only evidence at all against Ethel.

But Myles Lane also used the press to convict Ethel in advance of a trial. Following her arraignment he held a news conference at which he made this hyperbolic charge: "If the crime with which she is charged had not occurred, perhaps we would not have the present situation in Korea."[90] The next day, August 12, the *New York Times* included that statement in its story on Ethel under the headline "Atomic Spy Plot Is Laid to Woman." Two years later, a circuit court of appeals held in *Delaney v. United States* that similar behavior deprived defendants of their Sixth Amendment rights: where such material is "fed to the press by prosecuting officials of the Department of Justice," it is not only in violation of "due process of law" but fails to ensure "civilized standards of procedure and evidence."[91]

On March 15, 1951, the day of Ruth Greenglass's cross-examination during the trial, a front-page *New York Times* headline read, "Columbia Teacher Arrested, Linked to 2 on Trial as Spies." The article reported that the scientist William Perl would be a government witness in the Rosenberg espionage trial and quoted the prosecutor as saying that Perl's role was to corroborate statements of key government witnesses. This was a scare tactic, threatening the defense with another former member of the Communist party who might testify against the Rosenbergs to escape a perjury charge. It also served to provide the non-sequestered jury, whose members could not fail to have seen the widespread Perl publicity, with apparent corroboration of the Greenglass assertions against the Rosenbergs. Hoover had urged Perl's arrest prematurely because he thought it would aid both the prosecution and the FBI in its attempts to force the story of the spy ring; the prosecutor thus obtained a grand jury indictment while the trial was in session. Once arrested, Perl said nothing and did not appear as a witness. He was later convicted for perjury for denying that he had known Rosenberg and Sobell at the City College of New York (CCNY).

In the spring of 1953, when Judge Kaufman summarily denied a Rosenberg motion that because of Saypol's press conference about Perl during the Rosenberg trial, a new trial was in order, the motion was heard on appeal before the Second Circuit Court. Judge Swan asserted, "Such a statement to the press in the course of a trial we regard as wholly reprehensible." He added, "If the Defendants had then [upon the trial] moved for a mistrial, it should have been granted." Because the defendants had not so moved, however, the circuit court found that they had waived their rights to a new trial.[92] But six weeks later, on February 17, 1953, the circuit court stayed the March 9 execution until application for certiorari could be made to the Supreme Court on the basis of that potential error, defense failure to object notwithstanding.[93] When the government objected to the stay, Judge Learned Hand responded in open court that people do not execute people just because the defense failed to make the proper motion.[94]

Harold Urey, one of the senior scientists on the prosecution witness list, was present in the courtroom in May 1953 when the defense made a motion for a hearing based on the discovery of substantive new evidence. The judge refused to look at the evidence and denied the motion in a decision written before he had heard the oral arguments. Urey was shocked enough to say to a *New York Times* reporter who asked his opinion:

> Now I see what goes on in Judge Kaufman's courtroom, I believe the Rosenbergs are innocent. When I look in that courtroom I see no Kaufman but McCarthy. . . . What appalls me most is the role the press is playing. The judge's bias is so obvious. I keep looking over at you newspapermen and there's not a flicker of indignation or concern. When are you going to stop acting like a bunch of sheep?[95]

The next day the *New York Times* reported the denial of the defense motion without mentioning Urey's comments.[96]

These isolated but crucial instances of the manipulation of language and of the media by the FBI and the Department of Justice were among those that furthered the official story at the expense of due process and of rules of procedure and evidence. They cumulatively produced an extrajudicial conviction of the accused prior to any legal discovery of evidence. But these are also instances of media complicity in the uncritical production of words and silences that served the interests of one motivated narrative over still equally valid alternative versions of that same narrative, and, in this case, of media complicity in an extralegal trial.

Sign of Guilt

The Fifth Amendment grants a paradoxical power that rarely works as purely in practice as it was designed to do to protect the individual right to avoid self-incrimination and to maintain an official assumption of innocence. Refusals to declare innocence are inevitably tainted by a suggestion of guilt. Moreover, the right to require suspension of judgment to avoid self-incrimination cannot sufficiently articulate itself within the legal and moral parameters of an abstract cultural opposition between guilt and innocence that discounts the effects of historical context on any specific definition of guilt or innocence. People who used the Fifth Amendment during the HUAC and McCarthy era were labeled Communists; for Lieutenant Colonel Oliver North and Admiral John Poindexter in the Iran/contra hearings and trial in 1987 its use represented and dramatized a self-sacrificing and patriotic heroism.[97] Because almost everyone assumed that the Rosenbergs were Communists, no one was surprised that Julius and Ethel pled the Fifth as frequently as they did.

Ethel in particular used the Fifth throughout both of her subpoenaed appearances before the grand jury after Julius's arrest. Emanuel Bloch had advised her of her rights to avoid self-incrimination, she was especially vulnerable because of Communist Party affiliations, and she had no way of knowing of what she might be accused as a result of the Greenglass testimony. Without counsel present to guide her, she sought refuge in the Fifth Amendment, which she pled for almost every question asked her, questions of neutral and verifiable fact as well as of Communist party membership and alleged espionage activities. She refused to answer hundreds of questions "on the grounds that it might incriminate me," even if neither a positive nor a negative answer would have implied guilt of any kind. In the early stages of the Rosenberg story during which she found herself before the grand jury, it was impossible to differentiate between neutral and incriminating facts.

That the use of the Fifth allowed members of the grand jury and the trial jury to assume a defendant's guilt is understandable and unavoidable; the judge's charge to the jury is intended to neutralize such assumptions. But the judge gave the appropriate charge and then allowed and participated in turning Ethel's use of the Fifth before the grand jury into a sign of guilt before the trial jury.

The judge had previously charged the trial jury regarding the use of the Fifth Amendment: "You can't draw any inferences from the refusal to answer by the witness. . . . You can't infer that the witness has admitted anything from the refusal to answer." When Ethel took the stand, the prosecution secured her acknowledgment that everything she had told the grand jury was the truth. After questioning her, the prosecutor then went through her grand jury testimony and her immediately preceding trial testimony question by question, comparing her refusal to answer before the grand jury with her answers at the trial as a voluntary witness. He did this in order to ask her, with increasingly serious implications, if her response of possible self-incrimination was the truth, making the same point over and over, through some thirty pages of the trial record, until the judge finally stopped him.[98] Although Ethel was at first completely disarmed by this tactic, her answers gradually became an unwitting but increasingly astute critique of the limitations of abstract categories and legal formalism.

> Q. And everything you told the grand jury was the truth?
> A. Right.
> Q. Do you remember having been asked this question and giving this answer:
>   "Q. When did you consult with your attorney for the first time in connection with this matter?
>   "A. I refuse to answer on the ground that this may tend to incriminate me."
>   Q. Do you remember having been asked that and having given that answer?
> A. That's right.
> Q. Was that the truth?

Bloch objected, because he saw what was happening, and the judge responded that if the witness was willing to answer questions during the trial that she had refused to answer previously on the ground that it might tend to incriminate her, "might not that be something which the jury would consider on the question of credibility?" His ruling effectively canceled his charge to the jury and translated the assumption of innocence protected by the use of the Fifth into a question of witness reliability for jury consideration. The prosecutor continued, and I quote only the most damaging questions and the most astute answers:

> Q. Was this question asked of you and did you give this answer:
>   "Q. Do you recall ever having discussed the work of your brother, David Greenglass, the work that he was doing at Los Alamos, New Mexico?
>   "A. I decline to answer on the ground that this might tend to incriminate me."
>   Was that question asked and did you give that answer?
> A. Yes.
> Q. Would you care to state how that would incriminate you?
> Mr. Bloch: Just a second. I object to this question upon the
>   grounds that if this witness would ever answer that

question, it would vitiate and nullify all the rights
that every citizen is entitled under the Fifth
Amendment.

The judge sustained that objection but allowed Saypol to continue as long as he only asked Ethel if it were true that to answer
those questions before the grand jury would have incriminated
her:

Q. Do you remember this question and this answer:
   "Q. Did you invite your brother David and his wife to your
   home for dinner? I mean during the period while he was
   on furlough in January 1945?
   "A. I decline to answer on the ground that this might in-
   criminate me."
   Do you remember giving that testimony?
A. Yes, I remember.
Q. Was it true at the time you gave it? Yes or no.
A. It is not a question of it being true.

With this answer Ethel Rosenberg touched on the crucial issue
of a right that exists to protect individual citizens from polarized
and abstract categories, guilt by association, and judgments not
subject to due process. The protection is from anything that
might "tend" to incriminate the witness, and Ethel astutely recognized that a truth claim is not at issue in the use of the Fifth
Amendment, even though that was the import of the prosecution's line of questioning.

Bloch kept objecting, claiming that the prosecution's method
was destroying the privilege, but the judge insisted that Ethel's
use of the Fifth Amendment before the grand jury for questions
that she then answered at the trial created a question of reliability
for the jury to decide. He began participating in the prosecution
strategy by pushing Ethel to explain the discrepancy in her responses and dismissed Bloch with, "Oh no, no, I know you have
no quarrel with the Court; it wouldn't do you any good if you
did."[99] After another set of questions, Ethel responded,

My husband had been arrested on July 17 and I had been subpoenaed to come before the grand jury. It was not for me to
state what I thought or didn't think the Government might or
might not have in the way of accusation against me. I didn't

have to state my reason, but I did feel that in answering certain questions I might be incriminating myself until I exercised my privilege.

And after the next set, followed by "Was that the truth?" Ethel gave a simple but sophisticated defense of the Fifth Amendment:

When one uses the right [against] self-incrimination one does not mean that the answer is yes and one does not mean that the answer is no. I made no denial. I made no assertion that I did not know him [Harry Gold]. I simply refused to answer on the ground that that answer might incriminate me.

A little later, after another set and "Was it true [that your answer would have incriminated you]?" she said, "It can't be answered yes or no." And then, "It is not necessary to explain the use of self-incrimination. . . . Whatever reasons I may have had, I had them, and therefore I felt I had to take refuge."

This prosecution strategy was devastating to Ethel, and by supporting it the judge allowed the very inference that he had originally charged the jury to disallow: that every use of the Fifth Amendment was, by comparison with later testimony, an admission of Ethel's guilt on that question. Six years later, in *Grunewald v. United States,* the Supreme Court ruled that grand jury testimony is not allowable at the trial to show inconsistency, since there can be many reasons for taking the Fifth Amendment before a grand jury that are not necessarily inconsistent with later testimony in response to the same questions.[100] In 1962 Judge Thurgood Marshall asked the U.S. attorney appearing before the the circuit court of appeals to argue against a motion for a review of the trial made by Morton Sobell, the Rosenbergs' codefendant, "If Ethel Rosenberg were tried, say last spring, and we had her conviction before this court today, wouldn't we have to reverse on the authority of *Grunewald?*" The attorney's answer was, "This court would probably have to rule in favor of the defendant."[101]

Ethel as Lever

She was not "just a housewife": she was stubborn, intransigent, perhaps even the driving force behind her mild-mannered husband. With her stoic manner, her refusal to admit her "guilt" (even if such an admission would save her life, and spare her two young children from orphanage), and her final defiance of death, Ethel Rosenberg signified a denial of men's authority over women. Her alleged communist affiliations seemed allied with that denial in mutually reinforcing abnormality. In short, Rosenberg threatened the patriarchy that supported the social order of American capitalism.[102]

That Julius died without talking was a great disappointment to Hoover and Attorney General Brownell, but not a serious problem of conscience. Julius's file apparently contained a copy of a Communist party membership card and information that he was associated with a number of people believed to have been conducting industrial and military espionage for the Soviet Union.[103] The problem was Ethel, for whom no evidence of espionage existed, and who had been arrested and charged, convicted and sentenced to make Julius talk. The last question on an interrogatory prepared for Julius should he have decided to pick up the phone available on his way to the electric chair on June 19, 1953, indicates the degree to which high-level government cynicism operated toward Ethel to the end: "Was your wife cognizant of your activities?"[104]

A certain conception of woman was inherent in postwar ideology; Ethel Rosenberg was alien to it. Think of the fund of Madison Avenue and media images available to women in the United States in the 1950s, in an era of virtually unchallenged masculine representational authority—blond mothers in aprons or church clothes with their children or, according to the fashion plates of a burgeoning new postwar industry, in Christian Dior's "New Look"; the television mothers of "Ozzie and Harriet" and "Father Knows Best," the Hollywood versions portrayed by June Allyson and Doris Day; or the dramatization of domestic relationships by soap opera heroines.[105] Ethel was Jewish, the daughter of immigrants, lower Eastside poor, a labor activist and organizer in her shipping clerk union before her marriage, and a suspected communist. This was not the woman upon whom the Western order depended.

From the time of Julius's arrest, Ethel chose to assume the role of an apolitical housewife and to go through her three-year imprisonment, including two years in isolation at Sing Sing, with "courage, confidence, and perspective."[106] Her decision meant not giving anything away through facial expression, gesture, or language, which made of her a perfect projective screen for those representing her for their own purposes. It also meant not showing any signs of victimization that might have enlisted the sympathy and mercy of a masculist society and its institutional representatives. The media were discomfited by Ethel's emotionless presence and demeanor. At first they experimented with representing this lower Eastside Jewish housewife and mother accused of atomic espionage in the style of women's page social and fashion reporting. We know for example that for her first

Ethel Rosenberg on her way from jail to court as seen in Alvin H. Goldstein's 1974 documentary, *The Unquiet Death of Julius and Ethel Rosenberg.* (Photo: AP/WIDE WORLD PHOTO)

grand jury appearance she wore a powder-blue-and-white polka-dot dress and a modest straw hat. Each day of court appearance her size and dress were described; the day she wore the scarlet bodice, it was the only spot of color in the courtroom. But as the trial progressed, attention shifted to Ethel's refusal to demonstrate feeling, a refusal interpreted as a sign of arrogance, disdain, contempt, or absence of remorse, and increasingly read as evidence of guilt in a cold and unnatural woman.

Ethel's earlier letters to Julius, not written for publication, reveal her as a courageous, conflicted, angry, and often despairing woman; suffering from migraine headaches, back spasms, uncontrollable bouts of crying, and severe depression; and loyal to her husband and concerned for their children. After their first appeal was denied, Julius and Ethel decided to gain support from the people by writing letters for publication, which were then edited and published in part by the Rosenberg Defense Committee, the *National Guardian,* and the *Daily Worker.* In these letters Ethel wrote in a self-consciously elevated and allusive literary style, portraying herself as an ordinary middle-class housewife and mother of a happy family, committed to liberal democratic ideals and secure in her ability to face persecution with dignity.[107]

This use of sterile cultural images of the ideal 1950s wife and mother, liberal ideology stripped of conflict and feelings, and an acceptance of martyrdom, all expressed in high literary diction, elicited ridicule from the high-culture intellectual left and offered no effective counterengagement with the state's development of Ethel as master spy. These letters most clearly reveal the Rosenbergs' problem of effective self-representation. It is difficult to conceive of any position available to the Rosenbergs that could not have been used by the state for the representations it required.[108]

The government's story, which began with what certain officials considered to be Ethel's out-of-control behavior, veered out of control itself. What had been designed as a tactically political exploitation of the alien woman as spy turned or returned to require the murder of the woman and the mother, evoking the most primitive anxieties among its implementers.

Ethel's part in the story began the day of Julius's arrest, July 17, 1950, when FBI agents reported to Hoover on her disruptive female and Communist behavior: "Ethel, his wife, made a typical Communist remonstrance, demanding a warrant and the right to call an attorney. She was told to keep quiet and get in the other room with the children." After receiving this report, Hoover, who had a peculiar sensitivity to disruptive and subversive elements out of their place, endorsed the Justice Department's plan to develop a case against Ethel, suggesting she might serve as a "lever" to make Julius talk.[109] One month later, after Ruth Greenglass remembered that Ethel had been present at one of their espionage discussions, Ethel was arrested, and in FBI press releases printed verbatim by the media she was arbitrarily translated from an out of place Communist Jewish woman and mother to a Soviet spy of global importance.

Myles Lane of the Justice Department held a press conference on August 11, the day of Ethel's arrest, in which he blamed her for the Korean War, which had begun in June, noting also that "her crime jeopardizes the lives of every man, woman and child in this country."[110] In the August 12 *New York Times* headline on her arrest, "Atomic Spy Plot Is Laid to Woman," notice how the most mundane newspaper practice is implicated in a process of woman mythologizing or even demonizing. That the plan to steal the atomic bomb was the work of a woman is already hyperbolic, but by headline reduction it becomes a plot laid to mythic Woman.

On the other hand, how hyperbolic was this seven-word headline in terms of the narrative elaboration over time of the official Rosenberg story? Linguistically it confesses to a plot construction over time that its composers could not possibly have "known" at the time of Ethel's arrest. It contains an unusual use of the verb *laid* for attributed; as a participial adjective *laid* describes a fabric or paper made with only warp threads, lacking a woof and bonded together by a binding material. The official Rosenberg story—the one that prevailed—was a unidimensional (warp-laid) construction dependent on the binding material of background beliefs that were for the most part attributable to the motivated interpretations and constructions of conservative politicians, businessmen, and military figures, and their publicists, the mainstream U.S. media. The main ingredients of the binding material for the Rosenberg story were the constructed beliefs in a U.S.-owned atomic bomb that was stolen by U.S. citizens and given to the Soviet Union, in whose hands it would be used to destroy the American way of life, if not the world. An additional and essential binding ingredient for the Rosenberg story was first the instrumental assertion and then the belief on the part of the government—Attorney General McGrath; FBI director Hoover; federal prosecutors Saypol, Lane, and Cohn; trial judge Irving Kaufman; and finally President Eisenhower—that the woman was the "leader in everything they did in the spy ring."[111]

Hoover had at first hoped to produce an open-ended story with the Rosenbergs—from Los Alamos physicist Klaus Fuchs's arrest and conviction in England, to the arrest of Fuchs's self-confessed courier, Harry Gold, in Philadelphia, to Gold's implication of Greenglass, to Greenglass's implication of Julius, to Julius's implication of the entire spy ring. Ethel is absent from this series; it was just her body in prison that was intended to move Julius to do the chivalrous thing to save his woman. By the time of the trial, however, Julius had said nothing the Justice Department wanted to hear. So on February 8, 1951, Myles Lane held the meeting for members of the Justice Department, the Atomic Energy Commission, and the Joint Committee on Atomic Energy at which he stated his intention to secure a death sentence for Julius and a "stiff sentence" for Ethel to use her as a lever. Now two levers were operative: woman and death.[112]

It was typing that led to this. Until this February meeting a month before the trial began, and during the eight previous months of FBI interrogation, the only evidence implicating Ethel had been Ruth and David Greenglass's testimony that Ethel had been present when David's transmittal of information about the Los Alamos project was sought. The Justice Department felt that her presence alone was not sufficient for her prosecution. After the February 1950 meeting, however, Ruth and David remembered a number of occasions on which Ethel had typed or talked about typing David's notes for Julius. In her trial testimony Ruth described talks with Ethel about typing—Ethel's complaints about fatigue from staying up late to do Julius's typing, and Julius's reassurances to Ruth that Ethel would type David's illegible handwritten notes. In his summary argument at the end of the trial, prosecutor Irving Saypol portrayed Julius as the hub of a spy ring: "Imagine a wheel. In the center of the wheel, Rosenberg, reaching out like the tentacles of an octopus." Then he included Ethel, not at the center with Julius, but off to the side, at the typing table:

> Rosenberg got from [David] the cross-section sketch of *the atom bomb itself* and a 12-page description of this vital weapon. This description of the atom bomb, destined for delivery to the Soviet Union, was typed up by the defendant Ethel Rosenberg that afternoon at her apartment at 10 Monroe Street. Just so had she on countless other occasions sat at that typewriter and struck the keys, blow by blow, against her own country in the interests of the Soviets. [italics mine][113]

Irving Saypol had also been the chief prosecutor in the Alger Hiss case, as well as in the Brothman trial. In the government story he developed, it was Priscilla Hiss who typed the infamous "pumpkin papers"—an allegation never proven—and Elizabeth Bentley who typed Brothman's notes before handing them over to her Russian agent.[114] That is, Irving Saypol had a remarkably consistent plotting device culturally available to him: the woman as the spy's typist.

Lane's plan for stiff sentences for both Rosenbergs was effectively carried out by the prosecution, who convinced even the judge that they were guilty of apocalyptic treachery. Judge Kaufman declaimed in his sentencing speech: "Who knows but that millions more of innocent people may pay the price of your treason. Indeed you have altered the course of history . . . [in passing] this nation's most deadly and closely guarded secret weapon to Soviet Agents."[115] Kaufman singled Ethel out as a full-fledged partner who, three years older than Julius, was a moral failure as a woman and a wife in not having deterred her husband from his ignoble cause. He further castigated them both for sacrificing their children. In the two years before their executions, the brunt of this accusation came to bear primarily on Ethel as an unnatural mother. She was to become the moral and emotional focus of this story for both the right and the left. It was Ethel who fascinated the media, and it is Ethel who has inspired literary and biographical treatment in the years since the trial. She has become almost synonymous with "the Rosenbergs": a fifteen-year-old boy, for example, responded to a 1990 comment about the Rosenbergs, "The Rosenbergs—is that the lady spy who gave the Russians the atomic bomb, and they had to give her two extra jolts to kill her?"

The FBI and the Justice Department succeeded in convicting Ethel as spy, but they had not anticipated that the plan to use her as a lever would fail, that the Rosenbergs would maintain innocence and remain silent. Of course Hoover and certain members of the Justice Department knew that the representation of Ethel as atomic spy was instrumental and unsubstantiated. Hoover had actually signaled to the trial judge that he was not in favor of the death sentence in this case, especially for a woman and a mother. Hoover's relationship to his own mother served a defensive function in his obsession with the enemy within. His development of an extensive FBI apparatus for surveillance and apprehension of alien and subversive enemies within the state was, I believe, in part a displacement of his need to construct his own psychic security state. This public displacement, as well as a lifelong protective attachment to his mother, with whom he lived, worked to contain his phobias, including his apparent fear of the feminine. The possibility of the state murder of a mother was too unsettling to the elaborate defense system he had constructed for himself.[116]

But two reports in the spring before the June executions made it possible for Hoover to perceive Ethel as an unnatural mother, daughter, and wife. Ethel had refused to discuss her children with her own mother or to see her again after her mother's first two visits to Ethel in prison, two years after the trial. Mrs. Greenglass had from the beginning sided with David, the brother who had implicated Ethel with his trial testimony. During the second visit she had urged Ethel to support her brother by talking, even if it meant lying. In a letter, Ethel gave this visit and request as her reason for refusing to see her mother again. "I would still give anything for one kind word from her, though," she added. But for Hoover, Ethel's refusal to see her mother was clear evidence of a betrayal of her role as a good daughter.[117]

Even more helpful in allaying Hoover's anxiety about killing a mother—the Mother—was an unsolicited and so-called psychological report on the Rosenbergs prepared by American Civil Liberties Union cocounsel Morris Ernst without his having met or talked with either Rosenberg. At the time of their arrests, Ernst had suggested to Hoover that he represent them in order to pass on useful information to the FBI, but his offer was rejected. After receiving Ernst's voluntary psychological study just three months before the executions, FBI agent Louis Nichols wrote to Hoover that Ernst "has concluded that Julius is the slave and his wife, Ethel, the master." Phrases and paraphrases of this report would continue to appear in official reports, in statements by the attorney general, in Eisenhower's correspondence, and even today as misprisions in public statements and informal conversations about the Rosenbergs. This alleged inversion of the hierarchy between male and female, between natural authority and unnatural but ever-threatening counterforce, caused any anxieties on Hoover's part concerning Ethel's execution to revert to a moralistic advocacy of her death. It simply would not do to act in any way that might be interpreted as a sign of weakness toward this woman or toward the enemy within.[118]

The morning of the scheduled executions the Supreme Court vacated by a vote of six to three a stay issued the day before by Justice William O. Douglas, leaving presidential clemency as the only relief for the Rosenbergs. Ethel's manipulation and use by the government were unknown until the 1974 release of FBI documents concerning the Rosenbergs. At all levels of the appellate procedure the Rosenbergs had been considered as a unit; Ethel's role was at no time a matter for judicial review. But it was apparently a concern for Eisenhower. The day the Court vacated the stay, Attorney General Brownell encouraged Eisenhower to deny clemency, assuring him that the FBI had top secret documents proving both Rosenbergs guilty of treason. These documents had not been made available to the Rosenberg defense, however, and are still unavailable today—some forty

years after the executions and many years after the passage of
the 1974 Freedom of Information Act.[119]

Eisenhower's denial of clemency, issued immediately following
the Supreme Court decision and without the president's having
read the Court's majority or dissenting opinions that indicated
doubts and suggested clemency, reiterated in almost the exact
words of the trial judge's sentencing speech the heinous treachery
of the Rosenbergs, who were yet again deemed responsible for
the future deaths of tens of millions of innocent people all over
the world. Eisenhower, asserting the thoroughness of the judicial
review of their case, missed entirely the signals sent from every
level of the appeals procedure that remedy for certain contingencies and errors lay only with the Supreme Court or with
executive privilege.

Eisenhower may have held an unexamined belief in the absolute fairness of U.S. jurisprudence. To deny clemency, however,
he had to overcome his own discomfort with the state execution
of a woman. This he apparently accomplished, as did Hoover,
by means of the Morris Ernst report, and by a decision to concern
himself only with the statecraft, the *effect* of his action, as he
said, recalling the expedient of military executions for disciplinary purposes. He gave his rationale in a letter to his son, John:

> To address myself to the Rosenberg case for a minute. I must
> say that it goes against the grain to avoid interfering in the case
> where a woman is to receive capital punishment. Over against
> this, however, must be placed one or two facts which have
> greater significance. The first of these is that in this instance it
> is the woman who is the strong and recalcitrant character, the
> man is the weak one. She has obviously been the leader in
> everything they did in the spy ring. The second thing is that if
> there would be any commuting of the woman's sentence with-
> out the man's then from here on the Soviets would simply re-
> cruit their spies from among women.[120]

Eisenhower gives voice here to a dubious and often illusory
tradition of gallantry that would render femininity exempt from
the law. Moreover by defining the woman again as the stronger
of the two, and by translating her into the leader in the couple's

work, he recalls a contemporaneous social and economic situation: the wartime and postwar entry of women into the workplace, that is, into men's place. On top of that disruption, Ethel had introduced the possibility that women might take over the jobs of male spies.

Thus in the thinking and writing of all those involved in constructing Ethel's narrative she ends as more than a woman who was accused of stealing the state's main weapon. She has become a master of men, a threat to the espionage industry, a female lever manipulating the very men who instrumentalized her as lever, someone who must finally have the lever pulled on her. Nowhere is this clearer than in the report of one of the three media witnesses to her execution, Hearst reporter Bob Considine:

> Ethel wore a Mona Lisa smile. Her little minnow of a mouth was curled at the edges in the faintest possible way. She was dressed in a dark green print of cheap material, a prison dress that revealed her plump legs below the knee. Her dark brown hair . . . was set in an almost boyish manner. . . . As the hood was lowered over her eyes and the black strap placed across her mouth, she was looking straight ahead almost triumphantly. As the torrent of electricity swept through her body . . . from every pore there seemed to emanate a strange, unearthly sound made up almost exclusively of the letter Z. Now she seemed about to stand. Her hands contracted into fists. Thus she sat, lifted off her seat as far as the straps would permit, and I had the startled feeling that she would break those bonds and come charging across the floor, wielding those tight little fists. [After he comments on the two extra jolts needed to kill her, he continues.] She could relax now. Her face possessed the same quizzical half smile that had been painted upon it minutes before. [As she was pushed out of sight on a wheeled table her] right leg was flexed in an easy and almost nonchalant posture. It was a trying experience when, a few minutes later, briefing thirty-eight reporters from half a dozen countries, the first question asked was a shrill one from a lady reporter: "What did Mrs. Rosenberg wear tonight?" she called up to me. It just seemed so damned callous.[121]

A close reading is not necessary to hear in this report a figurative description of the maternal, as well as overt signs of a regressive and misogynist terror. Considine first takes Ethel's body apart to read in its fragments a seduction that is inscrutable, ambiguous, revolting, and marked by artifice. She wears a Mona Lisa smile that is painted on even in death; her mouth is a slippery little fish, her legs plump below the knees, her hair frowsy and boyish, and her fists closed tight and threatening; her eyes stare triumphantly. Considine has constructed his own viewing position as that of the boy and man disgusted at the sight of the mother's body. As she is wheeled away her leg falls loosely and suggestively to the side, and now he is seeing a prostitute, or perhaps the aftermath of the primal scene, or of a rape.

In describing Ethel's dying Considine's figured fantasies pitch themselves into a vision of a witchlike phallic mother.[122] Her body emits an unearthly "Z" sound as she tries to stand erect with the current running through her. Considine fears that she will break her bonds and charge him with her tight little fists. Now he has become the object of this woman's anger, which he depicts as the fury of a little child, the rage of a defiant and triumphant woman, and the threat of a charging animal. Considine tells us that it has been a trying experience. For Ethel certainly, for Considine in other ways trying, but that is not what he means. He is saying it was hard on him that in the briefing to the world press he gave after the executions a "shrill lady reporter" asked what Ethel was wearing. What this woman asked about was what he had just himself noted: Ethel's cheap little green death dress. With his contempt for the question and for the questioner, he manages a final flourish of displacement of his own hysterical misogyny onto a woman.

It is clear that the level of discourse has changed from one of public and institutional rationalization to one of primitive fears and fantasies of the woman out of bounds.[123] But more significant is the intimate and reciprocal relationship of these two levels of discourse that Ethel Rosenberg's story so clearly reveals. The postwar period was a time of atomic cold war–gaming among men. For the strategic purposes of this game, it was believed tactically necessary to produce Ethel as spy, depending on her as desired woman to move the man to reveal his secret. But this use of her, by the logic of the men's own rules, led to matricide, and thus their textual woman evoked a desire and fear complex of intrapsychic conflicts that were only too easily managed by increasingly regressive and projective rationales.

The normal and ongoing splitting and projective mechanism of meaning making became a regressive spiral, closed to interventions and driven to primitive limits by the excesses of its own production.[124] This regressive spiral, fueled by desire and fear, is a quite different dynamic from the operations of the momentary textual effects of a desire uncontaminated by fear, effects that some contemporary critics gender as feminine and read as working to interrupt discursive wills to knowledge and power, and intervening in drives that would silence, exclude, kill, or ignore.[125]

In the official Rosenberg story, it was the woman in the text—not a textual effect gendered as feminine—who provoked an exhibition of what we can today read as the usually private and unarticulated desire and fear component in public political discourse. Her foregrounding of this component and its regressive process makes her story a paradigm or microcosm of the regressive nature of the larger dynamics and operations of U.S. cold war ideology. But Ethel died of this text, our reading is belated, and the real ownership of the lever was never in doubt.

Legal Formalism and Extraformal Issues

As both the prosecutor's words throughout the trial and the judge's sentence show, although charged with conspiracy to commit espionage, the Rosenbergs were rhetorically tried and sentenced for treason. With no documentary evidence of any crime committed by anyone—the Rosenbergs or any other witness—conspiracy was the only charge the government could make. The government prefers such a charge when trying to make an undocumented case, as the usual laws of evidence and due process do not hold. In a conspiracy charge the prosecution must only show, by the uncorroborated testimony of one person, that the accused members of the conspiracy discussed the commission of an illegal act with intent to carry it out.

Julius and Ethel were accused by her brother David Greenglass, an army machinist at Los Alamos during the war under investigation for black market trading in stolen parts.[126] After

Harry Gold confessed to having been Klaus Fuchs's courier for information concerning the Los Alamos project, he said he had also received information from a GI in Albuquerque in 1945, whose name he later identified as David Greenglass. Under interrogation Greenglass accused Julius of having promoted and supported, through the agency of Greenglass's wife, Ruth, his conveyance of names of Los Alamos scientists and three sketches of atomic bomb design elements to Julius and to Harry Gold. Harry Gold testified in the Rosenberg trial that he was told to say, "I come from Julius," in greeting David Greenglass in Albuquerque; and Elizabeth Bentley, the ex-Communist professional government witness, said Soviet spies were indeed recruited and directed through the Communist party, and that she had taken phone call messages from a "Julius" to convey to her Soviet contact, Jacob Golos. One of Julius Rosenberg's CCNY friends, Max Elitcher, testified that Julius and Morton Sobell had tried on several occasions to recruit him for naval espionage purposes for the Soviet Union.

Despite the Rosenbergs' denials of the Greenglass testimony, the testimony of Gold, Bentley, and Elitcher established the crucial links, in terms of cause-effect, agency, and time span, for the government case against the Rosenbergs. Without those specific links and with just the Greenglass testimony, the case would not have held up. But with no Greenglass testimony, there would have been no story involving the Rosenbergs at all, and the asserted links were not the same thing as corroboration of that testimony. Judge Jerome Frank commented on this in his majority opinion for the Second Circuit Court of Appeals affirming the procedural legality of the trial and denying all defense motions: "Doubtless, if that [accomplice] testimony were disregarded, the conviction could not stand. But where trial is by jury, this court is not allowed to consider the credibility of witnesses or the reliability of testimony."[127]

The higher court may not rule on witness credibility or on testimony reliability in a federal jury trial because appellate judges are not in a position to evaluate nonverbal elements that contributed to the judgment of such issues.[128] But herein lies a logical inconsistency. Solely from reading the trial record the Second

Circuit Court judges felt confident in holding, in response to the defendants' charge, that the trial judge had not behaved prejudicially toward the defense and in favor of the prosecution. The charge was that Judge Kaufman showed bias in his tone, his diction, the orientation of his questions, and his rulings, silencing the defense and encouraging the prosecution. Such discriminations may indeed be spoken prejudicially without readily manifesting themselves as biased in the trial record, which consists of written words, sentences, and recorded actions that remain literally within the parameters of formally correct judicial behavior.

As I stated in the previous section, although no documentary evidence supporting the government claims regarding Julius and Ethel was available to the Rosenbergs or to their defense counsel during the trial, the prosecution, the trial judge, and President Eisenhower were all assured at various times by members of the FBI and of the Justice Department that unimpeachable documents in the Department of Justice files proved the existence of a spy ring headed by Julius Rosenberg.[129] If such documents exist, they have had to remain secret for national security reasons and for the protection of an informant, even though at the time such protection was also an abuse of the Rosenbergs' fundamental right to know the evidence against them, under the Fourteenth Amendment. When the prosecution and the judge share privileged information and reassurances relating to the defendants' guilt that are denied the defense and the defendants, the government's claims, rulings, agreements, rhetoric, and tone acquire extralegal significance that exceeds the prescriptions of any procedural formalism.

Under federal law the jury, properly charged by the judge to discount its own prejudices as well as any discernible biases of the judge, is solely responsible for deciding on the facts of a case. The federal judge, as "the only disinterested lawyer," has "unchallenged power to bring out the facts of the case. . . . He has no more important duty than to see that the facts are properly developed and that their bearing upon the question at issue are [sic] clearly understood by the jury."[130] A contradiction built into this description of the federal judge's function, based on an ideology of objectivity unique to the United States and thus inherent in the country's jurisprudence, lies in the semantic construction linking *disinterested* with *development of facts* and *understanding*. What is occluded in such a non sequitur posited as rational and normative procedure is the complex of background and assumed beliefs that inevitably structures the development of any facts, interpretations, or understandings. Also occluded in this case are Kaufman's beliefs concerning the Rosenbergs' guilt and the history and realities of atomic bomb development and production—beliefs based on ex parte assurances from the government that inevitably structured and oriented in advance any development of the facts on Kaufman's part during the trial.[131]

Once the jury had reached a guilty verdict based on its understanding of the facts as developed by the prosecution, defense, and trial judge, and once the judge had sentenced the defendants to death for treason—a rhetorical translation by the prosecution and the trial judge from the charge of conspiracy—the circuit court was in its own words "powerless" to call into question the credibility of witnesses, the reliability of testimony, the possible use of hearsay testimony, the defense failure to request an adjournment after a surprise witness impeached Rosenberg testimony, or the verdict and sentence, both of which fell within statutory boundaries.

In the first appellate opinion, delivered by Judge Frank for the Second Circuit Court of Appeals on February 25, 1952, is a message to the effect that, had the upper court had power of revision regarding convictions or sentences in this case, there were circumstances that would bear careful consideration: that the convictions depended entirely on the testimony of "self-confessed spies," and that the death sentence was based on evidence that came "almost entirely from accomplices." These statements, acknowledging contextual contingencies relevant to both conviction and sentencing, express a realistic and specific skepticism toward the general confidence in objectivity inherent in American rules of jurisprudence. But they also indicate that the circuit court judges were probably ignorant of the Justice Department assurances to the prosecution and to the judge of unimpeachable evidence of Rosenberg guilt. In fact, no Rosenberg historiographer has suggested that any appellate judge at the circuit court level was privy to the information shared by Judge Kaufman and Irving Saypol concerning secret evidence of Rosenberg guilt.[132]

At one point in the first circuit court ruling in 1952, Judge Frank qualified the court's claim to powerlessness to intervene in the trial court's decisions:

> True, we may, of our own motion, notice egregious errors to which there were no objections below, if they "seriously affect the fairness, integrity or public reputation of judicial proceedings." *Johnson v. United States,* 318 U.S. 189, 200–201; Criminal Rule 52(b). That exception might conceivably govern here if we believed the failure to object to this testimony resulted from the incompetence of defendants' counsel. But the record shows that defendants' counsel were singularly astute and conscientious.[133]

The latter part of this statement by Frank is an anomaly. The Rosenberg defense was so handicapped by relative lack of resources, information, courtroom skills, and adversarial skepticism toward the government story that among the most generous interpretations at the time of and following the trial was that the defense, as reputedly "leftist," was acting under orders from Moscow to sacrifice the Rosenbergs.

Judge Frank nevertheless, in the 1952 opinion and in an April 8, 1953, denial of a defense petition for a rehearing, found three problematic issues:

1. The trial judge had allowed the prosecution's assertion that two alleged conspiracies—Rosenberg/Greenglass/ Gold, and Rosenberg/Sobell/Elitcher—were a continuous one, without requiring the introduction of evidence or submitting that question to the jury for determination. The majority of the court agreed with Kaufman that the assertion of one giant conspiracy required no proof, but Frank found no evidence of such continuity.

2. Kaufman's death sentence was possibly a violation of the defendants' right to due process and freedom

from "cruel and unusual punishment." Although the majority held that precedent did not allow a higher court to modify a lower court judge's sentence that lay within the statutory limitations, Frank's reading of the statutes found that higher courts indeed had the power but had not exercised it.[134]

3. By being charged for conspiracy but rhetorically convicted and sentenced for treason, the Rosenbergs were deprived of the constitutional safeguard of the two-witness rule for treason. Frank noted, "As, however, the Supreme Court did not specifically discuss it, that Court [the Supreme Court] may well think it desirable to review that aspect [the translation of the charge into treason] of our decision in this case."[135]

The Supreme Court denied certiorari on all counts in October 1952, with Justices Frankfurter, Black, and Harold Burton dissenting, only one short of the four votes required for a hearing.

In February 1953, the Rosenberg defense came before the Circuit Court again with the motion, rejected by Kaufman, for a new trial based on the prosecution's use of the media to support testimony during the trial. The circuit court stayed the executions for the Supreme Court to review the circuit court's decision finding that "possible prejudice" had been present during the trial and that the Supreme Court should hear the defense's argument. Judge Swan stated, "Such a statement to the press [as Saypol made] in the course of a trial we regard as wholly reprehensible."[136] Judge Learned Hand, the Circuit Court's most cautious jurist, said in open court,

> People don't dispose of lives, just because an attorney didn't make a point. . . . You can't undo a death sentence. There are some Justices on the Supreme Court on whom the conduct of the prosecuting attorney might make an impression. . . . Your duty, Mr. Prosecutor, is to seek justice, not act as timekeeper.[137]

On March 25, 1953, the Supreme Court nevertheless denied certiorari without reviewing the trial record.[138]

The circuit court opinions contained messages to the Supreme Court and to the president that it lay within their power only to correct what might be found to be errors once the law was clarified by litigation, or to modify what might be an unjustified verdict or sentence. But in all the appeals, the trial record was reviewed only once, by the Second Circuit Court in 1952.[139]

The Supreme Court justices, however, were becoming increasingly politicized—in interpersonal relations as well as in terms of cold war ideology and contradictions. On June 19, 1953, the morning of the Rosenberg executions, the Supreme Court vacated Justice Douglas's stay of execution from the evening before, which he had granted in order to allow the Court to consider what he decided was a new and substantive issue: the question of applicability of statute—the 1917 Espionage Act, or the more specific 1946 Atomic Energy Act—to the Rosenberg charge, conviction, and sentencing. The Court had actually adjourned for the summer on June 15, before Douglas agreed to consider this new question posed to him that evening by two attorneys intervening and acting as "next friends" in the Rosenberg case: Fyke Farmer and Douglas Marshall, not members of the organized left but motivated by professional integrity to bring up what they considered to be a question of serious import.

The justices had on June 15 rejected a motion for the defense by another "next friend," John Finerty, based on Saypol's allegedly knowledgeable use of perjured testimony.[140] Justices Felix Frankfurter and Hugo Black had again dissented from the majority opinion. Then, according to notes made by Frankfurter and Justice Robert Jackson, the justices reached an informal and inappropriate understanding that no one of them would act alone to delay the executions by reopening the case:

> Jackson then went beyond what I had said [to Clerk Willey] by stating that it was perfectly understood at conference that in view of the Court's denial of *habeas corpus* no individual Justice to whom application was made would overrule the Court's determination.[141]

This entire addendum by Frankfurter appears also in Jackson's papers with the notation: "thereby making certain that the complete story is found in both records."[142]

Justice Douglas had disconcerted his associates by acting in an unpredictable and contradictory way on previous Rosenberg motions for writs of certiorari.[143] When, on June 17, he found merit in the new argument presented to him by Marshall and Farmer concerning applicability of statute and ordered that the question should be decided only after full briefing and argument beginning again with the trial court, he countervened the justices' informal understanding that no single justice would reopen the case. While Douglas was deliberating the grounds for this petition from Farmer and Marshall, Justice Jackson, whose enmity for Douglas was well known among his colleagues, had initiated and arranged a private ex parte meeting between Chief Justice Frederick Vinson and Attorney General Brownell. At this meeting, according to an FBI memorandum whose source was Judge Kaufman, in a highly incorrect reversal of accepted and constitutional judicial procedure the justices solicited Brownell's motion to reconvene the Court the next day in order to vacate Douglas's stay of execution should he grant one. "Jackson felt that the whole theory of listening to Farmer's motion was ridiculous and Douglas should have turned it down. . . . Vinson said that if a stay is granted he will call the full Court into session Thursday morning to vacate it."[144] This plan violated procedure in its decision—for the third time in the Court's history—to reconvene the Court immediately instead of waiting for the October session. In its call to vacate a fellow justice's action—an action that lay entirely within that justice's procedural discretion—before hearing his arguments concerning a new and substantive issue, and in its absolute foreclosure of the possibility for obtaining thorough briefs and hearing full arguments on the point, the plan was an egregious abuse of the Supreme Court's function.

By then some of the justices were deeply into illegal behavior, in violation of the Court's obligation to remain open to substantive issues raised regarding procedural correctness—Justice Douglas's stay—and in violation of the canons of judicial conduct prohibiting ex parte communications and impropriety or the appearance of impropriety. Attorney General Brownell—the highest lawyer in the land—by his participation in those ex parte communications, and by his request to Chief Justice Vinson that Vinson require Douglas to bring his point before the full Court where he would be defeated by the majority, was also violating the canons of conduct for attorneys.[145] The attorney general felt strongly that the executions should proceed without delay; thus his urging that the adjourned Court reconvene to vacate the stay, his assurances to Eisenhower that clemency should be denied without further delay because of secret documents proving the Rosenbergs' guilt, and his advance of the Rosenbergs' executions from 11:00 P.M. to 8:00 P.M. of the day on which the Court vacated Douglas's stay and Eisenhower denied clemency.[146] The vacating of the stay by a vote of seven to two that occurred at noon June 19, two days after the Brownell-Vinson meeting, was an unprecedented and irregular action on the part of the Court.[147]

The private and public papers of the last weeks of court skirmishes reveal the Court's implication in cold war ideology, the paralyzing contradictions of anticommunism, and political infighting among the justices themselves, especially in frustration with and animosity toward Justice Douglas.[148] In three previous Supreme Court denials of Rosenberg defense applications for writs of certiorari, dissenting Justices Frankfurter and Black had called for Supreme Court review of the record and of the circuit court's decision, a review that, consistently refused by the majority, never took place.

Frankfurter, a principal speaker for judicial restraint and a conservative on First Amendment issues, recognized the anticommunist double bind in which political and judicial decision making was caught: issues were being raised by the appellate judges that "arouse disquietude in minds that are fiercely hostile to Communist dangers as are Messrs. Jenner, McCarthy, and Velde, but who are also concerned for those American traditions which make them hostile to Communism."[149] He had reminded his colleagues on the Court on May 20 that "the Court's failure to take the case of the Rosenbergs has presented for me the most anguishing situation since I have been on the court." He had decided that to dissent from the Court's May 25 denial of the application for certiorari based on Saypol's extralegal use of the media during the trial would be to provide words to be distorted by radicals or for Communist propaganda, and to lead "high-minded and patriotic laymen who do not understand these things to believe that I implied that the Rosenbergs were convicted though innocent."[150] Frankfurter's concern for protecting the institution overrode the purpose for which that institution existed. The justices were trapped in the symbolic polarization at work in the inaugurating events and developing narrative of the cold war—that is, in both its reality and

> in its symbolism as well. Justice Frankfurter's memoranda indicate how a normally bold jurist, outraged by the prosecutor's tactics, could be intimidated by the prospect that words of dissent could be used against the nation in its global battle against communism. The Rosenbergs were thus finally left at the mercy of . . . a Supreme Court openly split by ideological divisions and torn asunder by personal feuds and hatreds.[151]

But in joining the majority opinion for vacating Douglas's stay of execution on June 19, an action that he had promoted before the stay had been granted, even Justice Jackson included his reservations about the sentence:

> Vacating this stay is not to be construed as endorsing the wisdom or appropriateness to this case of a Death Sentence. That sentence, however, is permitted by law and, as was previously pointed out, is therefore not within this court's power of revision.[152]

At this last court hearing Frankfurter responded more directly in his addendum to the Court's denial of the Rosenberg defense motion for time to prepare a clemency petition:

> Were it established that counsel are correct in their assumption that the sentences of death are to be carried out at 11 P.M. tonight, I believe that it would be right and proper for this court formally to grant a stay with a proper time limit to give appropriate opportunity for the process of executive clemency to operate. I justifiably assume, however, that the time for the execution has not been fixed as of 11 o'clock tonight. Of course, I respectfully assume that appropriate consideration will be given to a clemency application by the authority constitutionally charged with the clemency function.[153]

And Justice Black, the only member of the Supreme Court to have consistently voted for trial review, wrote in his dissenting opinion:

> I do not believe that Government counsel or this Court has had
> time or an adequate opportunity to investigate and decide the
> very serious question raised in asking this Court to vacate the
> stay. . . . Judicial haste is peculiarly out of place where the
> death penalty has been imposed for conduct part of which
> took place at a time when the Congress appears to have barred
> the imposition of the death penalty by district judges acting
> without a jury's recommendation. . . . It is not amiss to point
> out that this Court has never reviewed this record and has
> never affirmed the fairness of the trial below. Without an af-
> firmance of the fairness of the trial by the highest court of the
> land there may always be questions as to whether these execu-
> tions were legally and rightfully carried out. I would still grant
> *certiorari* and let this Court approve or disapprove the fairness
> of the trials.[154]

But President Eisenhower had already issued a statement thirty
minutes after the Supreme Court's decision was announced, without time to consider the written opinions. In one case at least—
Frankfurter's, calling for appropriate consideration of a clemency
application—the dissent had not yet been written when clemency
was denied. Notable in the president's statement are the absence
of any signs of awareness of the uncertainties, qualifications, and
messages to the executive found in the appellate opinions, as
well as Eisenhower's close repetition of the trial judge's diction,
hyperbole, and displacement in his sentencing speech. Carried
in the *New York Times,* June 20, 1953, the statement also manifests, as did Judge Kaufman's sentencing comments, the "second,
recessed tier of arguments," the "already in place beliefs," that
determine what will be heard and "traded on":[155]

> I am convinced that the only conclusion to be drawn from the
> history of this case is that the Rosenbergs have received the
> benefit of every safeguard which American justice can
> provide. . . . I am not unmindful of the fact that this case has
> aroused grave concern both here and abroad in the minds of
> serious people, aside from the considerations of the law. In this
> connection, I can only say that, by immeasurably increasing the
> chances of atomic war, the Rosenbergs may have condemned to
> death tens of millions of innocent people all over the world.
> The execution of two human beings is a grave matter. But even
> graver is the thought of the millions of dead whose deaths may

be directly attributable to what these spies have done. When democracy's enemies have been judged guilty of a crime as horrible as that of which the Rosenbergs were convicted; when the legal processes of democracy have been marshalled to their maximum strength to protect the lives of convicted spies; *when in their most solemn judgment the tribunals of the United States have adjudged them guilty and the sentence just, I will not intervene* in this matter. [italics mine][156]

The circuit court justices had noticed and explicitly commented in their opinions on the limits of legal formalism, which in this case worked to protect what were legal but still questionable decisions and procedures by the government, the judge, the prosecution, and the defense. There was also the substantive question concerning the applicability of the correct law, a question that deserved the Supreme Court's deliberate consideration. But certain justices' uncertainties regarding the sufficiency of formalist reviews, as well as the unlitigated confusion over the applicable law, were to a great extent resolved by the pervasive feeling among more than a majority of them that cold war political concerns took priority over recognizedly problematic issues of judicial practice in the Rosenberg case:

1. applicability of correct law[157]

2. adequacy of defense

3. abuse of defendants' rights by the prosecution and the trial judge

4. severity of the sentences

5. rhetorical translation of a conspiracy charge to one of treason and ensuing abuse of crucial rules of evidence

In addition to these issues addressed by the appellate courts, there were the unremarked problems of:

1. improprieties on the part of the trial judge, justices of the Supreme Court, and the attorney general

2. failure to follow the longstanding rule of clemency in the case of a statute's provision for a lesser penalty than that specified by a previous statute covering the same offense[158]

3. influences and effects of context and intertextuality

Background political beliefs and fears, disseminated and assimilated symbolically and intertextually, not only organized and prevailed over more immediate and particular sociopolitical and juridical data; they also operated symbolically, in excess of the protections offered by legal formalism, to produce and sanction the official story, enabling its determinate conclusion and specific material and cultural effects. The official Rosenberg story became the version that occupied the public domain, continuing its crucial contributions to the ongoing cold war narrative and material history.

Closure and Open-endedness

On June 21, two days after the executions of Julius and Ethel Rosenberg, the *New York Times* ran this wrap-up of the story, contradicting its 1949 contention that the United States had no monopoly on the atomic bomb and demonstrating the rapid development of a national consensus around cold war ideology.

> In the record of espionage against the United States there had
> been no case of its magnitude and its stern drama. The
> Rosenbergs were engaged in funneling the secrets of the most
> destructive weapon of all time to the most dangerous antago-
> nist the United States ever confronted—at a time when a deadly
> atomic arms race was on. Their crime was staggering in its po-
> tential for destruction. It stirred the fears and the emotions of
> the American people. . . . The prevailing opinion in the United
> States . . . is that the Rosenbergs for two years had access to
> every court in the land and every organ of public opinion, that
> no court found grounds for doubting their guilt, and that they
> were the only atom spies who refused to confess and that they
> got what they deserved.[159]

Eight years later, in a June 1961 *FBI Law Enforcement Bulletin,* J. Edgar Hoover, apparently forgetting that the United States was the only country to date to have "caused the shadow of annihilation to fall" on the world, asked:

> Who, in all good conscience, can say that Julius and Ethel
> Rosenberg, the spies who delivered the secret of the atomic

bomb into the hands of the Soviets, should have been spared when their treachery caused the shadow of annihilation to fall upon all of the world's peoples?[160]

The media, with a few exceptions such as the *National Guardian,* the *Daily Worker,* the anticommunist *Jewish Daily Forward,* and the *Washington Star,* closed down the story through restatements of its official version as it had developed by the time of the executions and attempted to deny that the Rosenberg deaths would be the end of the atomic spy story. But it was the end of that story. All subsequent government attempts to achieve full revelation and plenitude of the larger spy story came to nothing. The project was abandoned in 1957. Instead new stories were written, dismantling the official story, substituting alternative legal, historical, biographical, fictional, theatrical, and visual arts versions, of which this rhetorical analysis has been one.

Because the immediate Rosenberg story coincides with and emerges from a radical period of silencing of the left, some specific issues are thus available from that story and time for analyzing the subsequent cultural uses of the Rosenberg story: the long-term effects of cold war politics; the cultural work of opinion making; the functions of leaders, the media, and the individual in a late twentieth-century masculist capitalist democracy; the use and abuse of gender, race, and class in such a democracy; legal formalism and U.S. jurisprudence; attitudes toward nationalism, foreign policy, and arms control in a global society; mass culture and democracy; loyalty and betrayal, affirmation and dissent; the function, performance, and potential of traditional and emergent politics since 1950 and at the beginning of the twenty-first century; objectivity; attitudes toward historical narrative past, present, and potential; and the individual as political and cultural agent in postmodern society.

This is a heavy agenda; cultural arts have no *responsibility* to address these issues, but it is impossible not to read the major cultural artifacts as social work. A critical reading of such work would entail interrogating them for their effective positions toward social and historical issues, as well as toward the narrative performance of social criticism. It would also entail evaluating their use of specific social fields and literary forms and techniques for critical, dissenting, and oppositional cultural activity in what Gore Vidal refers to as the post-Rosenberg era—an era in which explanatory narratives for state and institutional policies and master narratives of historical development have lost their credibility.[161]

Part II
The Rosenberg Stories: Culture

The one duty we owe to history is to rewrite it.
—*Oscar Wilde, quoted in Linda Hutcheon,*
A Poetics of Postmodernism

3

Culture as Critique
in the Post-Rosenberg Era

This study of the Rosenberg stories is an experiment in using the tools of literary analysis to study first a political and collective use of symbol and narrative to construct a specific history and then the cultural use of symbol and narrative in literature and the performing and visual arts to come to terms with that history. I began with a consideration of the context of what would become the official Rosenberg story, suggesting and foregrounding the possible motivations, manipulated rhetoric, potential fictionality, and historical effects of that narrative as it developed. Now I turn more directly to the arts, extending this literary history of the Rosenberg story to include two novels, a multimedia drama, a photographic collage, and a painting—all of which use the Rosenberg story as the occasion of their production—and to read them in relation to the sociopolitical world of the United States during the cold war.[1]

These readings—as do all private and public responses to art— have their own potential for relative social effect. They are continuations, in yet another genre, of the ongoing critical function of the Rosenberg story(ies). The arts—aesthetic, avant-garde, critical, commercial, and popular (not necessarily exclusive categories)—cannot adequately be explained solely as either a reflection of historical society, an ideological masking or manipulation of social reality, or a critical response to a given set of social relationships. Advertising, journalism, television programs, political speeches, press conferences, and critical articles and books can be interpreted as more one than the other kind of symbolic and crafted activity—more reflective and reproductive of specific social conditions, or of specific points of view, and overtly ideological.[2] But both the popular and elite arts in twentieth-century mass culture—fiction, music, poetry, the visual and performing arts considered in the broadest sense—tend more toward an openly mixed performance of all three functions: reflection, ideological representation, and critique, opposition, negation, or all three. Contemporary cultural practices—especially those that take place in the forms of a critical or historiographic postmodernism—tend to foreground the mixed nature of their production and effects, accepting and self-consciously exploiting the necessity to represent aspects of the real world in order to say anything about them, while calling into question the act of representation itself.

This rhetorical analysis of the Rosenberg story and the historical and social critiques offered by the Rosenberg novels and drama and by the contemporary visual and multimedia arts commissioned and collected by the Rosenberg Era Art Project for a touring exhibition, "Unknown Secrets," that opened in 1988, have in common their status as phenomena of the "post-Rosenberg age."[3] The official Rosenberg story coincided with and helped inaugurate and produce—despite official political intentions to the contrary—postmodernity: a historical period in which the traditional liberal Enlightenment narratives of liberal individualism, objectivity, and the rational progressivity of democratic capitalism or socialism—and the hubristic U.S. version of that narrative, the mandate for moral protection of a free (market) world—have lost their adequacy to function as they did during World Wars I and II, and as they have for forty-five years. Beginning in the 1950s, however, as soon as they had been firmly articulated in their cold war versions—they also began to break down as overreaching, metanarrative explanatory justifications for the actual decisions, actions, evasions, injustices, and contradictions of lived historical experience in countries on both sides of and beyond the iron curtain. Despite their rote repetition and ritualistic *public* use by political officials, business leaders, military officers, church leaders, teachers, and schoolchildren, they are no longer adequate to the actual but unrepresentable complexities of late twentieth-century global society on planet earth.[4]

As I have noted in chapter 1, there were already in 1945 great discrepancies between the U.S. narrative of moral purpose inherited from Wilson and Roosevelt and actual socioeconomic and political conditions and ambitions, but the power of the narrative was still intact and operative for its national audience, as was the Marxist version for Communists and socialists worldwide, despite enormous and horrendous contradictions between that narrative and the realities of the Stalinist state. The Rosenberg story could not have taken place as it did without the support of the Manichaean version in the United States of the Enlightenment narrative, and without national belief in the U.S. role in keeping the world safe for that narrative to realize itself in history over and against the evil forces of communism.

The post-Rosenberg era is one of epistemological skepticism toward and interrogation of such official explanatory narratives for actual domestic and global material circumstances and relationships. Such a degree of skepticism began—for the United States, at least—with the debatably necessary use of the atomic bomb on Nagasaki and Hiroshima and has intensified with each destructive—and irrational, by any egalitarian moral calculus— official action performed in the name of peace, freedom, and democracy: antilabor illegalities and violence, the Rosenberg trial, McCarthyism, racist and sexist violence and deprivation of rights, antistudent violence, discriminatory domestic laws and economic policies, Vietnam, Watergate, arms escalation, the Iran/ Contra affair, U.S. foreign policy in the Middle East, the Iraqi war, Wall Street in-house get-rich stock and bond manipulations, the massive and costly savings and loan and banking system corruption and public failure, and CIA support—for the sake of intelligence—of the corrupt and ruinous operations of a world bank, BCCI, involved in money laundering, embezzlement, and worldwide drug trafficking.[5]

A growing awareness of the inability of the traditional explanatory narrative to account adequately for these phenomena is pervasively evident in the language of television sitcoms, MTV segments, cartoons, pop art, films, rap lyrics and other politicized song forms, comic routines, performance art—that is, in all the forms of popular culture. Skepticism toward traditional explanatory narrative characterizes also the more avant-garde and often less accessible or disturbing and repellant practices of an interrogating and denaturalizing postmodernity in films, television, cinema, literature, and the visual and performing arts. These aggressively antinarrative and antihumanist approaches in the arts, along with the reappearance and reformulation of the Nietzschean critique of meaning and truth in philosophy and literary theory, have produced in the 1980s and 1990s a bitter division in the academic humanities, between a subject-centered humanism based on Cartesian objectivity and Enlightenment rationality, and the more or less radical critique of such a humanism and its material history that occurs in poststructuralist, materialist, and feminist cultural criticism. The effectivity of all of these practices of art and criticism in interrupting, disturbing, and foregrounding the gaps and contradictions both internal to the traditional explanatory narrative and between that narrative and lived experience is evident in the powerful counteroffensives of official and institutional reaction and censorship.[6]

Cultural criticism in this period consists to a large extent in reading various cultural phenomena analytically in order to distinguish between and to foreground elements that reinforce traditional narrative support of oppressive relationships of power, and elements that interrogate and interrupt the relationships between such narrative and social blindness to lived experience. This interruption inevitably engages and implicates the reading or observing individual. It is not that the liberal narrative of a just and democratic society must be abandoned because it doesn't fit actual circumstances; it is that its use as a justification for unjust and undemocratic practices must be interrupted and displayed as in conflict with and in denial of the social reality that the narrative promises. The central contradiction within such use is that between a theorized unrestricted "free-market" individualist liberty and the promise of a socially just world.

The project of interruption, of which the continuing Rosenberg story in historiography, biography, literature, and the performing and visual arts can be seen as paradigmatic, is what postmodern fiction claims to be accomplishing. But the paradox of a delegitimating fiction that takes as its referent an irrational social order resides in the extent to which any fiction, even antirealist fiction, represents that society positively (as in positivism), even in order to interrogate its irrationalities. As Adorno noted, with his usual cultural pessimism, this problem of complicity in perpetuating an unjust social order cannot be avoided: "For discourse to refer, even protestingly, is for it to become instantly complicit with what it criticizes; in a familiar linguistic and psychoanalytic paradox, negation negates itself because it cannot help but posit the object it desires to destroy."[7] But this totalizing and pessimistic claim depends on a decontextualization and a dehistoricization of linguistic reference, representation, and reception. It also ignores the potential effect of the critical orientation of a given representation that occurs through manipulation of contexts, genres, forms, and modes of expression. But Adorno is right in emphasizing the critical burden placed on reading to uncover complicities in social representation with that which is being interrogated and criticized.

A purposeful critical practice for late twentieth-century cultural criticism that remains suspended between a nontotalizing optimism or pessimism, while working to resist and rebel against oppressive life forms, often indeed reproduces some of the very conditions that enable those forms to persist. Thus in order to read the Rosenberg novels, drama, and visual artifacts as critical cultural projects, it will be important to take into account several crucial relationships and phenomena: the relationship between the work's concept of the individual and its critical or utopian representation of a given world order; an unwitting and uncritical replication of structures of difference that support the order being interrogated or critiqued; the development, uses, and effects of style, form, frame, and context—gratuitous and purposeful, intrinsic and extrinsic; and the nature of the constitution and implication of a reader, viewer, or audience for the work. All these categories of analysis—representation of the individual, structures of difference, effects of form, and manipulation of reception—have the potential for articulating and foregrounding form and content contradictions that work not only to undercut the work but also to intersect our own critical consciousness, thus splitting, compartmentalizing, and blinding our reading of social reality. But, by the same token, those contradictions can work to make us see, with a sudden shock of self-implicating recognition.

The critical function for this post-Rosenberg era, then, is to define and foreground in any cultural practice—the arts, historiography, pedagogy, journalism, religion, or any other symbolic activity—the differences between the reproduction of oppressive material and social relationships and forms of thought on the one hand and the critical interrogation and discovery of the same, on the other. In this way many artists, critics, teachers, and left political activists, may, for now, in the latter part of a postmodern twentieth century, share the same purpose.

4

The Book of Daniel

*The oversaturation of an age with history . . . leads an age
into a dangerous mood of irony in regard to itself and subsequently into the even more dangerous mood of cynicism. . . . in
this mood . . . it develops more and more a prudent practical
egoism through which the forces of life are paralyzed and at
last destroyed. . . . Modern man . . . has become a strolling spec-
tator and has arrived at a condition in which even great wars
and revolutions are able to influence him for hardly more
than a moment. . . . Thus the individual grows fainthearted
and unsure and dares no longer believe in himself: he sinks
into his own subjective depths, which here means into the accumulated lumber of what he has learned but which has no
outward effect, of instruction which does not become life. The
man [overwhelmed by history] can no longer extricate himself
from the delicate net of his judiciousness and truth for a
simple act of will and desire.*

Friedrich Nietzsche, Untimely Meditations

E. L. Doctorow's *Book of Daniel*, published in 1971, was immediately hailed as "the political novel of our age" and continues
to be regarded critically as unique for its treatment of historical
and political issues through the lives of individuals. Called "a
threnody on the agony of the American left," it is, as reviewers
and Doctorow himself have noted, not about the Rosenbergs but
about the *idea* of the Rosenbergs, "how they came into being,
why their trial was needed, what their legacy is and the mixture
of that legacy with the social-political climate today."[1] Doctorow's
second novel, it was the first to bring him critical attention.

Daniel was not a best-seller; it was, however, a Bowker's notable book for 1971, with Maya Angelou's *I Know Why the Caged Bird Sings,* Donald Barthelme's *City Life,* Saul Bellow's *Mr. Sammler's Planet,* George Jackson's *Soledad Brother,* Gabriel García Márquez's *One Hundred Years of Solitude,* Kate Millet's *Sexual Politics,* Charles Silberman's *Crisis in the Classroom,* Germaine Greer's *Female Eunuch,* Ivan Illich's *Deschooling Society,* Daniel Ellsberg's *The Pentagon Papers,* Walker Percy's *Love in the Ruins,* B. F. Skinner's *Beyond Freedom and Dignity,* Frances Fox Piven and Richard A. Cloward's *Regulating the Poor,* and Ramsey Clark's *Crime in America. The Book of Daniel* has been in continuous print since 1971 and is regularly taught in high schools, colleges, and universities. It has been published in England and the Western European countries. The democratization of Eastern European countries in the late 1980s and early 1990s, and the ensuing need for a rearticulation of the meaning and practice of the left in those countries, evoked new interest in *The Book of Daniel.*

Daniel is an early juxtaposition of two literary modes—realism and postmodernism—as a method for bridging the two historical eras in which those modes prevailed: the pre-Rosenberg period of the old left, and the post-Rosenberg period of the 1960s and the New Left.[2] This historical bridging would also necessarily entail dealing with the discontinuities between a theory of history governed by the liberal and individualist concept of the self as a free and coherent agent, and one based on the less coherent and even posthumanist concept of the individual as a multiply interested and motivated product, producer, and reproducer of contradictory social and material conditions and interactions.

As most of its reviews noted, *Daniel* is a book about a past period in U.S. history that informs the issues of the present, particularly in regard to the potential for left effectivity in the late twentieth-century United States. The book maintains two primary and interpenetrating narrative tracks. It attempts to account for the effects on a family and its individual members of becoming the object of the antagonistic and projective (scapegoating) forces of a society. Using the history of that family, and the son's efforts to connect his past with his present and to experience the immediacy of his world, it also attempts to account for the generational break of the 1960s, the shift from old left to new, and to articulate the differences, losses, and gains of that apparently disjunctive withdrawal and emergence. It suggests indirectly and through multiple literary techniques the possibilities and potentials for dissent and radicalism in a post-McCarthy society whose dominant cultural image is Disneyland.

Doctorow uses the techniques of realism and postmodernism in a complex and multivoiced, multimode, first-, second-, and third-person, self-referential counterpoint of historical synthesis and narrative, interrogation and delegitimation, and imaginative reconstruction. In tone variations he registers political and personal uncertainty, skepticism, despair, cynicism, insights, and hopes for futurity. He performs political, biblical, and theological historiography, as well as social, political, and cultural analysis and critique, sometimes simultaneously. He uses what is often considered to be the primary literary genre in the United States— the individual's quest for identity, the bildungsroman—for the book's linear, realistic narrative thread. And he interrupts, complicates, cancels, and contests this plot line with book knowledge, digressive and contradictory historical and personal memories, and lived experience—a process not altogether productive of a represented unity of point of view or character. This open-endedness of subject(ivity) and argument is purposeful, refusing and critiquing simple ideologies of the unified self and moral national purpose, always from the critical imaginary of a just world, an ideal that serves as the novel's fixed moral point in a critical rethinking of history and its subjects.[3]

Generations

Fifteen years after the Rosenberg trial, when Doctorow noticed similarities and differences between the Vietnam antiwar movement and the ineffective old left efforts to oppose the cold war, he began thinking about the Rosenbergs and the U.S. left. As he developed the idea of a novel about the subject, he decided that the Rosenberg children could embody for him the problematic of a generational and cultural rupture in a way that a confirmed member of neither the old left nor the New Left could do.[4] Irving Howe, a left critic with origins in the old left and cofounder and editor of *Dissent,* wrote in 1965:

> The thirties intellectuals, bound together by common problems and understandings, seem in danger of losing their dominant position in American intellectual life. . . . A younger generation of intellectuals and semi-intellectuals, perhaps not as well equipped dialectically as the older leftists, semi-leftists and ex-leftists, and certainly not as wide ranging in interest or accomplished in style, yet endowed with a self assurance, a lust for power, a contempt for and readiness to swallow up their elders [is] at once amusing, admirable, and disturbing. Thinking of themselves as "new radicals," these young people see as one of their major tasks the dislodgement of the old ones. . . . A *Kulturkampf* seems in prospect, and one in which, I must confess, my own sympathies would be mixed.[5]

A member of that self-assured, lustful, and contemptuous generation of "careless courage" responds:

> The 1950s were the turning point in the history of America. Those who grew up before the 1950s live today in the mental world of Nazism, concentration camps, economic depression, and Communist dreams stalinized. . . . Kids who grew up in the post-1950s live in a world of supermarkets, color TV commercials, guerrilla war, international media, psychedelics, rock 'n roll and moon walks. . . . This generation gap is the widest in history. The pre-1950s generation has nothing to teach the post-1950s.[6]

In Doctorow's book, Daniel Isaacson is the transitional figure who in the end refuses the reductive and ahistorical idealism of the New Left—at some cost in terms of his ability to act.

From his vantage point of cynical detachment, he is an effective, if immature, agent for an analysis and critique of both a past and a present—the pre- and post-1950s—in which he has been and is present. He grew up in an old left family that remained loyal to the narrative of Marxism and the Communist party after most of the left was disaffected by disclosures of Stalin's practices.[7] Along with their unwavering belief in the Marxist narrative of an inevitable historical progression toward a just society, the Isaacsons also possessed a liberal faith in the U. S. Constitution and institutions, as did most of the Communist old left. Despite the ideological reductions of Marxist theory as it was then interpreted, they practiced an ongoing and collective political analysis of contemporary life. They educated their children to specific operations of political and cultural power excluded from or occluded by mainstream historiography, and they pointed out daily discrepancies between the American dream and actual social and economic conditions and experiences elided by the constructions of formal education, religion, advertising, and the media.

The Isaacsons were executed in 1953 for the treason of having given the Russians the secret of the atomic bomb, after having been convicted and tried for conspiracy. Their son, as he narrates the book in 1967, is a graduate student in history at Columbia who cannot find a thesis for his dissertation: "How [do his abuse of his wife, the suicide attempt of his sister, and other family griefs] establish sympathy for me [as narrator]? Why not begin [instead] with Daniel searching, too late, for a thesis?" (8). Although Daniel is a transitional figure without allegiances, he shares certain generational characteristics with the emerging New Left. He is middle class, rebellious, and enraged, but without historical knowledge and without a father—that is, without a sense of generational continuity. He lacks a practical knowledge of the past and the knack of analysis necessary to develop a workable thesis or a political position; he is paralyzed, unable to choose a subject for his dissertation and unable to discover himself as a political subject or agent.

But motivated by love, rage, and guilt for his parents and sister as sacrificial political victims, willing to experience anything in the interest of more understanding, equipped with a historical imagination, and aided by an unannounced wiser older voice that speaks through him (narratively, not mystically), he is able to begin the laborious personal and political work of "making connections"—not necessarily the same thing as making narrative. In this he achieves a kind of historical wisdom and understanding of radical effectivity and its limits that make the exuberant and "careless courage" of the New Left impossible

for him. Tom Hayden, a coauthor of the 1962 Port Huron inaugurating manifesto of the New Left, said that becoming a radical
"was like giving birth to yourself."[8] But Daniel's birth is not into
the unified self of old or New Left liberal individualist humanism.

Traditions of Character

Daniel Isaacson is a postmodern, intertextual, and historicized
David Copperfield. Charles Dickens wrote to discover himself
through David Copperfield writing to discover himself in the
novel of the same name. Like David, Daniel is writing an autobiography in order to come to terms with a criminal father (and
mother) as well as with himself in an irrational society: "Let's
see, what other David Copperfield kind of crap [can I tell you]?"
he asks (117). Since this is also a Holden Caulfield line, Daniel
notes that "the Trustees of Ohio State were right in 1956 when
they canned the English instructor for assigning *Catcher in the
Rye* to his freshman class. They knew there is no qualitative
difference between the kid who thinks it's funny to fart in chapel,
and Che Guevara. They knew then Holden Caulfield would found
SDS" (117–18). This is a typical Doctorow fusion of individual
and history, both in its evocation in a quip by Daniel of the
censorship and enforced conformities of the 1950s, and in its
situating of small individual gestures within larger political
scenarios.

But Daniel as a defensively cynical intellectual and nonparti-
cipating observer is even more directly a descendant of the U.S.
autobiographer Henry Adams, the distanced fence-sitting observer of himself and history.[9] Daniel is also writing his disser-
tation/novel to acquire an education in understanding the
individual in history. In *The Education* Adams thinks of himself,
as Daniel intermittently does, in the third person, as a spider
having to construct a web of understanding from his own perceptions of sequence in an anarchic world. Daniel is an equally
distanced observer in search of understanding, forced into an
unwilling remembering of his past and reconnection with his
present by the influence of his angry, dying sister with whom

he feels an incestuous relationship of the heart and mind: "They were like the compensating halves of a clock sculpture that would exchange positions when the chimes struck" (10). "My involvement with Susan has to do with rage, which is easily confused with unnatural passion" (253), a rage evoked by her moral judgment of him as an evasive and unprincipled betrayer of his family and his past through passivity and cynicism. But as a self-styled "criminal of perception" since childhood, he is a natural critic: a transgressor of the rules and laws of perception, one who can see behind, beneath, and beyond the masking sequences, coherencies, and closures of the prevailing justifying narratives.[10]

Like Adams, Daniel has his own concerns with "monstrous sequence"—the effects of the cause-effect constructions of history through historiography—as well as with an apparent historical transition from unity to multiplicity, from the unity of Christianity of the Middle Ages, or of the unified subject and progressive history Enlightenment narratives of both right and left, to the early twentieth-century crisis in Cartesian dualistic subject-object epistemology—occasioning the reactionary responses of modernist aestheticism and technocratic utopianism—to the dissolving boundaries and multiple conflicting, partial, and constitutive points of view of the 1960s and after. Daniel also sees electricity (Adams's dynamo) as the dominant metaphor for a society motivated, managed, extended, and radically transformed by electronic technology.[11]

Daniel is concerned with education, remembering the training his father had given him in being a "psychic alien," teaching him to practice his own form of critical estrangement on the daily cultural cover-ups achieved by organized religion, advertising, the media, and politics. He critiques the efficient substitutes for education and historical knowledge provided for a mass culture by the diversions and evasions of Disneyland and television, which he considers uniquely suited to the educational requirements of a totalitarian society. Here is Adams on the same subject: "All State education is a sort of dynamo machine for polarizing the popular mind; for turning and holding its lines of force in the direction supposed to be most effective for State purposes.

The German machine was terribly efficient [in this]" (*The Education,*78).

In *The Education* Adams is working toward a coherent theory of contemporary (late nineteenth- and twentieth-century) history, which he finally understands in an altogether naturalistic way as a field of multiple and contradictory forces drawing the individual along like a fish on a hook, entirely disjunctive with a more coherent past, and ultimately requiring an adaptive and reactive—posthumanist?—social mind. As he tells us over and over, his is a story of personal and human failure in what is becoming a posthumanist age. Appropriate to such a totalizing view, Adams protects himself throughout by consistently adopting the stance of ironized viewer.

In this instance Doctorow, writing Daniel Isaacson of 1967 writing himself, departs formally and thematically from Henry Adams of 1905 writing himself. Adams interpreted his rapidly changing, technologically and commercially burgeoning world through an ironic but consistent perceiving consciousness, promoted by his willed choice of marginality and outside observer status in a family and generational context of elite material, social, and political entitlement. Daniel perceives his world—a complex intensification of Adams's prophetic description of the twentieth century—through an inconsistent and fragmented but equally ironic consciousness: ironic by virtue of his outsider status—through class, race, and as an unwitting player in mainstream history—and fragmented by the contradictions, irrationalities, and undecidabilities of the external world that intersect and constitute his perceiving consciousness.

Adams's narrative is still that of the unified consciousness of modernism, addressing issues of an irrational world through what he finally realizes as futile attempts to achieve an aesthetic understanding of a history becoming increasingly hostile to mankind. Daniel's narrative is the quest of the fractured postmodern consciousness informed by the recognition of self as both construct and agent of a contradictory, irrational, unjust, and ultimately unknowable world.

Despite Daniel's insights into the very phenomena predicted by Adams—alien technology, manipulative social and economic

forces, and imminent multiform potentials for apocalyptic catas-
trophe—Daniel's story is, unlike that of Adams, not one of absolute or self-advertised failure. Like Adams, he begins in cynicism
and irony, but Daniel refuses paralysis and despair for tentative
moves toward historical engagement despite uncertainties and an
awareness of the potential for futility.

Formal Ambiguities and Implications

Doctorow himself to some extent shares Adams's reservations
about the possibilities for individual agency in a postnuclear
society:

> The story of any given individual may not be able to sustain an
> implication for the collective fate. The assumption that makes
> fiction possible, even Modernist fiction—the moral immensity
> of the single soul—is under question because of the bomb. . . .
> The over-riding condition of things [is] that we're in the count-
> down stages of a post-humanist society.[12]

But unlike Adams, Doctorow maintains his own contradictory
and existential position as an Enlightenment humanist in that
posthumanist society:

> I'm a leftist. But of the pragmatic, social democratic left—the
> humanist left that's wary of ideological fervor. It's a very ex-
> hausting place to be. . . . I've been called an idealist and naive
> and a pseudo-Marxist. But in this country the reference has to
> be the Constitution. . . . If I was not in [the radical Jewish hu-
> manist tradition], I would certainly want to apply for
> membership.[13]

Here Doctorow gives voice to a division and even contradiction not uncommon to critical thinkers and political activists: a
pessimistic or tragic view of history from an Enlightenment individualist point of view, coupled with a willed and defiant "obligation to engage to construct a just world," through a "fusion of
moral engagement with critical epistemology."[14] This is Antonio
Gramsci's "pessimism of the intellect, optimism of the will."[15] It
is a willed commitment despite the narrative foreclosure and
political paralysis entailed by a radical posthumanism. Since

Doctorow also claims that "a political [literary] work, by its very nature, would usually end up acknowledging the ambiguities of what it's talking about,"[16] we could expect, in a determinedly political novel like *Daniel,* a certain confusion and mocking skepticism on the questing Daniel's part toward conventional notions of self and agency, and the possibilities for individual agency in the melioration of history. Such ambiguity first manifests itself formally.

The epigraphs invoke a progressively despairing view of history, ending with a complete abdication of history and self by the poet. The first of the three epigraphs is from Daniel 3:4, in which the oppressed people under Nebuchadnezzar are exhorted to fall down and worship golden images. The biblical Daniel offered the possibility, through his interpretations of the king's dreams, of sparing the people from the worst excesses of authority, but his visions became increasingly apocalyptic and hysterical. The second epigraph is from Whitman, playing the same kind of instruments that served in the biblical Daniel as a signal to Nebuchadnezzar's people to fall down in worship; but in Whitman's verse they serve as poetic commemoration of historical tragedy, of the "conquer'd and slain." The final epigraph takes us to the end of this downward spiral, with Allen Ginsberg's words to America, in the poem by the same name, "I can't stand my own mind / . . . Go fuck yourself with your atom bomb."

Doctorow is telling us that history is apparently a repetitive and worsening story of the corruptions of power and greed and the barbarisms that underlie every act of civilization.[17] But this time with a difference: the possibility of the *end of history,* by atomic holocaust, through human agency practicing corruptions and barbarisms in the name of civilization. The redemption offered by modernist art to a tragic world is no longer available. The shift from local to global destructive capacities with the development of the atomic bomb was accompanied in the 1950s and 1960s by a cultural break almost as radical: the shift from the historical narrative constructions of Hitler and Stalin, or Truman, McCarthy, and Eisenhower, with their assumptions of the potential for a conflation of narrative and material historical mastery in the name of progress, to history by Disney, politics by television, and society by consumption. "Rather than making the culture, we seem these days to be in it. American culture suggests an infinitely expanding universe that generously accommodates, or imprisons, us all."[18] So the irrepressible public performance "criminal of perception" Allen Ginsberg rejects history and art, and ultimately his own mind.

But the epigraphic progression through tyranny and oppression to the potential for atomic apocalypse and individual alienation and impotence is belied by the formal structure of the novel: a division—by time, image, or both—into four books, beginning with "Memorial Day" 1967, commemorating all the "conquer'd and slain" evoked by Whitman's lines; passing through "Halloween," the night of carnival and the eruption of dark forces ("that archetype traitor, the master subversive Poe, who wore a hole into the parchment [of the Enlightenment and the Constitution] and let the darkness pour through" (218); then "Starfish," the forgotten thirteenth zodiac sign signifying the unity of language with truth, life with justice, and belief with intellect, but also paradoxically a unity in death for Daniel's sister, Susan, who died from world withdrawal; and ending with "Christmas," a time of birth and hope—for Christians, but also, to some extent, for Daniel. A calendar of cyclical, repetitive time when the darkness breaks through and God becomes human. Not just once, but again and again, in order to advocate and practice an unrationalized and paradoxical form of communitarian and egalitarian justice that the political left in a posttheological—and perhaps posthumanist—age finds itself charged with defending and promulgating. Individuals—divided against themselves by the contradictions and oppressions of history—find a new kind of imperative and agency in this kind of collective and existential charge.

This divided and incoherent individual overwhelmed by history is most obviously expressed in Daniel's oscillation between first and third person narrative, a formal critique of unified subjectivity. The book has been criticized for what are considered to be gratuitous uses of postmodern formal techniques. Although it may be difficult to show the congruence of a formal with a thematic logic in specific instances, the multiple interrupting persons, voices, and modes are true to the historical, political, social, and personal uncertainties and arguments that make up the book. A schematic correspondence between formal and semantic disruptions would itself be problematic, offering an aestheticized narrative coherence that it is the book's purpose to interrupt and interrogate.

Not only Daniel, but also Daniel's readers are not allowed to rest easily in a unified subject position; they are instead directly invoked by and involved with different and conflicting voices, in a range of tones, and at different points of uncertainty or conflict in the argument Daniel is conducting with himself and his audience. The manipulation and production of participating readers complicit in twentieth-century modern history, with its contradictions, hostilities, terrors, and hopes, is pervasive and largely unintrusive, with occasional purposeful foregroundings of the narrative demands on them.

Daniel speaks in the conventional conversational vernacular of the twentieth-century United States, repeatedly and colloquially using the impersonal and indefinite second person "you" instead of "one," and drawing us in at a largely unconscious level. "We understand St. Joan: You want to fuck her but if you do you miss the point" (254). Concerning the primitive rationale for the cold war's economic and military policies, he manages to show how the disavowed and projected other resides in our own hearts:

> When you defeat an enemy you are required to eat his
> heart. . . . You consume the heart of your enemy so that it can
> no longer be said of him that he exists—except as he exists in
> you. (286)

He laments his loss of childhood hope and his disconnection with family and the past in a way that also acknowledges a sense of connection in which we all participate:

> All my life I have been trying to escape from my relatives and I
> have been intricate in my run, but one way or another they are
> what you come upon around the corner, and the Lord God
> who is so frantic for recognition says you have to ask how they

142

are and would they like something cool to drink, and what is it
you can do for them this time. (37)

There are occasional intrusive and challenging invocations to
you, the reader, or to other yous whose evocation is equally
startling and forceful. These direct addresses are sometimes angry
and hostile, sometimes empathetic, sometimes ironic, sometimes
tragic. Whatever the tone, the result is a more intimate engagement between Daniel, the reader, and the world. As he is com-
manding his wife to undress and kneel away from him like "an
abject devotionalist" so he can burn her buttocks with a cigarette
lighter, he interrupts the narrative to interrupt the reader's voyeuristic and prurient gaze: "Who are you anyway? Who told you
you could read this?" (74). He then goes on to speculate about
the differing effects of realism and symbolic imagination, citing
the example of a razor slicing through an eyeball in a Buñuel
film just when the audience has settled for the symbolic substitution of a thin cloud gliding across the moon.

This is a metafictional and seemingly gratuitous digression on
literary matters, but as Daniel and Doctorow make clear to us
throughout the novel, and as Kenneth Burke demonstrates in
Rhetoric of Religion, what is always already characteristic of our
interpretations of the world is a *literary* reduction of the raw
data complexities of history, and thus eventually even of that
reduction—our historical memory itself—into motivated and
symbolic evasions, exclusions, coherencies, and closures that are
no longer adequate to material circumstances: like the symbolic
substitution of a thin cloud gliding across the moon for the real
horror of a razor slicing through an eyeball. What seems merely
gratuitous cinematographic aestheticism on Buñuel's part becomes something more radically critical in a political sense when
considered as his symbolic discovery of the function of symbolism in history to mask the horrors of reality—realities such
as Stalin's purges, the U.S. government's knowing exposure of
government workers to high-level radiation, the Holocaust, or
the Highway of Death produced (but not for television) in Iraq
by U.S. fighter planes strafing returning soldiers and civilians
following the Iraqi cease-fire, just as the yellow ribbons, flags,

bands, and parades were beginning to fill the television screens at home.[19]

This symbolic narrative reduction is what Doctorow and Daniel perceived as having occurred in the belief system of the old left. Daniel comments that the old left "dwelt in a realm so mysteriously symbolic that it defied understanding" (27). Daniel's quest is partially to remember his parents' real story for himself, from his own memory, investigations, and critical intelligence, rather than to settle for the equally bankrupt right or left symbolic versions of the Isaacsons as traitors or martyrs.

Daniel's "you" brings into the circle of address more than just the reader: he appeals to the oppressed and imprisoned around the world with an ironic consolation that is at the same time a foregrounding of the contradiction between U.S. symbolic narratives—the rhetoric of freedom—and actual political and economic practices—the performance of oppression and violence:

A MESSAGE OF CONSOLATION TO GREEK BROTHERS IN THEIR PRISON CAMPS, AND TO MY HAITIAN BROTHERS AND NICARAGUAN BROTHERS AND DOMINICAN BROTHERS AND SOUTH AFRICAN BROTHERS AND SPANISH BROTHERS AND TO MY BROTHERS IN SOUTH VIETNAM, ALL IN THEIR PRISON CAMPS: YOU ARE IN THE FREE WORLD! (288–89)

And he laments to his own country: "My country! Why aren't you what you claim to be?" (47), refusing with this gesture the blindly loyal turn that the intellectual old left made in the early 1950s. His diction echoes and subverts the famous "Our Country and Our Culture," *Partisan Review*'s collective statement of reallegiance in 1952 to U.S. cold war values and policies.

To a sympathetic reader, someone who already knows the history he is telling, someone perhaps from the old left or a contemporary left intellectual, he establishes his most intimate and personal relationship: "Note to the Reader: if [this historical analysis] seems after all this time elementary . . . then I am reading you. And together we may rend our clothes in mourning" (67). Finally, referring to his parents' arrest as "one of the Great Moments of the American Left . . . artfully reduced to the shabby conspiracies of a couple named Paul and Rochelle Isaacson" (135), he challenges a now antagonistic and perhaps complicit reader with his angry determination to render a realistic—not symbolic—account of their deaths: "I suppose you think I can't do the electrocution. I know there is a you. There has always been a you. YOU: I will show you that I can do the electrocution" (359).

Silent Structures

The Book of Daniel, and the greatly diluted film version, *Daniel,* directed by Sidney Lumet and scripted by Doctorow, along with Louis Nizer's bestselling *Implosion Conspiracy,* are the only versions of the Rosenberg story known by the public at large. Nizer's book—the "true" story, according to the author—was written without benefit of now-available FBI records, and is blatantly biased, based on an absolute faith in U.S. institutions and justice. Nizer's attitude toward the Rosenbergs is condescendingly moralistic and arrogantly classist, racist, and sexist. The film, synonymous with the Rosenberg story for most of its viewers, is a bland, depoliticized, privatized, sentimental, and familial take on the story, the product of a conscious decision on Lumet's part.[20] It is fair to say, then, that Nizer's book and Lumet's film—with larger audiences than Doctorow's novel—in telling the Rosenberg story have also worked to reproduce specific symbolic configurations masking and denying specific historical abusive and oppressive relationships of power. Doctorow's book is a more faithful and provocative representation of the complexities, uncertainties, and political implications of the story for the present.

Doctorow made three significant changes in the historical Rosenberg story, in addition to turning Ethel's accuser-brother David Greenglass into Dr. Mindish, the family dentist: the substitution of Susan, the Isaacson daughter, for one of the two Rosenberg sons; the dramatization of left insensitivity to and exploitation of the sons for political purposes instead of the actual sheltering and care offered the children by the left; and the elaboration of complicated and metaphorically purposeful pathologies for Daniel and Susan as opposed to the engaged and healthy lives of the Rosenberg sons, Michael and Robert Meeropol.

The Rosenberg brothers were beneficiaries of the emotional, familial, and financial support of a communitarian old left. Their parents' attorney Emanuel Bloch appealed for and was able to establish a trust fund sufficient for their education. Members of the left carried on an extended and difficult, but finally successful, court battle for their adoption by members of the community, Abel and Anne Meeropol, whose name the Rosenberg sons took for their own.[21] Both Michael and Robert are activists who spend only a part of their time representing their parents to colleges, universities, and interested groups around the country. They also work with local community projects and national or international issues specific to their interests. In the Massachusetts town where they live with their children, Robert and his wife helped organize the local group supporting Central American autonomy. Michael finished his formal education with graduate work in economics at Cambridge and a doctorate from the University of Wisconsin and now teaches in a college in Massachusetts, where he and his wife live and work. Their children are grown. Robert practiced law until September 1990, when he founded and began operating the Rosenberg Fund for Children to provide financial support for the education of the children of U.S. political prisoners and victims of political abuse, terrorism, and violence. This foundation is the direct outgrowth both of his and his brother's experience as the children of parents defined as political criminals, and as the beneficiaries of a communitarian old left.

It is important to insist that this biographical information has absolutely no claims on Doctorow or any other fiction writer. But the narratives he used, while serving his purposes metaphorically and formally, literally undercut those same purposes. In Susan's case, it is not the gender change itself that matters; it is how the literal story then departs from the Rosenberg story and the story of their sons, Michael and Robert Meeropol, that assumes significance for a critical reading of gender ideology. In his use of the Isaacson children to critique first the opportunism and then the exhaustion of old left views, the abuses and injuries performed on the family and the individual by the state, and the impotent idealism of the New Left, Doctorow laid a narrative burden on the children perhaps too heavy for them to carry. But even more costly to his apparent purposes in remembering and envisioning a sacrificial but redemptive role for the left was the loss of a concept and practice crucial to the old left and to the health and well-being of the Rosenberg sons, as well as to any theory and practice of a nonindividualistic contemporary left: communitarianism.

One of the more complex relationships Daniel dramatizes in his book is gender relations and specifically the political function of women in regard to men. The historical narratives—of Stalin's purges and Bukharin's resistance, of the formulation of U.S. cold war policies, and of the development of mass culture—are exclusively men's stories in the novel, as indeed they were. But Daniel's personal history involves more women than men, although it is populated with a rich range of each gender, and in the novel's economy, the functions of men and women are split along gender lines between the autonomous public life and the dependent private one.

Doctorow's replacement of one of the sons with Susan Isaacson and the ensuing elaboration of each child's story reproduce uncritically a relationship that, although irrational in terms of a liberal democratic society, is thoroughly rationalized in the practice of twentieth-century masculist-capitalist society. His decision to portray one Isaacson child as dying of old left despair and a sense of betrayal by a hypocritical business-controlled government, and the other child as coming to terms with political positionality and participation in a New Left world was an effective means of metaphorizing and dramatizing the history and differences of old left and New Left, as was his portrayal of a senile and confused (old Communist left) Dr. Mindish at Disneyland. But his division of these stories with their different outcomes along gender lines reproduces the costly differentials of a masculist society.

Daniel's quest as a man is slow and painful, and he works to establish a sense of continuity for himself through a critical rediscovery of his past, an enterprise that keeps him both from a nostalgic return to outmoded forms of thought and from a total identification with the more reckless and naive or self-absorbed

New Left. The novel opens with Daniel's visit to Susan after her puzzling suicide attempt, explained only by the note to him, "They're still fucking us. Goodby Daniel. You get the picture." Susan is Daniel's other half, the feminine counterpart who enrages him while inhabiting his mind and heart. And she is dying from a belated allegiance to old left values, an allegiance possible only through what Daniel calls a failure of (political) analysis:

> Look at her lying there making a fool of herself. Teach her to play her stupid games. Look at the actress! Look at how just lying there, not saying a fucking thing, not doing a thing but lying there and picking up bedsores she can still be morally preemptive. . . . I can live with your death. . . . I'll [still] want a hamburger with everything on it. . . . [Your voice] is so familiar to me that I cannot perceive the world except with your voice framing the edges of my vision. It is on the horizon and under my feet. . . . It is the feminine voice that passes solidly through ontological mirrors. It lies at the heart of the matter, the nub of the thing, the core of the problem, in the center, on the bull's eye, smack in the middle. We understand St. Joan: You want to fuck her but if you do you miss the point. (253–54)

But how many readers also miss the point, made silently and unwittingly, that it is the woman in this pair who can't be analytical or effectively involved in the political world? That it is the woman who acts, even in death, as the moral voice inhabiting the man's head? That it is the woman who has to die of thwarted desires for an active life, while the man incorporates her program and begins its fulfillment in his own life? This use of gender, motivated perhaps at least in part by formal needs, is an unambiguous example of the potential in representational fiction for the reproduction and reinforcement of oppressive and destructive social and political roles and relationships. Susan's fictional role supports Myra Jehlen's contention that "[the novelistic process of generation, of the becoming of the self] may be so defined as to require a definition of female characters that effectively precludes their becoming autonomous, so that indeed they would do so at the risk of the novel's artistic life."[22] Could we have had a *Book of Daniel* without a Susan Isaacson?

Daniel gives us a powerful and tragic dramatic portrait of his enraged and deranged immigrant grandmother, driven mad by lifelong hardship and repetitive loss of hope, in a process that descends, by declension, through the three generations of women, from his grandmother's faith in God, to his mother's faith in politics, and finally to Susan's loss of faith and suicidal despair. This is a formal and semantic echo of the downward historical declension of the three epigraphs, but in the person of the woman rather than that of the male poet. Using the subliminal suggestions of individual pathology and etiology, Daniel describes an imagined photograph of the three women in a medical textbook, in diction that recovers exactly the objectification of (mad and nude) women by a male gaze:

> They all have triangles, but move your gaze upward. This is a medical textbook. The meaning of the picture is in the thin, diagrammatic arrow line, colored red, that runs from Grandma's breast through your mama's and into your sister's. The red line describes the progress of madness inherited through the heart. (88)

It is the women—the ones with triangles—who are the bearers and enactors of society's irrationalities. But in describing the feminine voice as passing through ontological mirrors Daniel grants Susan an ability to challenge the narrative coherence and abstract essentialisms that mask a more complex situational reality. In this, he accords the feminine voice a critical function that feminist criticism explicitly assumes as a crucial part of its work: to challenge essentialist notions of U.S. twentieth-century masculist capitalist society, notions of what is natural to a hierarchical society in which one gendered and racial class lives by excluding and exploiting the others. Doctorow's use of Susan, however, is an extension and replication of that society's essential and natural notions of women, and in this sense perpetuates an oppressive and maddening process of purposeful social definition of women.

State of the Family

Daniel's own attitude toward women is skewed toward sadistic sexual manipulation, and it serves a critical function in the novel. For Daniel every woman is first someone to fuck, usually in anger or with a distanced sense of power and manipulation. He cynically talked his wife, Phyllis, into sex when they first met by telling her fucking was a philosophical act. A descendant of "harem breeders" in Daniel's eyes, Phyllis is a "sand dune" (5) to be kicked around, someone to terrorize and abuse physically and sexually, and someone who he thinks is turned on by forgiving him, someone whose appearance is improved by suffering. Because of his self-conscious desire to talk about his behavior, and his awareness of it as disgusting, we can read Daniel as the abused child passing on the abuse in his own family.

But Daniel was abused by the state, not by his family. How do the effects of losing loving parents to state justice translate into wife and child abuse? Perhaps that is only too obvious: by a familial replication of experienced abuses of a masculist state power, which is Doctorow's critical inversion of the Marx-Engels historical analysis of the state as an outgrowth of the monogamous and masculist familial division of labor and power.[23] Doctorow would have us consider the masculist and abusive family as a product, structural and sustaining replication, of the relationship of the masculist-capitalist state to the individual. Daniel speculates that the radical revolutionary Artie Sternlicht would not act in the same ways as Daniel does toward his wife:

> I am thinking if Phyllis met him she would have gone with him, her rhythm liberated, and this revolutionary stud would fuck her and afterwards they would both laugh and feel good. And she would not be hung up. He is probably a champion fucker. He does not put a woman in bondage. (186)

Old Left and New Left

Doctorow effectively rehearses the historical demise of the old left and its political force by means of Daniel's exercise of critical memory and analysis. Figuratively, he replicates the oppression and abuse the old left suffered in the 1950s through Daniel's sexual pathology, and its failed political history through Susan's despair, withdrawal, and death and through Mindish's senility. But after attempting to talk with contemporary radicals and participating self-consciously in the 1967 march on the Pentagon (the march that is the subject of Norman Mailer's 1968 *Armies of the Night*) Daniel is equally critical of the New Left for its naïveté and self-dramatization. His awareness of history as tragic and his lifetime habit of self-conscious but to some extent earned cynicism interfere with his ability to participate innocently in what he experiences as the narcissistic theatricality of the New Left. "[The march on the Pentagon] seems to be an academic gathering. . . . What a put-on. But I have come here to do whatever is being done. . . . I played Washington when I was a kid" (307-9). Even in attempting to reassure Susan, who is unconscious in a fetal position in the hospital, that he is becoming politically responsible, Daniel cannot avoid a final distancing comment on his own theatrical cynicism toward political activism, as he tapes a poster of himself over her bed: "The poster is a black and white photograph of a grainy Daniel looking scruffy and militant. Looking bearded, looking clear-eyed. His hand is raised, his fingers make the sign of peace. It is a posed photo blown up at a cost of four ninety-five" (257).

After Daniel has found his parents' sole accuser, Dr. Mindish, in California, hoping to learn from him and his daughter attitudes and points of view missing from his own reconstruction of his family story, and after receiving an enigmatic blessing from the senile Dr. Mindish, he returns to the Columbia library (in 1968) and his novel/dissertation, hoping "to discuss some of the questions raised by this narrative" (367). Only to be interrupted by: "Close the book, man, what's the matter with you, don't you know you're liberated? . . . We're doin' it, we're bringing the whole motherfucking university to its knees!" (367). And Daniel, still the observer but also now as tentative participant, "walk[s] out to the Sundial [to] see what's going down" (367).

Social Fiction

Daniel's personal quest is inseparable from social and historical analysis, which he performs and dramatizes in various modes, reaching in each segment of analysis earned insights that serve as efficient summary critiques of many aspects of the left and of contemporary U.S. society: the crippling idealism of old left Marxism and utopian socialism; the terror of Stalin's reign; the U.S. Communist party's postwar role in the demise of a viable postwar left in the United States; the failure of Enlightenment rationality; the complicity of liberal moralism, for its failure of analysis, in working to reproduce undemocratic and unjust social relationships; education by Disney, television, and images; the attainment of political power through money and bureaucracy instead of representative democracy; the censorship of dissent; trial by media; the law as protection of privilege; racism and anti-Semitism; U.S. capitalism as defined by its other, communism, socialism, or both;[24] the theatricality necessary to the working of institutions such as banks, courtrooms, and churches; corporal punishment as a system of class definition and management; the moral failure of U.S. fiction to engage socially (as in the work of Henry James); madness (of his grandmother and sister) as a social, not private and idiosyncratic, response to the end of hope.

The dramatization of these ideas in social and historical situations and the relevance of such recollections and analyses to Daniel's quest work to vitalize a potential didacticism. Also, as a writer and intellectual attempting to reconstruct his own history, Daniel is able credibly to offer philosophical and sometimes metafictional critiques of subjectivity, objectivity, historiography, and fiction making. These epistemological analyses and critiques, deriving from Daniel's reflections on or interactions with people and groups of political positionality, achieve a conflictual or dramatic materiality that dramatizes the ordinarily invisible relationships between an era's epistemology and its historical phenomena: the relationship between old left U.S. communism and faith in a progressive history; or that between faith in a progressive history (the same Enlightenment narrative) and the rationales for and development of the cold war; or that between Martin Luther King's use of the same narrative, as expressed in the U.S. Constitution, to initiate the civil rights confrontations of the 1960s, with the ensuing proliferation of points of view, and the construction of multiple narratives and multiple political positionalities—all in a liberal democratic society.

Sacrificial Left

Daniel the protagonist is unable to provide us with the analysis of some of the issues raised by his narrative because he walks out of the library to join the revolution—or at least "to see what's going down" (367). But Daniel the narrator has provided us with a more critical and at the same time positive analysis of the possibility for left effectivity in the post-Rosenberg era than has Daniel the protagonist. He has discussed the role of God in past theological eras as that of "lay[ing] on this monumental justice," "seek[ing] recognition and help of righteous people," and testing each generation anew to discover who can learn and practice his justice. "The drama in the Bible is always in the conflict of those who have learned with those who have not learned. Or in the testing of those who seem that they might be able to learn" (12). The implication is that in a secular age, justice is the work of human beings, and it is political work. Not politics in the ersatz and farcical sense of U.S. electoral politics, but the work of attempting to know and analyze real social conditions and to envision workable alternatives, in order to disrupt and intervene in unjust practices of everyday life—asking again and again what is it you can do this time.

With the help of the radical Artie Sternlicht, Daniel analyzes the limitations of liberalism and of the New Left as inhering in a failure to make connections, a failure not confined to those on the left. But this is the paradox of narrative and of "making connections": explanatory narratives establish cause-effect and sequential relationships that mask and occlude cause-effect and sequential relationships. Responsible political work begins in foregrounding those connections that the hegemonic narrative— or any ideological narrative, for that matter—denies, negates, or hides, while understanding that any ensuing counternarratives or antinarratives necessary to left political positionality and effectivity always risk co-optation by more dominant and conservative powers in a capitalist mass culture.

> The radical discovers connections between available data and the root responsibility. Finally he connects everything. At this

> point he begins to lose his following. It is not that he has in-
> correctly connected everything, it is that he has connected
> everything. Nothing is left outside the connections. At this
> point society becomes bored with the radical. Fully connected
> in his characterization it has achieved the counterinsurgent ra-
> tionale that allows it to destroy him. The radical is given the
> occasion for one last discovery—the connection between
> society and his death. After the radical is dead his early music
> haunts his persecutors. And the liberals use this to achieve
> power. (173)

Daniel notes the frequency with which "radical" suggestions, like that of Eugene Debs for social security, or of Rosa Luxemburg for women's rights to their own bodies, become liberal and then con-servative policies. This sacrificial but analytic and prophetic role is the intellectual—ideological —function that Michael Harring-ton, Barbara Ehrenreich, Cornel West, and others have assumed for the Democratic Socialists of America in the 1990s.[25]

The failure Sternlicht and Daniel attribute to the left—that of failing to make connections not sanctioned by the master narra-tive—is the same failure that is operative in U.S. social fiction, a failure of second- and third-degree orders of thinking. A failure to imagine fiction that can dramatize the unnarrated social contra-dictions of twentieth-century U.S. society. A failure to apprehend and conceptualize invisible political, historical, economic, social, and cultural relationships of power and constraint that intersect, construct, and empower or constrain the lives of individuals. A failure that results in a national literature the rest of the world con-siders apolitical and unworldly, focused on private lives living in pure social groups in suspended time and space, and mindlessly replicating the traditional relationships that make a specific social order possible.

At the 1986 PEN International meeting in New York, Günter Grass and Salman Rushdie, among others, were unreticent in calling U.S. writing "insular, naive, and provincial." Grass com-plained that he couldn't say anything critical of the United States without first claiming that he was not a Communist, and the *New York Times* confirmed this by reporting his comment and noting that Grass had not publicly criticized a Communist gov-ernment in the past eighteen years. Salman Rushdie commented that "Americans seem unaware of the effect of the United States on the rest of the world." But John Updike, in his defense of U.S. writers in response to this critique, cited George Washington's warning against foreign entanglements and described his own experience of the nation as a pastoral.

Doctorow, reporting that 1986 meeting in the 120th anniversary issue of the *Nation,* comments on the "love it or leave it" attitude of many critics and readers in the United States and claims that "the loss of a social dimension in much of the otherwise impressive fiction being written today has been widely noted. Horizons have diminished." He emphasizes the critical and cultural costs to the United States of the cold war linkage of dissent with communism and anti-Americanism: "That the argument [over social fiction] should surface now, with each insufficient side of it divided fairly neatly between America and the rest of the world, suggests the possibility that we are suffering some state of mind not apparent to ourselves."[26]

Working to analyze and develop self-awareness toward these national states of mind not apparent to ourselves—the unified free liberal subject, U.S. objectivity and moral superiority, the evasions of an elite aestheticism, and an ignorance of history— is the accomplishment of *The Book of Daniel.*

5

The Public Burning

Robert Coover's magnum opus about the Rosenberg story, *The Public Burning,* was finally published in 1977. His previous books, *Origin of the Brunists* (1966), *The Universal Baseball Association, Inc., J. Henry Waugh, Prop.* (1968), a collection of short stories, *Pricksongs and Descants* (1969), and a collection of plays, *A Theological Position* (1972), had secured him a primarily academic reputation as an intensely powerful postmodern writer. *Public Burning* brought him a measure of popular acclaim.

Having noted at the time of the Rosenberg executions the unusual aspect of the state execution of a female spy, Coover became interested in the story again in 1966 after reading Wexley's 1955 *Judgment of Julius and Ethel Rosenberg.* He read for several years, following the multiple directions in which the story led: biographies, newspapers, histories, court records, letters, essays, and articles, and finally the censored and unsorted jumble of released FBI records obtained by the historian Allen Weinstein in 1974 under the Freedom of Information Act. Begun in 1966, *The Public Burning* was almost finished in 1973 when the Watergate scandal broke, resulting in front-page and editorial displays of Nixon biographical material that Coover had spent seven years developing for his use of Nixon as narrator and prime actor of the book. This unexpected and unwelcome scoop served Coover ultimately as encouragement for a figural and thematic intensification of his Nixon material.

The book was promised for publication in the bicentennial year 1976 by Coover's Knopf editor, Robert Gottlieb. But Random House (Knopf publisher) and RCA (Random House owner) attorneys, worried about potentially libelous material, pressured Knopf to reject the book as immoral. As Gottlieb explained to Coover, "What if you had written a book like this about Eleanor Roosevelt?" The book then went from house to house, finally to be published by Richard Seaver at Viking in 1977. By then, editing decisions and legal opinions had become inextricably intertwined, and Coover felt the house lawyers were doing "everything they could to pressure me to emasculate the book." He began resisting requests for revisions and cuts "in fear that I was being asked for the wrong reasons to take it out. The book's probably still informed a bit by that anxious tenacity."[1]

By the time of publication *Public Burning* had received publicity about the delay over potentially libelous material, and it quickly became a best-seller. But the first week *Public Burning* reached the *New York Times* best-seller list, Viking abruptly stopped all commercial publicity and promotion. After publication in paperback by Bantam, the book quickly went out of print.

Frequently compared to *Gargantua and Pantagruel, Moby-Dick, Ulysses, Giles Goat-Boy, Catch-22,* and *Gravity's Rainbow, Public Burning* was reviewed with the energy and passion it deserved. Donald Hall called it a "monstrous, obscene, impossible, valuable fantasy. . . . But what is one to *do* with it? I cannot tell if it will survive its setting. If it survives it will survive as a monster—but then American literature is a collection of monsters." Robert Tower wrote in the *New York Review of Books* that "excesses and miscalculations hobble *Public Burning*'s course like a pair of dropped pants." Paul Gray in *Time* called it a "protracted sneer," and Norman Podhoretz called it, in so many words, an anti-American partisan revisionist fiction that, hiding behind "the immunities of artistic freedom," was a "cowardly lie." But Tom LeClair claimed that *Public Burning* "was too important a book—too total and significant a vision—to be denied by taste or ideology."[2]

Coover's fear that the RCA–Random House lawyers would succeed in emasculating his book were well founded: *Public Burning* is in every way a man's book. It is constructed by male voices and by what are conventionally assumed to be masculine points of view, masculine tones, masculine humor, masculine characters, masculine workplaces, and masculine behavior. The constant use of the generic "man" to generalize to society as a whole offers rhetorical support to the dramatization of this man's world. Coover wanted to replicate "all the sounds of the nation," to construct "a text that would seem to have been written by the whole nation through all its history."³ In this he falls considerably short, for the sounds of his whole nation throughout all its history are white, male, and masculist. A few women are present, more psychically than physically, but they are shadow figures of morality, reproach, and rejection, or fixated objects of (infantile or projective) male desires.

In this 534-page collection of the nation's voices, often referred to and critiqued as a novel of excess, the only women's voices we hear—through Nixon—are those of his wife, Pat ("Why don't you grow up, Dick?"), his Quaker grandmother Milhous, his mother (who taught him to want emotional resolutions to unresolvable conflicts and to feel sorry when people have to die), and Ethel Rosenberg (who is an object of erotic fantasy for Nixon, as well as someone with whom he identifies). Julie and Tricia Nixon and Eleanor Roosevelt are mentioned (Tricia's bottom and the whack Teddy Roosevelt gave to Eleanor's, to be specific); as are Oveta Culp Hobby (who was laughing so hard at Nixon she was showing her khaki drawers [474]) and Clare Boothe Luce, the mother of *Time* magazine; as are the generic "girls" of whom the young Nixon was ignorant and afraid; secretaries (one of whom is raped on the "Good Neighbor Special" train to the executions, inspiring Nixon to attempt to alter the course of history by visiting Ethel in Sing Sing); Marilyn Monroe, Christine Jorgenson, Bess Truman, Elsa Maxwell, Teresa Wright, and the ladies in the Mormon Tabernacle Choir who are all at the executions; and Betty Crocker—sprung Athena-like ("full-formed and all buttoned up" [453]) from the head of General Mills—who is invited by Uncle Sam to introduce the government officials, entertainment stars, and VIPs present at the Times Square Rosenberg execution ceremony. "'Okay, get your sweet buns out there, dumplin' and preparest a table before me in the presents a mine inimies!' He whacks her lovingly on her corseted butt" (457).

By now it should be clear that the relative absence of female voices is purposeful. *Public Burning* is an outrageous parody of the hegemonic American Manifest Destiny Man's World in the formative stages of the cold war: a racist, classist, sexist, hierarchical, exploitive, aggressive, violent, and obscene world. That is, Coover sets up this world in order to interrogate, cruelly mock, and radically undercut its values, while exposing its contradictions and costs.

If Coover has written a parody of a man's book, then one could expect that gender might be a primary category for interrogation, manipulating this manifestly sexist book into what functions effectively as a feminist critique of masculist society. I am not at all sure that the prevalent twentieth-century U.S. ideology of objectivity or positivism has not shifted the general reading audience so far to the literal side of reception that it is difficult for us as a culture to read parody as parody. Coover's book is a devastating critique of masculist hegemony, but many readers object to this work as pornographic and sexist, and as a dramatic replication of and complicity in that which Coover attempts to subvert. As Brecht asked about literature that fails in its critical function, is it the text or the audience that needs to be rewritten? That is not a rhetorical question.[4]

Postmodernism and Perfecting Myths

Empirically I sanction dialectic; time and development, never without a principle of transcendence, an upward way that, when reversed, interprets all incidental things in terms of overall fulfillment toward which development is SAID to be striving. . . . But [human beings] will forget this and assume that words are positive and erect systems from them. . . . And empires will be built on what seems to be a positive: mine, which is implicitly a negative command, leading to guilt, yearning for a sacrifice to cancel the guilt and allow the same conditions to continue.[5]

Coover, like Kenneth Burke (author of the preceding quotation), reads the immediate postwar period as an extreme example
of the theological, mythological, ritualistic, and violent scapegoating (projective) nature of political order keeping in history.
And Coover's critical project, like Burke's, is to expose the motivations, rhetoricity, and irrationalities of historical order-justi-
fying narratives, "perfecting myths" reduced from "sociopolitical
raw data" to inaugurate and rationally maintain a certain order.[6]
Coover is a Burkean critical fiction writer, the writer who most
consistently practices Burke's strategy of "perspectives by incongruity," or acategorical juxtapositions to unsettle the "natural," mythic (often the same thing), and rational categories that
structure systems of knowledge, power, social relationships, and
common sense—the categories, that is, that structure our everyday life.[7] Such planned incongruities, constituting both a methodology and an epistemology, constructing new ways of seeing
material and cultural relationships, will necessarily "violate 'good
taste,' critical decorum, and what he calls the 'proprieties of
words.'"[8] Burke advocates and practices, as does Coover, Daniel's
"criminal perception."[9]

While it can be easily shown that all fiction—even antirealist
fiction—is to some extent realistic, postmodern fiction claims to
operate in opposition to classical realism and its pretensions to
transparency and objective naming, in favor of language and juxtapositions that attempt to upset the supporting assumptions and
constructed unities of such a positivist mimesis. The distinction
between a positivist rational realism and a more irrational critical
realism is central to debates on the politics of literature, beginning
with the debates among Georg Lukács, Theodor Adorno, Walter
Benjamin, and Bertolt Brecht in the 1930s on the cultural and
political effects of literary realism.[10] Coover shares with Kenneth
Burke a suspicion of what Burke calls the "liberal ideal" of supposedly neutral naming, in favor of a double method that inter-
rogates what it invokes, subverts what it inevitably installs, and
in so doing, makes perceivable and thinkable phenomenal relationships, disjunctions, or contradictions neither susceptible to
conventional perception nor readily nameable within the discrete
categories of rationalized experience.

Such a double method is also a scrupulously open process, unable to hide its operations behind assumptions of objectivity, transparency, neutrality, or omniscience; and it refuses its readers any subject position of identity or coherence, at worst constructing a confused and disaffected reader, at best requiring a reader as active participant in the development of a point of view and of a critical position. The classic realist text allows and even encourages passive consumption; the postmodern text requires a critical completion by the reader. This is a dangerous, discomfiting, and unpopular practice. As Burke says, "One must violate the tenor of one's own culture as the members of his culture know it" in order to undo conventional structures of perception and thought.[11]

This Coover does purposefully, with great moral passion, bitterness, and grotesquerie. He only too successfully sustains "the dis-ease that constitutes the critical condition," producing the kind of postmodern fiction that many critics call sacrificial, a fiction that can be distinguished, in intention but not in the limitations on its effectivity, from a more aestheticized high-culture or elitist fiction.[12]

Although Coover construes the "fiction-maker's function [as furnishing] better fictions with which we can re-form our notions of things," *Public Burning*'s work is ultimately a dark and bitter symbolic formalization and simultaneous de-forming and denaturalizing of what he calls the U.S. civil religion and its operations by, on, and through individuals.[13] The book offers no positive vision, no "better fictions," no possibilities of redemption or recuperation, the salvific claims for male postmodern (and Coover's) fiction notwithstanding.[14] It is a historically specific human comedy, Rabelaisian in its exuberance and freedom of expression, and Swiftian in its scatology and pessimism.

Coover's conviction that we have come to the end of an epistemological tradition in the ways we look at and adjust to the world is entirely consistent with poststructuralist philosophy's claims for the twentieth century as the beginning of a posthumanist era. Poststructuralist philosophers use linguistic categories and operations to call into question the rational and polarizing categories of Enlightenment epistemology, objectivity, identity, truth, and the unified subject. From the vantage point of a master fictionist Coover critiques those same categories of liberal ideology as inadequate mythic and fictional constructions that have outlived their usefulness and relevance to contemporary lived experience, fictions that nevertheless reproduce themselves through conventional narrative practices and continue to serve ideological functions of order keeping:

> Our old faith—one might better say our old sense of constructs derived from myths, legends, philosophies, fairy stories, histories, and other fictions which help to explain what happens to us from day to day, why our governments are the way they are, why our institutions have the character they have, why the world turns as its does—has lost its efficacy.[15]

This epistemological revolution—with inevitable ontological implications—theorized variously in the 1970s and 1980s as an encompassing global phenomenon called postmodernism, finds its motivations in the twentieth-century experience of rationalized history as irrational, the existence of the mutually exclusive but individually coherent and logical explanatory accounts of wave and particle physics, and complex, interpenetrating global socioeconomic conditions that seem to defy rational conceptualization or manipulation. Despite the commonsensical Newtonian ways in which we continue to approach daily life, we find ourselves in a disorienting and alienating epistemological transition or revolution, without confidence in the usual explanatory methods and practices, and before we as a political culture have found and assimilated new and more adequate general languages and methods of apprehension and communication.[16]

Postmodern fiction is a symptomatic but also constitutive component of this interperiod. Its practitioners and supporters describe its political function as that of performing politically useful disruptions of worn-out categories, rationales, fictions, and myths, the stories that continue to throw their weight around with shaping authority when their explanatory adequacy to actual social conditions is nonexistent. Coover's sense of these worn-out fictions working as "dogma, invading the world and turning it to stone," is his non-Marxist or neo-Marxist version of Lukács's elaboration of Marx's concept of reification, a contradictory yet systemic rational solidification or concretization of specific human relationships (inevitable in modern capitalism, according to Marx) that conceals their actual spatial-temporal-affective nature. For Coover and neo-Marxists, reification, or "turning [the world] to stone," is a collective product of the order-seeking mind working symbolically to achieve worldly understanding in ways that, contradictorily, alienate the thinker from her world.[17] As a fictionist Coover finds it compelling and necessary to interrogate such dogmatic explanatory narratives on their own grounds, relying on narrative strategies to undo narrative fixities homeopathically.

Commitment to Design

Coover initiates his writing with "an arbitrary commitment to design," not from a belief in cosmic or Platonic underlying order, but, on the contrary, from "a delight with the rich ironic possibilities that the use of structure affords."[18] This use of design is also consistent with his understanding that every effort to make meaning of the world requires a narrative shaping of data and language in a "kind of fiction-making process." Games and numerology are important metaphors for this inevitable and necessary process:

> When life has no ontological meaning, it becomes a kind of game itself. A metaphor for a perception of the way the world works, and also something that almost everybody's doing. If not on the playing field, in politics or education. If you're cynical about it, you learn the rules and strategies, shut up about them, and get what you can out of it. If you're not inclined to be a manipulator, you might want to expose the game plan for your own protection and ask how it can be a better game than it is at present.[19]

The symmetrical and numerical design of *Public Burning* follows a historical sequence of the three days leading up to the Rosenberg executions. Each of the four parts contains seven sections. Seven plays a significant role in the biblical apocalypse, the Book of Revelations, and it is also on "the seventh occasion [the seventh court appeal by the Rosenbergs] [that] the great hand of Uncle Sam shall finally subdue the Phantom [the Soviet

Union]" (108). These twenty-eight sections are narrated alter-
nately by Nixon and an anonymous, multivoiced narrator. The
four parts are divided by three dramatic intermezzos: a radio
broadcast by Eisenhower in which he conflates faith in God and
freedom with the U.S. role of protecting foreign resources important to U.S. interests; a dramatic dialogue by Eisenhower and
Ethel Rosenberg of selected passages from her clemency appeal
and from his denial of that appeal; and an operetta sung by Julius
and Ethel refusing the Justice Department's last-minute offer of
freedom in exchange for talk. There is a prologue in which the
official Rosenberg story and all other major personae and plot
elements are announced, and an epilogue providing an ending
word on politics and fiction—in a situation of painfully induced
skepticism about form, closure, and endings that leaves the reader's "critical dis-ease" fully intact.

The arbitrary and mathematical symmetrical design of the
book (whose numerological implications can be unpacked for
further intimations of apocalyptic and redemptive meaning)
serves to contain the centrifugal energies produced by the book's
raucous interrogation of mythic meaning systems in the United
States. This interrogation occurs formally, at levels of rhetoric
and plot, as well as narratively and directly in the skeptical but
ambitious and self-doubting investigative work of the book's *histor,* Richard Nixon.[20] The narrative line is at least a double one:
that of the Rosenbergs and that of Nixon, to whom Uncle Sam
has put the test of researching the Rosenberg story, interpreting
it politically correctly in order to pass the presidential test, and
successfully representing, to the public gathered in Times Square,
the Rosenberg executions as an occasion for national renewal
and redefinition.

The alternate unknown narrator sections provide a social, historical, and ideological context for Nixon's quest, voiced at first
by an Archie Bunker worst-case U.S. male using multiple ver-
naculars, dictions, and modes and frequently quoting Uncle Sam,
also known as Sam Slick the Yankee Peddler. This voice slips
sometimes into a more intelligent and moderate critical voice
supplying (verifiable documentary) background data for the story
line as well as two set pieces, one on the *New York Times* as

the maker of a monolithic history of the commonplace and one on *Time* magazine as the National Poet Laureate, a consummate stylist who celebrates what he understands and belittles what he does not. By the ending sections, the unknown narrator's voice has become that of an intelligent and well-informed literary parodist. This slippage is confusing, but the voice is consistent in its maintenance of a bawdy, sexist, racist, classist, and masculist point of view.

Public Burning's first title was *The Public Burning of Julius and Ethel Rosenberg: An Historical Romance,* but Coover's editors rejected the notion of the book as a historical romance. *Public Burning* is indeed generically (comic) historical romance in the medieval sense, similar to the fourteenth-century (comic) epic romance, *Sir Gawain and the Green Knight,* with Richard Nixon setting forth to test himself in the political and affective world against his ideal self-image. It is also a mock epic, with Nixon as the questing hero, finally returning home wiser and three days older, to be embraced not by Pat, who spurns him, but by Uncle Sam proclaiming "I Want You" (530).[21] Coover has deliberately structured *Public Burning* as a comedy, rather than the tragedy it continually threatens to be, because he thinks of "tragedy as a kind of adolescent response to the universe—the higher truth is a comic response. . . . There is a kind of humor extremity which is even more mature than the tragic response."[22] The happy ending, with the main couple joined in an embrace, provides a formally correct ending to this dark and bitter novel, but the degree of its "humor extremity" achieves an intimation of the collective human tragedy of polarized semantic and political orders. The ending serves both as a specific historical critique of the cold war period and as a universal critique of rigidified belief systems that violate human, social integrity.

Any attempt to write about *Public Burning*'s design is as limited by the sequentiality of language as it is overwhelmed by the novel's surplus of form and content. There are four separate but interrelated narrative sequences: the three days leading up to the Rosenberg executions, the Rosenberg story, the Nixon story, and the formally correct story with its narrative closure and its arbitrary design of twenty-eight episodes with prologue and epilogue. But there are also the three metanarratives, commenting throughout on the motives and methods of rhetoric, narrative, and historiography. And all seven virtually inextricable stories (again the redemptive or apocalyptic number seven) coincide in a literary, historical, and ethical critique of all (the) stories.

Planned Incongruity

Public Burning's language, consistent with the book's parodic mode and its purposeful unsettling of categories and assumptions, performs provocative incongruities on three linguistic and structural levels: rhetorical and stylistic, logical and semantic, and dramatic and structural. A formal, semantic, and thematic continuity through narrative levels—from rhetoric to drama—rehearses and foregrounds the largely unperceived continuum of rhetoricity that is operative in shaping, motivating, and interpreting actual historical events.[23]

Truth claims, codes, and boundaries between fact and fiction break down incrementally and consistently through every level of linguistic operation. Incongruities begin at the level of rhetoric and style and intensify as they are articulated and replicated semantically and structurally. Illogical semantic shifts modulate into logical self-cancellation or outright paradox. Semantically garbled language achieves meaning contextually, or plain language becomes contextually nonsensical. Reflections, analyses, conversations, speeches, and arguments are laced with effusive and irrepressible returns of the repressed.

The third level—dramatic and plotted juxtapositions—utilizes all the resources of contradictory rhetoric and logic to reinforce the unsettling value of its situational and shocking dark humor. As ideological commentary and critique, each dramatic episode has its own effectivity emerging directly from the specific incongruencies of the situation. Highly dramatic situations juxtapose the most unlikely characters in the most unlikely situations, calling into question conventional social roles, interactions, and boundaries based on rationalized categories of economic, ethnic, and sexual difference. Nixon's visit to and assault on Ethel at Sing Sing provides a clash between classes, genders, desires, powers, politics, ethics, and ambitions. The staging of the Rosenberg executions in Times Square enacts an aspect of the story that lies outside the realm of historiography: the official U.S. ritualistic and reintegrative scapegoating and justification accomplished by the Rosenberg trial and executions. Uncle Sam's unique selection and initiation of Nixon at the end dramatizes the national ideology as a masculist and invasive violation of its own people that seeks to reproduce itself, through men, from generation to generation.

Such a carnivalesque linguistic performance is intellectually challenging, stimulating, and pleasurable in its own right in a purely formal sense, but it also always poses a disconcerting challenge to received meanings. These challenges, saturating the novel on all levels, are intensified by the formal and thematic repetition of another dimension of incongruity, a consistent production of epistemological confusion and uncertainty along the axis of fact and fiction. This production of uncertainty is an aspect of postmodern fiction attacked by cultural critics for its tendency toward repetitive and empty assertions of a radical epistemological undecidability. *Public Burning,* however, uses destabilizing literary techniques not for a totalizing critique of meaning, but for the production of a skepticism toward specific historical truth claims for meaning, in this case as a challenge to the cold war Rosenberg history and its motivations, values, effects, and masking myths.

There is much talk of codes in *Public Burning.* Nixon understands that political and social life are coded, and that if "you knew the code, life was relatively easy" (406). Any member of an old boys' network, a street gang, or a humanities faculty understands this reality at a pragmatic level. In *Public Burning* Coover thwarts any pragmatic or facile reception or use of such codes within the world of the book, as well as between the book and its reader, by conflating and confusing words from different and antagonistic codes. Nixon's attempts to make sense of his historical world, and the reader's attempts to make sense of *Public Burning*'s representation of that world, are disrupted by juxtapositions revealing affinities and continuities of supposedly incongruous motives and effects, as well as contradictions and discontinuities of ideologically coherent motives and effects.

Public Burning's most pervasive conflation of codes is the one Burke analyzed in *The Rhetoric of Religion,* that between theology and dominion, between religion and politics. In a nation established on the separation of church and state, the U.S. vernacular in *Public Burning* gives voice to an ethnocentric civil religion that is based on concepts of Calvinist election (irrational privilege), uncontingent freedom, and economic individualism as the surest means to the common good. *Public Burning* purposefully confuses political and religious terminology to foreground the religious (irrational, mythic, and primitive) aspects of this national ideology. The Statue of Liberty is our *Regina Coeli;* Times Square is the ritual center of the world and a place of national rebirth; Uncle Sam, like Athena, "popped virgin-born and fully constituted from the shattered seed-poll of the very Enlightenment" (6).

The traditional and prevailing historiography of the United States is "a hierology of free enterprise, football, revival meetings, five-card stud, motion pictures, war, and the sales pitch" (83). It functions as a divine code, continually "bringing the Glad Tidings of America's election, and fulfilling the oracles of every tout from John the Seer and Nostradamus to Joseph and Adam Smith" (9). Imperialism is preordained, like gravity; and the United States is the Hope of the World, but the electric sign at Times Square bearing this aphorism transmutes *Hope,* letter by letter, from *hope* to *rope, rape, rake, fake, fate, hate, nate, nite, bite, bile, pile, pule, puke, juke, JOKE* (36-41). The Phantom (the Soviet Union) is darkness, evil, and Satan personified, and dissent from U.S. imperialist and cold war policies is heresy, apostasy, and an embracing of the anti-Christ. The accused and accursed Rosenbergs are to be electrocuted, for "it is written that 'any man who is dominated by demonic spirits to the extent that he gives voice to apostasy is to be subject to the judgment upon sorcerers and wizards'" (3).

These rhetorical juxtapositions of codes, modes of speech, and realms of practice fall into a seemingly random juxtaposition, of fact and fiction, to the extent that even the most historically well-informed reader is not able confidently to maintain a distinction between the two. The result is the promotion of a habit of doubled or multiplied reading: "Treasury Secretary George Humphrey has let it be known that there is 'no reason to fear peace, U.S. military spending is still necessary, armistice in Korea or no'" (214). The reader can take this as fictive, nonsensical, or paradoxical wordplay (fear of peace?) completely in character with the outrageous linguistic performance of the book, while receiving it as what it also is, an actual quotation of the U.S. secretary of the treasury. The shock of this doubled reception lies in the unconscious awareness that it is reality, not fiction, that is nonsensical and paradoxical at the same time that it is real and rational: large sectors of the American public do fear and resist peace, for rational, economic reasons.

Nixon's linear narrative chapters are composed almost entirely of his self-doubts and reflections, family memories, fantasies, desires, and political and historical speculations. The anonymously narrated chapters give voice to more synchronic phenomena of the postwar years. Interwoven with their ideological rhetoric, code mixing, and tall tales are large amounts of historical data of the Rosenberg case and of cold war history during Eisenhower's presidency. Words, phrases, aphorisms, sentences, and paragraphs of these sections are as likely to be recontextualized matter from verifiable historical documents—speeches, memorandums, newspaper reports, letters, sacred texts, sermons, or information taken from historiographies and biographies of the period and of its main actors—as they are to be imaginative constructions and reconstructions by the narrator, or the contradictory rhetoric of U.S. ideology. Fact, fiction, speculation, ideology, humor, and farce are formally indistinguishable in *Public Burning,* producing for the reader a disorientation of the commonsense relation of language to a supposedly objective reality. In such a context, the motivated and constructed nature of interpretive facts is foregrounded, as is the relative adequacy or inadequacy of figures and fictions to experienced reality.

Figures and fictions in this confusion of language codes, by escaping or exceeding the usual generic boundaries of fictiveness, acquire their own peculiar resonances with reality. The career of J. Edgar Hoover, U.S. Top Cop, is contemporaneous with that of Mickey Mouse, and Hoover and Walt Disney are the nation's masters of the spin-off (15, 281); FBI agents are soldiers in Christ; the free press cries out with one voice (66); the nine Supreme Court justices file in "under a frieze of Truth, holding up a mirror to life" (69); and the country is governed by "ilictions" (75). Figure and fictions, while undercutting myth and ideology, begin to claim their own authority to speak a different kind of truth that amuses, challenges, provokes, and offends.

Readers, whose mental categories are increasingly disrupted to the extent that they begin to read with minds open to the semantic implications of what appear to be alternative or mutually exclusive categories, become more and more adept at "criminal perception": the perception of ideologically undercutting "truth effects" from jarring and irreverent conflations of codes, blatantly bombastic and fabulist passages, and alarming linguistic returns of the (politically) repressed. Bunyanesque tall tales and Puritan, Enlightenment, and Yankee aphorisms suddenly give voice to real socioeconomic relationships masked by U.S. liberal ideology:

> I am Sam Slick the Yankee Peddler—I can ride on a flash of light
> nin', catch a thunderbolt in my fist, swaller niggers whole, raw or
> cooked, slip without a scratch down a honey locust, whup my
> weight in wildcats and redcoats, squeeze blood out of a turnip
> and cold cash out of a parson, and out-inscrutabullize the heathen
> Chinee. . . . We hold these truths to be self-evident: that God
> helps them what helps themselves, it's a mere matter of marchin';
> that idleness is emptiness and he who lives on hope will die with
> his foot in his mouth; that no nation was ever ruint by trade; and
> that nothin' is sartin but death, taxes, God's blowin' Covenant,
> enlightened self-interest, certain unalienated rights, and woods,
> woods, woods, as far as the world extends! . . . A Freeman, con-
> tendin' for Liberty on his own ground, can out-run, out-dance,
> out-jump, chaw more tobacky and spit less, out-drink, out-holler,
> out-finagle and out-lick any yaller, brown, red, black, or white
> thing in the shape of human that's ever set his onfortunate knick-
> ers on Yankee soil! It is our manifest dust-in-yer-eye to overspread
> the continent allotted by Providence for the free development of
> our yearly multiplyin' millions, so damn the torpedoes and full
> steam ahead, fellow ripstavers, we cannot escape history! (7-8)

Nixon as Representative Man

As Coover worked with his initial concept of the Rosenberg executions as a circus narrated by "all the sounds of the nation," he felt "the need for a quieter voice." Of all the characters that auditioned for the part, "Nixon, when he appeared, proved ideal."[24] Nixon's prosecution of Alger Hiss, even though it achieved only the limited success of a conviction for perjury, not for espionage, had provided him with a number of crucial photograph and television opportunities to dramatize the threats of domestic communism. He apparently staged an interrupted vacation to announce his discovery of the "pumpkin papers" implicating Hiss, exploiting the occasion to the fullest for its anticommunist political potentials.[25] For many people ignorant of the actual course of the trial, Nixon's television appearances about Hiss had the effect of establishing the connection between the domestic left and espionage upon which Hoover had insisted since the 1930s.

But Nixon's role in the Rosenberg story was more direct than that. Along with Hoover and the media, he helped set it up, establishing the genre, roles, and audience expectations before the story had been filled out. In a political attack on Truman in response to the Soviet atomic bomb test in August 1949, Representative Nixon of HUAC had stated for the media, "If the President says the American people are entitled to know all the facts—I feel the American people are also entitled to know the facts about the espionage ring which was responsible for turning over information on the atom bomb to agents of the Russian government."[26] This is a Coover-like semantic shift that conflates a fiction with an empty concept of fact in order to translate a fictional hypothesis into apparent material reality.

What a satisfying irony then for the author of a novel about the Rosenbergs to use Richard Nixon as his surrogate, as open-minded *histor* sorting through the enormous numbers of documents constructing and relating to the Rosenberg story, interrogating the official story in the process of trying to define the correct version that will demonstrate to Uncle Sam that he,

Nixon, is presidential material. The biographical Nixon was perfect for the part: his self-consciousness, his need to analyze everything, his suspicious view of the world, and his understanding of the strategies and powers of rhetoric were positive qualities for Coover's narrator. And Coover wanted someone who clearly resided and operated *inside* the national mythology, while feeling alienated and slightly off center: the self-aware critical observer.

Both detractors and admirers of *Public Burning* comment on the sympathetic character of the Nixon figure, a figure with whom most readers experience, to some degree, an unexpected and unsought identification. This, for many, is the supreme accomplishment of the book, the depiction of the humanity of Richard Nixon in such an unlikely historical and generic context. Coover anticipated this reaction, even before he had constructed his Nixon:

> And, of course, I also had it on faith from the beginning that any exploration of Nixon, this man who has played such a large role in American society since World War II, would have to reveal something about us all. It was another quality, though, that first called him forth in my mind—this was in 1969, just after he'd been elected president—and that was his peculiar talent for making a fool of himself.[27]

The Coover-Nixon identity is a more immediate one than this quotation would suggest. Nixon, known as Iron Butt for, among other qualities, his thoroughness, was famous and respected for the scrupulous preparations he made for a trial or hearing, or to inform himself about an issue for a political appearance. He accumulated reams of notes based on his reading of massive amounts of materials. This of course is what Coover found himself doing as he attempted to deal with the complex and unknowable Rosenberg story. Here is Nixon struggling with all the information:

> I was sitting on the floor of my inner office, surrounded by every scrap of information I could find on the Rosenberg case, feeling scruffy and tired, dejected, lost in a surfeit of detail and further from a final position on the issue than ever. (79)

And Uncle Sam, who has dropped in for a visit, catching Nixon masturbating in a fantasy about Ethel:

I ain't seen so much shit piled around in one place since we
cleaned out Harry Gold's basement! . . . I know how much your
famous Iron Butt means to you, and I reckanize it gets you
more votes than your face does, but you don't wanta get muscle-
bound in one joint while the rest just withers away! (333)

And here is Robert Coover writing *Public Burning:*

I like to completely exhaust an image—the white whale syn-
drome, as you might call it. As a consequence, each book is
supported by tons of debris. . . . I could have saved myself two
or three years had I had [a computer when I wrote *Public
Burning*]. That book is a good page-by-page example of a tre-
mendous amount of preparatory material adding up to a few
lines of text. Well, not so few, as it turned out—but that was
the perfect kind of project to have done with the help of a
computer. Instead I had thousands of little slivers of scissored
paper spread out all over the floor and furniture—and watch
out if the cat got in![28]

Both attempts to organize, shape, and manage all the information—Coover's story and Nixon's story within the story—are
inadequate to the raw materials. In both accounts there is an
excess of data to meaning, a reality of human existence and
history that *Public Burning*'s text manages to keep open, un-
reduced, and unresolved, despite the book's formal and seven-
fold commitment to design, and despite its definitive narrative
closure. No positive statement is made that isn't contested, qualified, undercut, contradicted, mitigated, or parodied. The result,
paradoxically, is not canceled meaning or radical skepticism toward meaning or affirmation of meaninglessness in what Adorno
calls a "positivism of meaninglessness."[29] It is rather an elaboration of multiple motivations and perspectives for a set of historical feelings, perceptions, interpretations, and actions—a
multiplicity that overflows formal explanatory boundaries, making all the more evident the exclusionary nature and costs of
purified cold war codes and systems of meaning, including the
professional code ultimately chosen by Nixon.

More elusive than the Coover-Nixon identity are the points of
contact for the reader's identification with Nixon, who is an
absurd and finally humiliated character. I would argue that this
reader identification occurs to some extent whether or not it is

a conscious one, as it often does with a first-person narrator. To the degree that we are all culturally prejudiced subjects, Nixon's blatant, outrageous, and comic expressions of classism, racism, and sexism have the potential always to evoke laughter and more or less unconscious responses of recognition on the part of the reader. Undoubtedly these representations have the double potential of providing reinforcement for the socially destructive attitudes they foreground for their irrationality and cruelty. But a reader who experiences complicity in these attitudes is also set up for the discomfiting experience of identification and complicity in the painful and degrading resolution of Nixon's search for meaning and sociopolitical identity.

An equally complicated kind of Nixon-reader identification occurs at the level of Nixon's self-expressed conflicts and vulnerabilities: confusion in the face of conflicting data and desires, needs and fears that appear effeminate in a masculist world, and a pervasive sense of individual helplessness before the demands and affronts of history. Nixon lets us in on his most private fears and fantasies, and at some level of intimacy he truly becomes representative of the contemporary human situation, despite the absurd and parodic intensification and exaggerations of his personality. His sexual fears, his family history, his ambitions, his need for approval and his desire for love, his sense of himself as an outsider, his (realistic) political skepticism, his dividedness and vulnerabilities, and above all his desire to make sense of it all, of himself and of his place in the world—all of these self-confessed elements work both as a critique of masculism and as points of identity with a general reader. Coover has managed to construct a parodic version of the biographical Nixon, whose self-awareness and conscious, performative self-construction also operate a humanizing critique of the Nixon persona in the process of becoming Nixon.

Class and Race

Since there is much more information than Nixon is able to shape into a story that satisfies his motivations and ambitions, the readers' less restricted point of view gives them a larger critical horizon in which to view Nixon's and the Rosenbergs' story. But at the same time, the readers' felt identifications with Nixon and through Nixon with the Rosenbergs also allow a concomitant sense of participation in the complicities, contradictions, and implications of U.S. ideology. That is, the reader, theoretically free from the narrated limitations of the narrator and able to assess more impartially the surfeit of data that exceeds any narrated structure of the book, is in a superior position for critical judgment. Through identification with the narrator, however, the same reader also feels a discomfiting sense of the potentials for complicity in a passive reception and even unwitting or active reproduction of a classist, racist, sexist, and violent society.

Despite his gestures toward open-mindedness and critical self-awareness, Nixon is an ambitious, power-hungry U.S. male politician, with serious limitations as a self-aware narrator. His fears of being the scripted actor instead of the director of his life keep him from being able or willing to comprehend or commit himself to the complicated and ambiguous, even paradoxical, middleness of responsible historical engagement. His limitations come from an announced inability to tolerate anything but the certainty of opposites:

> I'm no believer in dialectics, material or otherwise, let me be absolutely clear about that, I wouldn't be Vice President of the United States of America if I was, it's either/or as far as I'm concerned and let the best man win so long as it's me. But I want these emotional resolutions. . . . it feels good to indulge in emotions when it no longer matters. (48)

> What were the Phantom's dialectical machinations if not the dissolution of the natural limits of language, the conscious invention of a space, a spooky artificial no-man's land, between logical alternatives? I loved to debate both sides of any issue, but thinking about that strange space in between made me sweat. Paradox was the one thing I hated more than psychiatrists and lady journalists. (136)

He vacillates instead between extreme and contradictory abstractions of the free and unified liberal individual, or the captured man of history who thinks he serves his country by serving his own desires—in Nixon's case, a desire to be at the center of power.

His purchase on Uncle Sam's Manichaean division of global reality allows him a self-serving and illusory reconciliation of the conflicting ideals of the liberal state. In the mythic American Dream, the pursuits of individual interests coincide to produce the common good. He can thus interpret his own country's social reality under a rubric of reason, light, and sacred purpose, and that of the Phantom under a rubric of satanic ignorance and evil. But he experiences contradictions in this American dream when he attempts to accommodate the perceived differences between his fate and that of the Rosenbergs to the nation's civil religion. It appears to him that he and the Rosenbergs had similar family (class) histories and shared many of the same ambitions. How then did the poverty, beatings, and other hardships of his childhood allow him a Ragged Dick (Horatio Alger's protagonist) kind of access to the American dream, leading him into the light of success, power, truth, and freedom, while Julius and Ethel, also wanting success in a better world, wandered into the darkness of communism, criminality, imprisonment, and death. He understands the positional nature of his limitations: "The one thing you could never understand was the thing you were intimately a part of" (427). But he is unwilling to risk his position as next in line for the presidency and his ambitions to manage the world long enough to pursue the critical evaluation and understanding his information, experience, and perceptions are making possible.

Instead, in his continual attempts to explain and justify the fates of the Rosenbergs as well as his own success, he unwittingly gives voice to the dark underside of the national practice of Enlightenment liberalism: failure and guilt were finally matters of class and race. The only explanation for the Rosenbergs' having stayed in the ghetto and remained poor in the land of opportunity was a "failure of imagination on their parts." Or perhaps they were simply faking it as a cover for their Communist beliefs and illegal activities. But "you only had to look at them [to know they were guilty]"; for "dowdiness *was* guilt" (127, 122). Of course their guilt was also revealed by their inability to play the absurdly phony middle-class roles they had chosen for the trial: "deep in their voices like an indelible stain ran irrepressible un-American accents, the sour babble of steerage passengers and backpack peddlers. The electorate, needless to say, were not fooled" (128). But, as Uncle Sam explains, the main guilt is derived metonymically:

> No, bein' a Jew ain't it, though it probably didn't help them
> none either. Their kind of depravity is something deeper even
> than that, something worse. You don't see it so much in the
> shape of their noses as in the way they twitch and blow them.
> You see it in how they shuffle and squat, how they bend,
> snort, and grimace. You see it in their crummy business, their
> greasy flat, their friends—even their crockery betrays them,
> their lawyers, their pajamas, their diseases. It's no accident,
> son, that they've been nailed with such things as Jell-O boxes,
> console tables, and brown wrappers—and it coulda just as easi-
> ly been the studio couch they slept on, their record player,
> medicine chest, or underwear—they stink with it, boy, it's on
> everything they touch! (88)

Then Uncle Sam makes the common disjunctive translation of this kind of metonymic guilt (by class and race) into an implied political (and, by linguistic conflation, moral and religious) guilt: such people were "violators of the Covenant, defilers of the sanctuary . . . Sons of Darkness!" (88). "Phantom-seed brought from the Old World like lice in an old hat brim" (129).

Class and race are constant subjects throughout *Public Burning:* as blatant bigotry or return of the repressed in the anonymous narrator sections, and as the subject of a mixture of serious reflection and unconscious but motivated racism and classism on the part of Nixon. These two narrators, prejudiced and blinded by their own empowered positions, nevertheless speak directly to the reader the split ideology of ethnocentric liberalism: a belief in an abstracted common humanity of equals whose different histories can only be explained by tautologies of inherent and self-fulfilling predictors such as class, race, gender, and failure of imagination.

Gender

Nixon's two cherished political notions—pure individual freedom in an open-ended (U.S.) history, and the common good as the

product of (his) individual interests and ambitions—are contradictory ideals and self-serving illusions unified and reconciled
by the American dream myth to which he subscribes. He perceives their antagonistic nature, however, in the way he imagines
them as gendered alternatives embodied by the loving mother
and the stern, punitive, angry, and violent father. Despite his
graphically described gynophobia, he fantasizes his mother and
all women as a potential haven for uncontingent love, unity, and
freedom from time. He experiences his father and the old powerful men he encounters in his political world as the male authority whom he must please and obey in order to survive and
succeed in the world:

> Jesus! he could really set your ass on fire, he scared the hell
> out of me early on and I learned how to avoid the beatings,
> even if I had to lie or throw off on others, but he pounded
> Don's butt to leather and I used to worry he'd broken poor
> Harold's health and crushed little Arthur's spirit, I still have
> nightmares about it. . . . I suppose I've got something of both
> of them in me—"The Fighting Quaker." (49-50)

With gender as with class and race, Nixon's problem is one
of attempting to preserve his identity and position in the complex
of interwoven and conflicting social-sexual-political phenomena
he experiences in his daily life. As is his habit, he attempts
management through polar separations and compartmentaliza-
tions of his experiences, a nonresolution that is unstable, unsa-
tisfying, and costly. He alternates between the poles of maternal/
paternal, feminine/masculine, passive/aggressive, fear/desire, pri-
vate/public, failure/success, means/ends, and moral/practical. He
wants to be a healer, a bridger of rifts, a unifier as he "keeps
moving to find out who [I am] and what the world is" (366). He
understands that "you create character as you go along" (295),
and his desire is for some kind of mediation of the psychic
oppositions he experiences in himself and in the cold war world.
This is thwarted by his preference for the clear either/or. But
his experiences in the three days leading up to the executions
have been a serious challenge to such a bifurcated view of the
world.

His dilemma is embodied in the figure of the 3-D film viewer who has left a showing of *House of Wax* with his Polaroid glasses still on, who can't get his two disparate views of the real world to coincide as they did in the art, technology, and manipulation of the theater. Nixon has left the ideologically focused and rhetorically secure world of Congress and the political elites to investigate the Rosenberg story and to experience life in the streets. And he has found that he can't coherently and consistently assemble all the raw data and all his experiences under the unifying myth of the American way. Nor can he seem to achieve a fit between his ambitions to be the president of the American dream and a sense of himself as a scripted product of that dream who wishes to escape its manipulations and irrationalities to find a more humane and open-ended kind of existence.

When for public purposes he needs to appear to manage ambiguities for a coherent argument, Nixon resorts to rhetoric and formalism: "[Debate taught me] how to manipulate ambiguities when you don't have the facts and aren't even sure what the subject matter is. I learned in debate that the topic didn't count for shit, the important thing was strategy" (295). But in his personal meditations he swerves back and forth between a complex and disorganized private self and a carefully controlled public Richard Nixon, a manipulated two-dimensional reduction, obsessed always with achieving the right gesture, tone, and camera angle: "Maybe the caricature came first and the face followed" (187). The private Nixon wants love, unity, and freedom (available, he thinks, from a woman), while the public Nixon wants to be at the center of power in a masculist world "for the future of my country and the cause of peace and freedom for the entire world," he tells himself (308).

The private Nixon continually conflates Pat and Ethel with his mother, especially when he is feeling a need for warmth, comfort, and soothing: "If only I were home and [mama] and Ethel could take care of me" (68); "[Pat] looked at me like my mother used to when I came in from playing touch football in a muddy field. . . . Why was it, whenever I was at home, I felt guilty?" (203). But Pat and Ethel are also parodies of the fair and dark women Leslie Fiedler finds so often in U.S. literature, women who embody the opposites of asexual moral purity and dangerous, forbidden erotic sexuality.[30] Pat, whom he married as the "win" he needed to complete himself for politics, and with whom he never quite understood "the mating part," although a stretch in the Navy helped,

> had simplified my life, brought it all together for me. Not by doing anything. Just by being Pat and being mine. Without having to say a thing, she became my arbiter, my audience, guide, model, and goal. Sometimes she felt she did have to say something, but it was usually better when she kept quiet. She looked good in photographs. I understood myself better when I looked at those photographs. She was the undiscovered heroine whom I could make rich and famous and who would be my constant companion. (55)

Pat, completely and cruelly objectified by Nixon, serves her instrumental gendered function for him even better in photographs than in person. He fantasizes her death and wonders, "Was I ready for that? Tough, of course. It would hurt. I'd be lost without Pat. It'd win a lot of votes, though" (204).

Ethel is a more complex and projective figure for Nixon, since he knows her not at all. She is able to embody the fantasized dark lady, the exotic, erotic Jewish alien other who is sexually uninhibited: "The Rosenbergs had no doubt tried everything. Since they were little kids maybe in the ghetto, being Jews and all" (143). And, as Nixon admits, "My weakness, I knew, was an extreme susceptibility to love, to passion. This is not obvious, but it is true" (298). This susceptibility is rather severely hampered by his ignorance about and abhorrence of genital sexuality. But his initial assault on Ethel when he visits her at Sing Sing gives him an unexpected sense of erotic empowerment:

> I pushed my tongue between her lips as she jerked and twisted helplessly in my arms—I was glad I hadn't shaved, I was glad it was rough for her! I felt mean and bulky like a bear . . . but erotically powerful at the same time. I'll be goddamned! I thought. This *was* what I'd been planning to do all along! (437)

Until his meeting with Ethel, Nixon had uncomfortably resided within his own clearly drawn opposition of male to female, with

its concomitant and troubling aspects of homophobia, gynophobia, and, in Nixon's case, a fascination with buttocks. He was a
"normal" man who always assumed he would keep a wife beside
him and have children. Marriage and children would tell the
world something about him and be good for his career. But in
his moment of erotic abandon and aggression with Ethel, and
despite his fears of being "swallowed up, lost, and disoriented,"
unexpected linguistic slippages, identities, confusions, and reversals of gender begin to occur in his elated responses to himself
as a "new man."

For the first time he no longer feels "inadequate" or "incomplete," and he "opened" himself to her as he never had to any
other person. While she is still his narcissistic object, his "perfectly reflected image," through a sudden rush of images as he
is grasping her bottom he also somehow begins to understand
the individual injustices and cruelties of history. As he gazes at
the cleft between her buttocks, he feels the peace and warmth
of "brotherhood." Feeling great affinity with Ethel and with their
similarly deprived pasts, he "let [his] hair down" with her as
with no one before, and "jerked her hard into [his] body." He's
always wanted to be this free, to say what he feels, to be a bum
(437–42). He finds himself experiencing feelings of wholeness,
power, freedom, and empathy:

> I thought: all strength lies in giving, not taking. I wanted to
> serve. . . . In this long chaste embrace, I felt an incredible new
> power, a new freedom. . . . I had escaped [both Uncle Sam and
> the Phantom]. I was outside guarded time! I was my own man
> at last! I felt like shouting for joy. . . . We patted each other's
> bottoms. We rubbed noses. It was a bit prominent her nose.
> (442)

Consistent with the loosening of thought produced by his
disorienting experiences of the past three days, Nixon in his
openness and abandon with Ethel feels a gender confusion manifest in a linguistic collapse of conventional gender categories.
He gives voice, through pronouns and images, to a bisexual
combination of conventional-wisdom aspects of both femininity
and masculinity. This is Nixon's moment of carnival, confusing
and breaking down the masculist boundaries upon which he

rigidly relies as a defense against such eruptions and returns of the repressed feminine and homosocial. This linguistic and emotional liminality for Nixon could have resolved in a number of ways, given the range of sexual feelings and experiences now available to him. Not surprisingly, however, given the book's and Nixon's obsession with anality, Ethel's and Nixon's encounter ends in a realm of a pre-oedipal anal logic.

An unwilled and recurring image of Ethel has appeared to Nixon as he has been trying to understand the Rosenbergs and their story: that of little Ethel as a child bending over by the kitchen stove to pull up her underpants. Nixon obsessively prefers bottoms, butts, buttocks to female genitalia.[31] He has responded to the sight of Pat's bare bottom in bed, slack and inviting, with a free-associative meditation on his revulsion for female genitals. His passionate assault on Ethel slows into a "chaste embrace" while they rub each other's bottoms. Ethel's urgings to him to take off his pants in order to take her sexually evoke nothing but regressive fear and reluctance on his part: "I cried, Damn it, I was doing my best! I seemed to hear my mother getting me ready for school. You're going to be late!" (445). But Ethel's ploy to get his pants off is to make possible the final gesture of autonomy and resistance on her part; just before she is led off for the execution, on the pretense of cleaning his "filthy bottom," she lipsticks "I AM A SCAMP" across his buttocks.

Nixon next finds himself "front and center" on the execution stage at Times Square, pants down around his ankles with Ethel's message prominently displayed as he tries to summon his debate skills to salvage his career. He is confused by what he has just experienced but can only fall back on the code of his lifelong ambitions:

> Christ! I thought. . . . I can't even remember my name! I fought to recover that name, that self, even as I grappled with my trousers, hobbling about in a tight miserable circle, fought to drag myself back to myself, my old safe self, which was—who knows?—maybe not even a self at all, my frazzled mind reaching out for the old catchwords, the functional code words of the profession, but drawing a blank. I ought to quit, I knew, but I couldn't. I didn't know how. I only knew how to plunge forward. (471)

He triumphs, co-opting Ethel's rebellious gesture for his own ambitions by asking everyone in the audience to "drop his pants for America." Compliance is enthusiastic, and the ritual orgy of national renewal ensues.

Nixon instinctively knows, despite his erotic and political confusion when he decides to visit Ethel, that faced with what he construes as a choice between feminine freedom and masculine power his allegiance lies with the paternal or patriarchal:

> [Mom] was the one I'd turned away from back there in Penn Station, and if I was walking with either one of them now, it was the rebellious and hot-blooded old man, not her. (359)

His choice of allegiance to the violent, racist, sexist old man of U.S. history following his visit to Ethel is finally a definitive splitting of his complex personality in favor of the hegemonic masculine, producing a closure to his quest for identity as well as to *Public Burning,* an ending that radically calls into question the exemption of men from the violence of a society governed by masculist extremes.

The book-long fascination with buttocks—by all narrators, including Uncle Sam and especially Nixon—more than adequately prepares for the book's resolution of the sexual and gendered ambiguities and oppositions. But the resolution also takes place in political terms and on political grounds, emphasizing once more the inextricable implications of sex, gender, and politics, as well as the metaphorical usefulness of sexual imagery and relationships to explore relationships of power and abuse.[32] Nixon believes, with some regret, that he is choosing the masculine and political at the expense of the feminine ethical and sexual. But he underestimates the costs of his choice. Following Nixon's persuasive performance at the executions, Uncle Sam shows up at his house to let him know he is the chosen one in an economy of masculist sexual politics:

> "Come here, boy," he said, smiling frostily and jabbing his recruitment finger at me with one hand, unbuttoning his striped pantaloons with the other: "I want YOU! . . . Speech me no speeches, my friend, I had a bellyfulla baloney—what I got a burnin' yearnin' for now is a little humble toil, heavenward

duty, and onmittygated cornholin' whoopee! So jes' drap your
drawers and bend over, boy—you been ee-LECK-ted! . . . You
heerd me!" he roared. "E pluribus the ole anum, buster, and on
the double!" . . . "No!" I shrieked, giving way. And in he came,
filling me with a ripping all-rupturing force so fierce I thought
I'd die! This . . . this is not happening to me alone, I thought
desperately, or tried to think . . . but to the nation as well! . . . I
felt like a woman in hard labor. (530, 532–33)

Uncle Sam leaves Nixon "rolling about helplessly on the spare-
room floor, scrunched up around my throbbing pain and bawling
like a baby" (534).

So ends this comedy of the masculist state, in a sexual embrace
between its two principal males—Nixon and Uncle Sam, the
country's representative figures of the individual and of its masculist ideology. The embrace is homoerotic, anal, and violent,
reducing the individual to the abject position of helpless hu-
miliation, despite and because of his choice of allegiance to the
national civil religion. His ambitions to be at an unambiguous
and masculine center of power have implicated him in a costly
web of divisions and requirements that strip him of agency except as it coincides with the national ideology and interests.
Without occluding the greater costs of white male dominance
to women, minorities, and underclasses, *Public Burning* demonstrates the reproduction of ideology and power as a violent
penetration and impregnation of the psyche and body, even
of men.

6

Closure

Anal Logic and Masculist Society

The emasculation figured and dramatized in *Public Burning* is not men's castration by women, even though gynophobia and misogyny pervasively characterize its masculist world; it is rather the degrading anal aggression of a violent penetration and occupation by the hegemonic masculine, getting fucked by masculist history and the masculist capitalist state. The threat and practice of this kind of political violence produce a nongendered emasculation that manifests itself as a kind of individual impotence before such invasive power; men, women, and children are all equally vulnerable, albeit within a hierarchy structured by class, race, and gender. As Uncle Sam says, "There ain't nothin' to fear but fear itself and a dry hole."

Misogyny, gynophobic homosocial bonding, and narcissistic anal aggression are predominant in *Public Burning* as figures for U.S. cold war states of mind. The other novel that takes the Rosenbergs, the cold war, and the left as its subjects, *The Book of Daniel,* also uses misogyny, homosocial bonding, and anal aggression as evidence of the costs to the individual, the family, and the society of state abuse. One manifestation of Daniel's displacement of the effects of family abuse by the state is his misogyny toward his wife and sister. While his aggression often takes the form of fantasies of erotic genital violence, in the cruelest moment in the book he makes his wife kneel away from him while he prepares to burn her buttocks with a cigarette lighter. There is at least a formal homology to *Public Burning*'s ending in the blessing, in the form of a kiss, that the senile Mindish gives Daniel, ending Daniel's family history quest. Doctorow has carefully developed Mindish as an ambiguous and unknowable figure. Possibly a tool of the state and a traitor to Daniel's parents, he might also be a tragic member of the old left, called upon to betray his close friends in order to protect the Communist party. In either case, he is a representative of a masculist power that claims ownership and mastery of history, and Daniel's search for identity, as does Nixon's, achieves a tentative resolution in an embrace with that power. Gore Vidal's novel *Myra Breckinridge* (1968), about the post-Rosenberg generation, uses anality and anal aggression as its structuring theme for a parody of the masculist mass culture society of the United States in the second half of the twentieth century.

Such figurative analogies between postwar U.S. history and aspects of anality have their own kinds of metaphoric and cognitive descriptive power, even if the relationships are not easily demonstrable in the rubric of the social sciences. Fredric Jameson's comment is relevant: a cultural phenomenon like postmodernism—and in this case a predominant literary theme of anality—must be articulating something about what is going on in the world.[1] This is especially true when we consider other major postwar and postmodern U.S. novels that depend to some extent on anal logic and anal aggression for narrative development and resolution, such as William Gaddis's *Recognitions* (1955), John Barth's *Floating Opera* (1956), Norman Mailer's *American Dream* (1965), and Thomas Pynchon's *Gravity's Rainbow* (1973).

According to psychoanalytic theory, the anal stage, occurring generally from one to three years of age, follows without canceling the oral stage and prepares for the Oedipal, genital stage. If negotiated relatively successfully, it results in the development of first a body ego and then a psychic ego, with a sense of body and psychic boundaries, and a capacity for both defenses and openness at the will of and in the best interests of the individual. The anal stage is critical to the development of a degree of autonomy that can tolerate and deal with the ambiguities, aggressions, and excesses of the internal and external world; it is crucial to the cognitive development of ways of knowing and ways of not knowing.[2]

At this stage, attempts to manage one's own newly discovered aggressive and libidinal feelings and capabilities—the need to learn how to control destructiveness—are marked at first by an unpredictable alternation between extreme opposites: yes/no, passivity/aggression, withholding/attacking, closure/openness, submission/resistance. "The world that is dominated by anal psychology is full of opposites, reversals, and contradictions. . . . In the second and third year of life, an easy reversibility . . . can approach a cancelling out of meaning."[3] This phenomenon is one that Derrida critiques as inherent in an epistemology founded on binary logic: "When the middle of an opposition is not the passageway of a mediation, there is every chance that the opposition is not pertinent. The consequences are boundless."[4] The tendency to resort to a binary logic allows the development of "various ways of disregarding, disowning, or negating external and psychic reality."[5] I want to suggest that the coordinates of an incomplete anal stage, or of an anal fixation in extremes of owning/disowning (both materially and psychically) and containing/attacking, have at least metaphorically a homological correspondence to both the extremes of rhetoric and of the material practices of the anticommunist, consumer-driven national security state that developed during the cold war period.

The rhetorical excesses of the articulation of the cold war I have discussed in part 1 as the ordinary operations of language being put to exclusionary extremes of polarization and closure to provide the dominant group with a sense of certainty and positional security in a time of aggressive threats (internal and external), socioeconomic disruption, and unsettling liminality. But the socially retarding and destructive costs of the reassuring cold war narrative with its long-term unnegotiable plot strictly governed by an either-or closure were enormous, cumulative, and enduring. Again at least an analogy exists between the social costs of this situation and the psychic costs of anal fixation: "A concomitant of the need to achieve an illusion of closure, fixity, and stability (without which there might be no feeling of identity) is the danger of fixation. . . . Unless in the course of maturation the illusion of closure becomes subject to doubt, full humanity will not be achieved."[6]

Discounting the notion of what even the author of these words would probably admit as an illusion of an achievable plenitude of humanity, the anal-stage necessity of learning and then practicing skepticism toward closure is most definitively a requirement for a reality-based democratic politics presumed to be oriented toward the goal of a just society—as it is a requirement for critical intellectual practice. But the cold war period was a lengthy practice of a politics of acquisition, containment, holding, and withholding, based on a fixed and polarizing narrative of historical closure. It solidified and realized itself and its ideology in specific global political and economic relationships, producing a domestic society devoted to mindless consumption and waste and a national security state devoted to power through arms and secrecy.

And finally, the cold war national security consumer state was the product of male networks of power in which women, minorities, and the working class served functions of exchange value for white male interests. Coover's book is a critique, using anality as its predominant metaphor, of this masculist system and of its social costs to everyone, not just to the visibly exploited and oppressed. Nixon, preferring a clear either/or, chose the definitive closure of an extreme masculist U.S. ideology, and closure is what he got. Not unlike George Orwell's *1984* protagonist who feels love for Big Brother, in Coover's *Public Burning* Nixon's attitude ultimately becomes one of submission to and identification with an idealized oppressor and aggressor. Nixon's first sentence here is an oblique critique of the ideological construction of his own desire:

> Maybe the worst thing that can happen to you in this world is to get what you think you want. And how did we know what we wanted? It was a scary question and I let it leak away, unanswered. Of course, he was an incorrigible huckster, a sweet-talking con-artist, you couldn't trust him, I knew that—but what did it matter? Whatever else he was, he was beautiful

(how had I ever thought him ugly?), the most beautiful thing in all the world. I was ready at last to do what I had never done before. "I . . . I love you, Uncle Sam!" I confessed. (534)[7]

Open-endedness

The oxymoronic or apocalyptic concept of historical closure has always been a theme of history and historiography, predating of course the atomic bomb and the twentieth-century awareness of global limits. But despite the atomic bomb, the reality of global limitations, and apocalyptic poststructuralist totalizations of a postindividual collective culture, there has been a concomitant and not inconsistent development of the notion of the individual as cultural and historical narrator and participant in the construction of social reality.

Certainly we have seen individual narrators making contributions to a collectively written history in the construction of the Rosenberg story, as we have seen authors like Doctorow and Coover add their own critical narrative revisions of the cold war stories we told, heard, and performed as a nation. Until the end of history, we are all apparently to some degree engaged in producing an ending to history, the revelation of which remains deferred.

I mentioned that all seven of the stories operative in *Public Burning* come to a close together. Doctorow's book appears to end in greater uncertainty, with Daniel recounting three possible endings, capped by an admonition from the biblical Book of Daniel to "Go thy way, Daniel: for the words are closed up and sealed till the time of the end" (368). We need to consider the endings of these two books that are manifestly critical social fiction dealing with contemporary U.S. history and with the modes and potentials for dissent from and oppositional politics within that history. Both books dramatize the social and personal costs of adherence to dogmatic narratives of history; both formally insist upon that complicated middle ground of life and experience in which the closures of meaning necessary to thought and action are always also necessarily thought as part of the flux and points of departure for more useful versions.

Daniel's three proposed endings for his novel/dissertation do not, as some critics have maintained, affirm a postmodern uncertainty and undecidability. They follow instead a progressive logic in the context of the book and its subject of left politics, having to do with saying goodbye to outmoded forms of life and stepping down into the world from the security of a purely mental and reflective environment in order to "see what's going down" (367). Daniel's future is unknown; while his skepticism and cynicism may hold him to the role of observer, his tentative reflections on left analysis and politics always seem to be a source of energy and optimism to him. Through his reflections, as well as through the book's formal design, we begin to put together a modest and sacrificial but always potentially historically significant program for left politics. It is for the left to perform the hard work of analysis, of making connections not visible through naturalized or masculist versions of society. It is also for the left to assume and articulate positions based on such analysis and believed to be productive of social justice. This is an always provisional practice, requiring resistance toward one's own tendency to totalizing narratives and simple binary explanations of social reality. It also requires a willingness to persist, despite being ignored, rejected, misstated, misused, or co-opted. Not unlike the work of artists or prophets unhonored in their own time, the relevance and value of articulated left positionality can only be judged in retrospect, almost always as subsumed and enacted under a liberal or conservative agenda.

Public Burning is criticized for offering no positive vision, but in its pervasive engagement with the issue of closure, it presents an ethical challenge for critical participation in history. Coover elaborates this challenge thematically and figuratively at key moments in the text, and formally by the ending of both the Rosenbergs' story and Nixon's. The argument is figured, in typical Coover fashion, in terms of open-endedness and rape. An innocent or absolute open-endedness is a crippling vulnerability to assault, abuse, and co-optation:

> They's a political axiom that wheresomever a vacuum exists, it
> will be filled by the nearest or strongest power! Well, you're
> lookin' at it, mister: an example and fit instrument, big as they

come in this world and gittin' bigger by the minute! . . . So
clutch aholt on somethin' and say your prayers, cuz I propose
to move immeejitly upon your works! (532)

Dogmatic closure, figured by rape, is by definition aggressive,
abusive, and exploitive, working a deliberate violence on its
vulnerable victims. Nixon's Ethel learns this lesson when she is
a high school member of the Clark Street Players. To an older
cast member walking home with her, arguing that life means
adopting a role and sticking with it, "She said, no, life is more
open-ended than that. Then he jammed her up against a wall in
a dark doorway, dragged up her skirts, and pushed his knee into
her crotch. Some argument" (104).

Uncle Sam admonishes his audience to "Go forth to meet the
shadowy future, without fear, and with a manly heart on," his
masculist dogma operating to organize data and human behavior
into what is best for him: "It ain't easy holdin' a community
together, order ain't what comes natural, you know that, boy,
and a lotta people gotta get killt tryin' to pretend that it is, that's
how the game is played" (531). Nixon is confused, though, until
he finally gets it at the end. He has it in his mind that freedom
in the United States means the absence of script and plot, and
that the real struggle against the Phantom is against the "lie of
purpose" (363), while Uncle Sam remains for him "The Super-
chief in the Age of Flux" (341). He extends the analogy—illog-
ically, and in accord with the American dream—to equate
freedom, flux, and open-endedness with U.S. capitalism (called
free individual enterprise); and plot, social engineering, and historical closure with socialist oppression. "Maybe in Russia History had a plot because one was being laid on, but not here—
that was what freedom was all about!" (362).

By the time of these speculations, the motivated and constructed nature of the Rosenberg story has become apparent to
Nixon; as he noted from a lawyer's point of view, a story that
cohered perfectly in lock-step cause-effect sequence when you
walked forward through it began to unravel when you worked
your way backward from end to beginning: "Hoover was in many
ways a complete loony, arbitrary in his power and pampered
like a Caesar, and if he dreamed up a spy network one day, then

by God it existed. . . . It was an agent's job [to carry the Rosenberg case] to successful conclusions" (371). This doesn't fit his
concept of free flow in his country: "How do such things
happen?" He speculates that the Rosenberg truth lay somewhere
in the middle, that territory of dialectics, ambiguities, and uncertainties that he cannot tolerate. It is ultimately Nixon's intolerance for this ground and the naïveté of his insistence on the
reality of the opposites U.S. openness/Communist closure that
leave him open to impregnation by the U.S. "lie of purpose."

The ethical challenge to dogmatic closures is posed by the
paradox inherent in the seven endings. The microhistory of the
seventy-two hours leading up to the executions has come to a
temporal end, as has the twenty-eight-part mathematical series,
an arbitrary and fashioned design with predetermined closure.
Hoover and the state have ended the Rosenberg story, but this
book is also demonstrating by its very existence that the story
is, despite their deaths in June 1953, still open-ended, still being
narrated. Uncle Sam has violently satisfied Nixon's quest, but
only because Nixon has made himself entirely vulnerable to ideological co-optation by believing, against the evidence of a more
complex and motivated political world, in a pure form of openness as the moral property of the United States.

But three of the stories, although they each stop arbitrarily in
the last word of the book, "good-bye!" (534), cannot end until
history ends: the play of words (language), narrativity, and history
itself. *Public Burning* has told metastories—words about words,
narrative about narrative, and history about history—that all demonstrate the ongoing and oscillating constructive and destructive
activities of symbol-making, -organizing, and -enacting, activities
that are always potentially liminal moments of political agency.
To resist the dangers and costs of rigid formalized closure, *Public
Burning* demonstrates the critical potential of an alternating postmodern literary discourse that can move within and work the
middle of a historical epoch, interrogating opposites, exploring
ambiguities, uncertainties, and contradictions, figuratively evoking skepticism toward final words, and providing a point of
departure for more useful narratives. But more useful for whom?

7

Framed Arts

All living phenomena can be viewed as content occurring in the framework of a container which circumscribes and describes the content, and, reciprocally, the content has great influence in transforming the nature of its container.

> James S. Grotstein, formulating Wilfred Bion's
> concept of the container and the contained, in
> "Who Is the Dreamer Who Dreams the Dream and
> Who Is the Dreamer Who Understands It?"

In reading United States cold war history and society through the critical categories offered by the postmodern factual/fictional novel we have depended upon formal structures that, by framing and organizing the material of the novel, also orient our readings: the temporal boundaries of the books' topical subjects; the material boundaries of the bound book itself, beginning and ending within a cover; and the interpretive frames established by the complex and multiform shaping and delimiting performed by language and its artful constructions.

We have considered the ways in which the postmodern form serves Doctorow's purposes in critiquing the naive and self-destructive liberalism and ideological rigidity of the Communist old left, as well as, for the second half of the twentieth century, the liberal categories of the unified or coherent subject as agent, objectivity, and progressive history. Doctorow's announced personal ambiguity toward the role of the individual in a post-humanist history is well served by his chosen and crafted frames.

The historical period encompassing the demise of the old left and the emergence of the new leads him to that consideration of the transition from the concept of liberal individual to the more complicated emergent cultural and political concept of the subject as neither free nor unified, but as a contingent product and producer of history and social relationships. The bound book encloses a nonorganic narrative that explicitly refuses coherence and formal closure. Daniel interrupts—and ends for the purposes of the book—his narrated search for social and political self-definition with his decision that he will "walk out . . . [to] see what's going down." He then provides his own metacommentary on his narration: "A Life Submitted in Partial Fulfillment of the Requirements." The bound book contains only a partial—in both senses—life story, not the whole or complete story, which, like Scheherazade's endlessly lifesaving stories in *Arabian Nights,* is coterminous with narrative itself. Doctorow provides a final metametacommentary, quoting from the biblical Book of Daniel, offering delivery at "the time of the end" to those who are "found written in the book": written as historical participants, but in what differential combination and potential of writer/written? Daniel has just written himself into his own book, but any concept of himself or his book is inseparable from the larger narrative of history itself—which cannot be known "till the time of the end." The last words in the book provide the most definitive linguistic ending available: "the end" at the end of the last sentence. But their linguistic context cancels them out as closure in favor of the uncertain futurity of going on: "Go thy way Daniel: for the words are closed up and sealed till the time of the end."

The crafted formal structure of the book most congruently mimics Doctorow's contradictory and willed assertion of humanist obligation as ambiguous ethical participants in history, despite our being "written" in a postatomic posthumanist age. As elaborated in chapter 4, this structure refuses tragedy by countering the historical declension of the power of the individual as figured in the epigraphs with an ongoing redemptive change through time in individual consciousness and practice.

This onward movement is figured both by the ensuing elaboration of a nonorganic narrative, and by the formal progression of the book's divisions from a remembering of the past, through an acknowledgment of the dark side (the terrors of history), to a rejection of a vicariously experienced unity that is death, into a sense of futurity that requires continual reiteration in word and deed.

We have considered in chapter 5 the ways in which Coover establishes and at the same time exploits *The Public Burning*'s frames as an integral part of the message. No period in U.S. history serves more sufficiently or dramatically Coover's constant obsession with the costs of individual and collective adherence to motivated fictions—perfecting myths and ideologies—than the cold war anticommunist period. He chooses carefully the specific situation to be defined and represented by his book and announces it symmetrically at the beginning and again at the end: a historically situated story in the arbitrary form of a comedy.

His epigraphs, in addition to introducing us to the historical situation (the Rosenberg story and the cold war), some of the main characters (Nixon and Ethel), and themes (narrativity and the law of the nation-state, male homosocial bonding, objectivity, and ideology), establish a formal context for the reception of the book. In two short quotations he both asserts and performs ironic situation comedy as the way in which the book is to be taken. He first quotes the biographical Ethel delivering one of her lines in the play *The Valiant:* "That's what I'm counting on most of all—the stories," and then the biographical Nixon claiming, "All my humor is situation stuff." It was stories that did Ethel in, but it is also through stories that those stories, their supporting structures of power and authority, and their historic and cultural effects can be analyzed, criticized, and changed in time. All stories are "situation stuff." Despite the potential paralysis of such an irony—that stories imprison us and stories set us free in material and daily life—stories are what we have to count on and to keep on telling. But, as Nixon tells us, even in a choice of comedy over tragedy, we can never escape the situation. I argue that it is ultimately the situation—the context, the frame—that is the critical object.

The first two sentences of the first chapter of *The Public Burning* perform a sequential ironic transmutation of history into culture, of literal fact into figured fiction, and of narrative into demonized symbology. They situate us—the readers—somewhere in the everyday middle between the theoretical extremes of fact and fiction:

> On June 24, 1950, less than five years after the end of World War II, the Korean War begins, American boys are again sent off in uniforms to die for Liberty, and a few weeks later, two New York City Jews, Julius and Ethel Rosenberg, are arrested by the FBI and charged with having conspired to steal atomic secrets and pass them to the Russians. They are tried, found guilty, and on April 5, 1951, sentenced by the Judge to die— thieves of light to be burned by light—in the electric chair, for it is written that "any man who is dominated by demonic spirits to the extent that he gives voice to apostasy is to be subject to the judgment upon sorcerers and wizards." (3)

After 534 pages of a seemingly infinite number of such multilevel formal permutations, convolutions, inversions, and figurations that work to interrogate any received and coherently mythic notions of cold war history, and after the darkly comedic closure of the linear narrative by Uncle Sam's rape of a Nixon who's been "asking for it," Uncle Sam ends the book by saying "good-bye": Nixon is "scrunched up around [his] throbbing pain and bawling like a baby," but Uncle Sam insists that he is leaving "'em laughing as [he] say[s] good-bye." Coover's critical and darkly cynical view of the power of dominant ideology has the last word, in a blatantly cruel and sadistic inversion of the situation, a formal and figurative construction of comic incongruence that makes the terrors of history momentarily visible and perceivable—through the evocation of our own pained but ironic, perhaps even critical, angry, and implicated, laugh at the cruelty of a contradiction which we all—in our own ways and to differing degrees—support.

In summary, we can say that Doctorow's contextualizing frame or horizon is that of ambiguity and contradiction, and Coover's is that of situated comic irony. Each orients us as readers, telling us how to take its particular narrative subject: in Doctorow's novel, the problematic and never-ending quest for self-definition and agency in history; in Coover's, the uses and abuses of ideological narrative in the service of power. And each, with the various strategies we have considered, manages to implicate the reader in the situation framed by its orienting context. In neither does the constructed limit to or horizon of understanding—ambiguity, contradiction, and situated irony—produce paralysis. On the contrary, such doubleness of point of view is proposed as the only possibility for an already situated and complicit—written—person's purposeful engagement in the uncertain and risky but inevitable process of historical change. And integral to each narrative—central in Coover's case—is the deadly cost to individual and history of the unrelentingly single and theoretically unsituated point of view.

But what of arts that are also delimited by the seemingly more arbitrary and fixed boundaries of the stage and the frame? What of arts and performances that appear to stand alone, in a visually framed formal coherence or incoherence, or a contained human performance that proves—or does not prove—a message or challenge right there, on the spot, in that arbitrarily bounded time and space? Drama and painting are more immediate presentations than narrative and poetry on the page; in being more immediate both must necessarily establish their contextualizing or orienting context in a more efficient simultaneity with presentation. This simultaneity occurs also in language arts, but I am, for the purposes of an argument concerning the operations of critical art, noting a difference of degree between narrative and performing and visual arts, in their relation to their frames and their dependency on an explicit orienting context or form. Visual and performing arts, like literature, can be so historically stylized, ritualized, and culturally naturalized as to *appear* to require no contextualization, as with Greek drama for the Greeks, or impressionist or abstract expressionist painting by the late twentieth century.

But contemporary critical and avant-garde arts have not yet achieved historical integration into everyday life. They still invite and require interpretation, while at the same time inviting a domesticating commodification by a self-sustaining circuit of

aestheticizing exchange among certain critics, dealers, and elite
and radical-chic consumers and collectors. The critical apparatuses evoked by the relatively autonomous and objectified status
of contemporary, late twentieth-century art have tended toward
formalist readings that render art harmless, critical readings that
attack such art for its elite aestheticism or abstraction and sustaining participation in the commodity circuit, or readings that
work to recuperate a critical or oppositional function for art in
its inevitable context of social injustices and terrors.[1] The latter
kind of politicizing reading of the arts is at the forefront in the
academic humanities in the 1990s, leading to political critiques
of traditional cultural forms and techniques that the cultural and
political right has had to disparage, defensively and without irony,
in terms of "political correctness"—the left's own ironic warning
to itself against the political inconsistencies and dangers of the
single view. In any case, careers are often made for critic and
artist by the drawing of contemporary decontextualized make-
it-new art into a persuasive, coherent, and commodifiable context, regardless of its purported and relative critical valence. In
all of this activity, it is a single point of view of artist, critic, or
both—expressed by or in terms of uncomplicated formal unities,
diffuse fields, or meaning-resistant juxtapositions, or allowing
(even promoting) a facile objectification of the artifact through
an undisturbed gaze—that lends itself most readily to co-optation
through interpretation and consumption.

A dramatic presentation or an image tends more than verbal
language to block out its opposite and alternative images and
representations, and to foreclose countermemory and associa-
tions. The immediate arts convey a positivity and affective force
that written language cannot achieve. This is to suggest that a
single image or a single message—while it can be informing,
ordering, mobilizing, or reconciling—without an orienting context cannot be critical. By itself, a yellow ribbon or an American
flag cannot perform a critical function in regard to the U.S.-Iraqi
war or any other social or political situation, but one can imagine
all kinds of ironizing contexts for this image that would evoke
a critical disturbance in the viewer's mind—no matter what her

attitude toward the war—a context that would force a phenom-enological awareness (perhaps subliminal) of the contradictions, costs, and complicities involved in the use or representation of a yellow ribbon or a flag in order to say one thing.

I am building toward the generalization that critical art, given that it calls attention to itself as art(ifact), requires an orienting context—internal, external, or both—while aesthetic art can appear to stand alone in its formal, technical, or performative immediacy, wholeness, and perfection or near perfection. My concern in this study of the Rosenberg stories is with art that self-consciously sets out to be and announces itself as critical work. I am convinced, by the works under consideration, that a critical work or artifact will call attention to itself as referential and disturbing, originating in and returning to the social world of lived relations; provide the reader with a critical orientation that resists or refuses the liberal subject-object or audience-artifact split; risk rejection by disturbing single points of view and passive or pleasurable aestheticized reception; and thus resist, at least for a moment, commodification and co-optation.

Disturbatory Art

Arthur Danto calls visual arts that work in these ways disturbatory art and criticizes it—sometimes with nostalgia—for its aggression, for its victimization of the viewer, and for its complicity in performing and embodying the problem that it wishes to critique. He suggests that the energies spent in crafting a disturbatory critical work of art might be better spent in direct political activism than in destroying art by attacking its viewers. Danto complains that at the 1991 Whitney Biennial the viewer was a target of the political works collected on the fourth floor:[2]

> The viewer is cast in a very different relationship to these works than to those on the other two floors. . . . The viewer is put on the defensive. The viewer is a target. And since the whole fourth floor is a kind of attack, one wonders, in sustaining it, whether the works are after all not merely weapons, and the true agents of aggression the curators who chose them.[3]

But he also acknowledges in the same article that an art that is not "eager to please"

> rais[es] the hardest questions that can be raised about art today and mak[es] us face the hardest truths. It does a great deal more than show what is happening in art: It shows what is happening to art in a world in which we are all players.[4]

In a more optimistic mode in 1989, he accorded contemporary critical art the potential for changing consciousness:

> Disturbatory art is intended, rather, to modify, through experiencing it, the mentality of those who do experience it. This is . . . art intended . . . to modify the consciousness and even change the lives of its "viewers."[5]

Undoubtedly these are the claims any self-consciously critical artist would want to be able to make for his or her mode of representation: the potential for bringing the viewer to a perceptual crisis productive of newly critical self-awareness.

Donald Freed's *Inquest*

I want to consider three "framed" Rosenberg stories in terms of the criteria and critiques they evoke and produce: Donald Freed's 1969 multi-media play, *Inquest;* Martha Rosler's 1989 photographic collage, "Unknown Secrets"; and Peter Saul's 1989 acrylic painting on paper, "Ethel Rosenberg."[6]

Freed's play opened in Cleveland in 1969, enjoyed an extended run for nine weeks there, and then opened in a revised and abridged version at the Music Box Theater in New York on April 23, 1970. Both Clive Barnes and Walter Kerr reviewed the play for the *New York Times,* and Barnes claims it as his only experience with attempted but unsuccessful censorship.[7] For its technical staging and human peformances they greeted it as successful, even powerful theater; for its single and uncomplicated point of view they tended to consider it as failed political—critical—drama. Judge Kaufman, however, the Rosenbergs' trial judge, greeted it as politically threatening procommunist propaganda. FBI records show that he contacted J. Edgar Hoover about the play and its two reviews in the *New York Times*. In a subsequent letter, Kaufman thanked Hoover for supplying him with background information on Donald Freed. The FBI obtained a copy of the script and decided that the matter would be "followed closely."[8] But this opposite and equal reaction, on the part of the Rosenberg trial judge, to a one-sided political version of the story is not an effect that would qualify the play as disturbing, critical art.

Freed describes his purpose in writing plays as establishing antimyth to oppressive and terror-producing or terror-masking (or both) perfecting myth, in this case the cold war myth and its necessary anticommunism. He proposes to accomplish antimyth through a combination of the Artaudian theater of cruelty and the theater of fact—a combination that he calls the grammar for a twentieth-century popular drama attempting to address the terrors of history. Such a grammar, through intensification, ruptures of decorum, distortion, and grotesquerie in the first case— not unlike Brecht's alienation effect—and through a stark presentation of unaestheticized and unpublicized historical data in the second, can break certain social and political realities away from their naturalizing and moralizing context and reveal them for what they are: abuses of humanity in the name of a certain kind of order.

To this end, Freed chose the theater of fact, in a multimedia presentation that could situate both the Rosenberg story and the audience in the cultural and political atmosphere of the (atomic) end of World War II and the 1950s. The visual projections and sound reenactments through slides, photographs, newspaper reproductions, posters, music, radio shows, and other taped voices and sounds began outside the theater and continued through the lobby and throughout the staged dramatic presentation. The backdrop for the side-by-side performing stages—one for documentary representations, and one for "reconstruction from events"—was an eighteen-panel screen on which were projected some 3,500 images: pictures of the Japanese reacting to the atomic bomb explosions in 1945; of Truman, Eisenhower, Hoover, McCarthy, Supreme Court justices, Nietzsche, Marx, and Freud;

of Einstein, Milton Berle, Walter Winchell, newspaper headlines, prosecution exhibits during the trial, and the Rosenberg family.

The staged drama consisted of an alternating series of selected documentary reenactments of the public record of the official Rosenberg story and imaginative reconstructions from events— incidents before, during, and after the trial that Freed felt were persuasive indicators of the extent to which the innocent Rosenbergs were framed. Freed was limited by writing before the release of selected FBI documents relating to the case that would have supplemented and reinforced the line of argument he was establishing. The audience was cast, from the beginning, in the role of jury—to the successful extent that when the actor/clerk first entered the stage/courtroom, many members of the audience stood for the pledge of allegiance. The roles of Julius, Ethel, and their attorney Emanuel Bloch were played powerfully and persuasively, according to the critics, by the accomplished actors George Grizzard, Anne Jackson, and James Whitmore.

Freed put together the formal elements and dynamics of critical art: the play announces itself from the beginning as referential art or artifact. It establishes a putatively critical contextual frame, situating and saturating even the audience in a 1950s political and cultural environment. It interrupts and disturbs the audience's passive reception of entertainment by actively engaging its members as jury. But despite the correct formal recipe for critical postmodern art, as critical work the play fails in two crucial ways. In evoking audience participation, what it constitutes and invites is an objective moral assessment, by the untroubled consciences of coherent liberal individuals, of an unambiguous factual representation of state corruption and injustice toward two specific individuals, in a context that both requires and explains such an event. It also fails, despite the richly textured historical context evoked by the multimedia presentation, to establish a critical context that disturbs and calls for more than a liberal and sympathetic identification with the victims of that injustice or a righteous anger at the state. That kind of affective and moral identification with the victim and against the oppressor does not necessarily entail or require a critical response, a re-cognition of the self, the individual, and its systemic implications in the social order being represented to us, a newly complicated—or simplified—sense of the connections that inhere in a social order that we support with our daily lives.

A measure of the degree to which Freed's own critical point of view was ideologically domesticated during the 1950s, when he was in his twenties, is his strategic division of the drama into the public and private Rosenberg story. The public version consists of the literal reenactments of documented public conversations and trial records; the private version consists of brief alternating pieces of more private moments, in which the Rosenbergs encounter each other, their family and children, and their attorney, and in which their concerns are primarily local and domestic. Freed's strategy is to use the apolitical, familial innocence of the private lives as evidence of a larger innocence in the realm of the law. Such personae were, of course, the public roles chosen by the Rosenbergs for the trial and thereafter in their public letters, a misbegotten appropriation of the dominant ideology of self-representation, an identification with the aggressor that deprived them of a critical standpoint. But in Freed's design, as it was—in part at least—in the Rosenbergs' self-representation, it was the apolitical familial innocence that was imaginatively reconstructed. Intending to produce evidence for the jury in a theater of fact, Freed has reproduced not a plausible version of a lower Eastside Communist Jewish family in the 1950s on trial for their lives for giving away the secret of the atomic bomb, but the 1950s family of the dominant media and advertising ideology, a family whose economic, marital, parental, and social concerns are solely domestic and private, intersected and structured neither by those of the imperialist, national security anticommunist state being represented on the screen, nor by the problematic Marxist and Stalinist loyalties of much of the old left.

Freed thus reproduces his blindness to the connections between his own membership in the Silent Generation, "totally uninvolved and unaware of the case," as he said, and the ways in which the Rosenberg history took place.[9] And he allows the audience the comfort of this same blindness, reassuring them of their engagement by providing viewing positions from which they can sympathize with the persuasively performed victims at the same time that they objectify the story, assign it an absolute moral value, and go home without being confronted with or disturbed by their own writing and being written in that same story, simply by the witting and unwitting practices of their everyday lives.

Freed's audience leaves more informed, but reconfirmed in the integrity of their liberal selves.[10] His elaborate contextualization—split stage, multimedia juxtaposition of image, text, and sound—is an add-on, a gratuitous, mystifying affectation to make complex and aestheticize a relentlessly single idea. The context sets a mood and evokes a merely iconic past; it fails to establish a critical orientation or require a critical response.

The "Unknown Secrets" Exhibit

In 1988 Rob Okun, editor and publisher of *Workplace Democracy,* and Nina Felshin, a free-lance curator, completed a five-year project collecting art and commentary about the Rosenberg era under the auspices of the Rosenberg Era Art Project: an exhibit, "Unknown Secrets," and companion book, *The Rosenbergs: Collected Visions of Artists and Writers.* The book includes excerpts from the Schneirs', Coover's, and Doctorow's books; from Freed's play and Arthur Miller's 1953 play, *The Crucible;* from a fictional biography of Ethel Rosenberg by Tema Nason; and poems by Adrienne Rich, W. E. B. Du Bois, Allen Ginsberg, Louise Bernikow, and Ethel Rosenberg. The exhibit comprises fifty-seven single and multimedia works; a third were executed in the 1950s, and a third were newly commissioned for the show. Two hundred and fifty galleries were invited to exhibit the show; of the nine that accepted, seven were university and college galleries or alternative spaces.[11]

The work divides along a 1950s–1980s axis. The 1950s work is generally memorial, iconic, and even lyrical (in the drawings by Picasso and Leger)—with the notable exceptions of two paintings by the U.S. urban immigrant primitivist Ralph Fasanella, *McCarthy-Era Gray Day* (1963) and *McCarthy Press* (1963), Louis

Mittelberg's poster of Eisenhower, *His Famous Smile* (1952), and a painting by Alice Neel, *Eisenhower, McCarthy and Dulles* (1953). The subject of most of the earlier paintings is the Rosenbergs as Jewish victims of U.S. injustice. The 1980s work announces itself by its postmodern formal complexities, its multimedia composition, and its shift in subject from the individual figures of the Rosenbergs to the postatomic anticommunist cold war context. The exhibit provides an occasion for the analysis of basic and necessary elements, operations, and potential effects of critical art. It also provides an opportunity to consider the potential for reciprocal critical relationships among artifacts exhibited in a group, and between the works and the chosen space and form of their group presentation: traditional gallery or alternative space; high, popular, or street culture context; and linear wall-mounted or interactive and confrontational presentation.

Hilton Kramer, the formulator of the predominant critical apparatus for abstract expressionism, formalism, spoke at the opening of "Unknown Secrets" in September 1988, at the C. W. Post campus in Brookville, Long Island. According to Kramer, the bulk of the work in the exhibit was a "total loss," "garbage," "sheerest propaganda," and "political kitsch . . . in sympathy with Communist causes," with the only "art" (my quotation marks) that of Picasso and Leger. Of the university exhibiting gallery he said he was "embarrassed that adults should behave this way, especially in the name of education." Lucy Lippard, a social art critic, responded, "If Hilton Kramer called this art 'garbage,' it has to be good, and it is." George Will saw the show in Chicago and complained that it "mixes lugubrious martyrology . . . and loathing for America."[12] To evoke and provoke that kind of abstractly polarized and ideological reaction on the right, these works—especially those that are critically specific, not rigidly and abstractly ideological—must be impinging effectively on some well-defended, and defensive, belief systems.

For the purposes of my argument about the operations of critical art I will consider only two works—one by Martha Rosler and one by Peter Saul—from "Unknown Secrets." Although a number of works would enrich and complicate this analysis, Rosler's and

Saul's images are the two that disturbed me—and my stand-point—the most, and that have stayed with me, continuing to work since I first saw them. Also I could have analyzed them as critical art without having seen them more than once. This is not insignificant in any consideration of critical art, because, although critical art by definition requires reading, not just an objectifying look, its effect will be limited to the degree that it depends on a prolonged scholarly or critical commodifying study of it. But among other critical works of art in the Rosenberg exhibit, I include, in addition to the Fasanellas, the Mittelberg, and the Neel, Margia Kramer's *Covert Operations* (1987–88), Paul Marcus's *The Greatest Show on Earth* (1987), Sue Coe's *Needs of the State* (1987), Leon Marcus's *Roy Judas Cohn* (1986), Deborah Small's *Witch Hunt* (1987), Marina Gutierrez's *Remembering the Rosenbergs* (1987), Robert Arneson's *2 Fried Commie Jews* (1987), Adrian Piper's *Xenophobia* (1987), and Kim Abeles's *Other* (1987).

Martha Rosler's *Unknown Secrets*

Martha Rosler uses video, photography, audio, performance, image, and text in densely layered and multiple-framed configurations whose organization establishes an opportunity for a self-implicating critique of the ensemble.[13] She disturbs and makes strange—and impossible—any natural way of taking her ostensible object: the Bowery, female norms, hunger, Ethel Rosenberg. She uses whatever media and formal organization are necessary to destabilize the chosen object—and our unified objectifying perception of that object—according to her politics, her understanding of the systemically gendered and materially invested world of social relationships. Her respect for any given project as "stemming from and returning to lived relationships" calls for the hard work of both allowing and forcing the object to reveal itself as critical.[14] This results in a nonprogrammatic, nonrepetitive range of work of great flexibility, as well as an unpredictability and freshness of critical demands and effects on the viewer altogether appropriate to Rosler's different critical objects.

Because her intent is to destabilize any facile perception of a unified object by a unified subject, it is a false but linguistically necessary start to identify her 1989 photographic montage/stage

Martha Rosler, detail of three-part installation entitled *Unknown Secrets*, 1987–88. 90¾ × 85 inches. (Reproduced by courtesy of the artist. Photo by Eric Weeks)

set/essay, *Unknown Secrets,* as being about Ethel Rosenberg. Ethel Rosenberg is indeed the major and focal image, life-size, posed for the news camera as a housewife in her kitchen the day after Julius's arrest. With only that image before us, and taking it straight, we can easily settle for a mindless objectification of her, depending on how much and what kind of historical information we have, as feigning spy or framed and pathetic victim. Those were the choices the government and mainstream media, on the one hand, and the Communist party and its media, on the other, gave us in the 1950s, replicated by Freed's play. But Rosler's construction of a contextualizing frame around Ethel's image complicates such a simple and absolute polarity while seducing us into a critique of Ethel's representation from any point of view.

Rosler surrounds Ethel's image with a montage ("jumble," in one definition of montage, like Burke's "jumble of plot" residing in a metaphor) of photographic images from advertising, war data and propaganda, politics, and the Rosenberg story. Admittedly, it takes time to read Rosler's work, to take in all these images while making the connections that inhere among them. But it is harder to let them provide us with a mood, or an iconic memory, as Freed's framing context did, because they make cognitive and affective demands on us that seem at first unrelated to the central image. They stimulate feelings of desire, identification, inadequacy, anxiety, and alienation through Madison Avenue images of body-building men, of female models in veiled hats, bathing suits, brassieres, and corsets; they invite us to self-parody in their reproduction of images that we—or our parents—allowed to set goals, standards, and parameters for us: domesticated WASP husbands, wives, and children exuberantly enjoying the freedoms of the modern appliance-filled household; they attract and repel us with the power and obscenity of war maps, strategies, weapons, and bomb recipes; they give us the guilty, gossipy, prurient, *People* magazine thrill of seeing photographs of Klaus Fuchs, Harry Gold, Julius's arrest, the Rosenberg sons, Ethel in a hat, Ethel and Julius kissing, Irving Saypol, Irving Kaufman, a Jell-O box, Ethel and Julius in their coffins, and Richard Nixon and Murray Chotiner.[15]

What is the subject, and what are the connections? It may be that the subject in a montage is the reader-viewer, and that it is the reader-viewer who makes the connections.[16] What Rosler's *Unknown Secrets* is about is a phenomenological object that takes shape in the viewers' consciousnesses as they begin both to feel and to consider—not in an altogether comfortable manner—the various connections between all these images, with themselves as the circuits through which they pass. An advertising image attracts—on the strength of its rhetorical capacity for the construction of desire—and then ironically reflects on the social and historical reality of Ethel Rosenberg by means of the viewer's now performatively complicit consciousness. All the surrounding images work in this way, only able to connect with and interpret the central image through the mediation of the acquisitive desiring and fearing individual viewer. In the aggregate and while still uncritical, such mediations make a certain history—the cold war, for example—possible. Performed again at the insistence of art, they make possible a newly critical standpoint toward both that history and the present.

Rosler's image of Ethel Rosenberg framed by a border of juxtaposed images resides in yet another frame, staged by four props: a towel rack and shelf, a Jell-O box on the shelf, a towel over the rack printed with Eisenhower's explanation to his son John that Ethel had to die because she was the "leader in everything they did," and a textual montage essay by Rosler composed of quotations from a wide range of books, articles, headlines, names, dates, and events, composing a complex and contextualized argument concerning the Rosenberg frame story of the atomic cold war. With this setting Rosler establishes yet another framing category of analysis: the relationship of gender to politics and oppression. Eisenhower's speech in the Rosenberg kitchen displays the contradictory exploitations of Ethel Rosenberg as housewife, mother, typist, spy—all in the service of a masculist cold war politics.

Peter Saul's *Ethel Rosenberg in Electric Chair*

Rosler's carefully thought out and executed complex formal organization, with its multiple and layered juxtaposing and framing, directs the reception of her work. Peter Saul's work operates almost entirely at the level of affect. Robert L. Pincus, reviewing the exhibit "Unknown Secrets" for the *San Diego Union,* notes a "troubling parallel between the attacks on supposed communists in the 50s and recent congressional attacks on individual artists," such as Robert Mappelthorpe, Andres Serrano, and performance artists like Karen Finley.[17] He sees a San Diego exhibit, "No Stomach," protesting government censorship of the arts, as a companion piece to the Rosenberg show. At least one of the works in the Rosenberg show could easily have participated in the "No Stomach" show: Peter Saul's portrait of Ethel Rosenberg in the electric chair.

This will come as no surprise to people familiar with Saul's grotesque, obscene, pornographic, bad-taste art. In the 1950s, in painterly but unpretty attacks on the madness of consumerism and the pretensions and aesthetic commodifications of high culture, Saul found a gallery sponsor, patron, and legitimate showcase in Allan Frumkin and his New York gallery. When Saul returned to the United States from eight years in Europe in 1965, his subject shifted toward domestic racism, Vietnam, and elite taste. His imagery became more focused, explicitly topical, and at the same time more violent and contorted, in paintings such as *Angela Davis at San Quentin, Typical Saigon,* and in the parodic knockoffs of high art, as in *Double de Kooning Ducks, Francis Bacon Descending a Staircase,* and *Donald Duck Descending a Staircase.* Originally antiformalist and painterly messy, he became—in an age of disdain for slick representational art—deliberately committed to slick painting, in grotesque and garish colors including Day-Glo pigments, of intensified three-dimensional representations of bulging, protruding, and contorted but recognizable human forms and appendages intricately implicated with metonymic objects of violence, obscenity, and terror. One can imagine the exponential intensification of effect that would be accomplished by a William Burroughs and Peter Saul collaborative word-and-image venture. Saul's unspeakable Reagan series provides a *Mad* comics parodic "jumble" and anticipates the possibilities of a future Bush series.[18] Distinct from Rosler, whose materialist-feminist politics meticulously inform

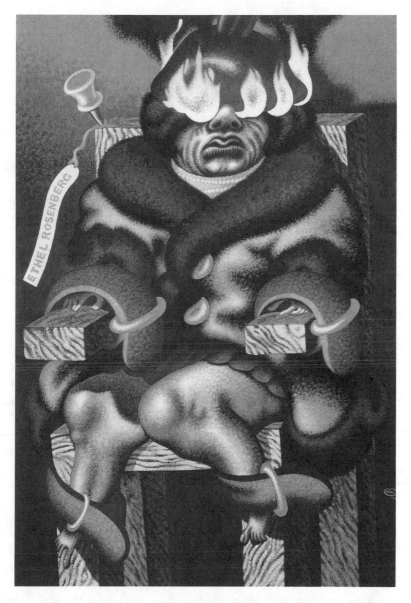

Peter Saul, *Ethel Rosenberg in Electric Chair*, 1987. 60 × 40 inches, acrylic and oil on paper. (Courtesy of Frumkin/Adams Gallery, New York. Photo by eeva-inkeri)

every detail of her work and indeed organize its critical analysis, Saul's energies and motivations are those of a rebellious adolescent more interested in breaking taboos and getting attention than in working within the rubric of any notion of political correctness—even on his own terms.[19] No coherent political program can be constructed or inferred from his work, much of which is only too vulnerable to a critique of representation as a reproduction of undesirable relationships and ideologies.

Woman in the House (1989), for example, is an intense and grotesque apparently single image in which a woman extrudes through the walls and windows of her mansion while detaining her husband with a distended hand around his neck. The subject of this painting appears to be the psychology of the wife, a ubiquitous monster-oppressor of a helpless victim, her husband. Precisely because of the compelling force of Saul's presentation as monumental art in a comic-cartoon form and technique of what he intends as antiart (which as an opposition cannot escape the category he attempts to escape), his humorous attack demands to be taken seriously as a representation of wives. Absent a critical reading, the image works to represent and reproduce a specific kind of heterosexual marital relationship in which the woman dominates, grotesquely. Chaucer's humorous representation of the bawdy, bossy Wife of Bath was a psychological portrait of a wife, but one that was irretrievably implicated in a sophisticated, complex, and humane social analysis of gender relations and oppressions. In an uncritical and culturally conventional reading of *Woman in the House,* Saul appears instead to be reducing a socially produced personality (in terms of gender and class, in this case) to one that is the result of biology alone.

But Saul's painting, upon closer examination, is not a relentlessly single image foreclosing critical purchase. The "Woman in the House" is a particular sort of woman—white and living in a mansion—who has outgrown her house; it now immobilizes and imprisons her. This woman needs to get out of the house in a bad way. Is she attempting to hold her husband back as he drives away, or to make him let her out, to take her along too: "Going somewhere, dear?" The visual ingredients for a social critique of a specific twentieth-century form of institutional power—

marriage—are present in the painting, but the critical hermeneu-
tic burden is on the viewers. We must bring to *Woman in the
House* an awareness of the dialectics of power—the differential
and dependent relationships that exist between oppressor and
oppressed, and the nature of power and the potential for abuse in
both directions in an oppressive hierarchy, such as that which has
been the dominant model for marriage for most of the twentieth
century. Saul's painting offers, for the viewer who can see, the
two-sided story of power in marriage.

I have suggested that art that relies on the single image cannot
achieve the at least ironized structure required for critical art.
But an analysis of Saul's *Ethel Rosenberg in Electric Chair* in
terms of inadequate intrinsic critical structure and orientation is
inadequate to the complex operations of that awful image. Nor
is it in any way sufficient to the operations of the work to read
it in terms of a psychologizing sexism or of a gross misogyny—
both of which would lead us to a critique of the individual painter
and his politics, as well as his implication in and reproduction
of a certain social ideology. It would—and should—also lead to
a critique of Saul's work as pornography, a category that will
always be determined to some degree by the context in which
and the purpose for which Saul's paintings are publicly displayed.
But I argue that the image of "Ethel Rosenberg," while subject
to such criticism, and fruitfully so, exceeds the reach of that
criticism both because of its cold war historical referent and
context, and because of its purposeful execution for and situation
in the exhibit "Unknown Secrets."

Ethel is strapped into the electric chair in a feminine pearl
choker and bathrobe coat with a shawl collar in garish Day-Glo
colors of purple, red, green, yellow, chartreuse, and orange.
Flames and smoke are engulfing the top of her head and coming
out of her eyes. Her skin is red, mottled, and inflamed; her thighs
and knees bulbous and distended; her hands and feet tiny rac-
coonlike claws; her porcine face distorted and masculinized, with
grossly exaggerated lips and nose. The electric chair has an identifying tag stuck on with a map pin: "Ethel Rosenberg." Laura
Caruso, reviewing the "Unknown Secrets" exhibit for the Boulder, Colorado, *Sunday Camera,* writes:

Many of these works are disturbing, but again, it is a show stronger as a whole than in its parts. The only picture I actively disliked is Peter Saul's grossly tarted-up Ethel Rosenberg in the electric chair, her head engulfed in flames. Mostly I looked and shrugged. But I left the exhibit feeling, like Sylvia Plath's heroine in *The Bell Jar,* that "all I could think about was the Rosenbergs."[20]

The excesses of Saul's depiction and its affective force do not allow us an easy iconic objectification of the image in terms of our historical memory. Nor does the image allow an easy projective explanation of it as the artist's private vision. The image is unspeakable: descriptive, formalist, or critical discourse about it is a taming reduction, and its charge cannot adequately be translated into words. Decorum has been breached, by a self-styled breaker of taboos—a "criminal of perception," like Daniel Isaacson. But in transgressing the civilized rules of perception, what has Saul dis-covered? And what are we to make of it?

What his image dis-covers is the primitive and regressed state of mind of a perpetrator-executioner-witness of the official Rosenberg story, for here also, Ethel Rosenberg stands—and burns—for the story. Unlike the internal and often complex, even narratable, actions of most of Saul's other paintings, the only action here is between the depicted state of mind and the viewer. The visual representation of the primitive version of that official state of mind places a certain unwelcome demand on the viewer, simply because she stands in the place of—for—the perpetrator-executioner-witness. Saul's depiction of his criminal discovery provokes a crisis of perception and horror at the unsought empathic acknowledgment or even recognition of such a state of mind. In transgressing the "acceptable limits of representation," Saul produces a theater of cruelty in which the viewer experiences an unspeakable aspect of political reality through the shock of recognition.

This is sacrificial and dangerous art, risking rejection, doubling as pornography, and refusing co-optation. The viewer can refuse the engagement defensively, as Caruso did, by shrugging and moving on—but the painting was not without effect for her. It is her example of work that disturbed her, and she cannot stop thinking about the Rosenbergs. As is always the potential with the representation of regressive extremes of human behavior, the viewer can accept the painting's demand for response in order to repeat, once again, the pornographic pleasure of a stimulated and perverse imagination. But Saul's painting refuses easy evasion or voyeuristic enjoyment. It demands that we situate ourselves in relation to a specific state of mind—defensively, pornographically, or critically. Naming the painting *A Cold War State of Mind* might have made our work easier for us, by providing a more sufficiently ironizing critical context. But it also would have allowed us to stand outside the critical circuit.

Epilogue
Political Projection and Gathering the Splits

In this consideration of the official Rosenberg story and its cold war frame and of the cultural critiques of that story and its supporting period, we have in each case reached transgressive moments where the repressed—that which is split off and (unsuccessfully) denied or projected—has returned. It manifested itself unwittingly in the language of the trial judge, the prosecution, Hoover, Ernst, and Eisenhower, and most dramatically in the eyewitness report by Bob Considine of Ethel's electrocution—a report for which Saul's image is an almost perfect visual and tonal embodiment. It manifested itself imaginatively and purposefully in the Doctorow and Coover novels, as motivations and metaphors for the injustices and terrors of a specific history. It manifested itself analytically in Martha Rosler's careful displaying of unrecognized connections between Ethel Rosenberg (in her synecdochic function) and the requirements of a militaristic consumer society. And it manifested itself with horrible affective immediacy in Peter Saul's visual dis-covery of the cold war state of mind that was articulated piecemeal by the various narrators of the official Rosenberg story.

There is of course a residual and inescapable defensive splitting and projective process that is and will continue to be inevitable, useful—even necessary—and at times costly to the individual, even after the historical and constructed nature of the individual's experience of reality is (theoretically) taken into account. Splitting and projection are interlocking mechanisms that are primary and fundamental to language as well as to human consciousness. They are our only way of knowing and assimilating reality, as they are the sole instruments of intuition, imagination, and empathic feelings. They are also, however, our way of not knowing and of dividing and categorizing reality in the necessary interests of understanding, protecting ourselves, and achieving a sufficient degree of mastery to persist.

While one might want to consider the extent to which this residual process works through the individual to produce the political interactions of society at large, to consider that as an adequate explanation of a given historical reality is to ignore both the socially constructed nature of consciousness and the reciprocal effects produced between macrocosm and microcosm, between a given political society and its individuals. It is also to ignore the phenomenon that in any political society that group with the greatest power over the uses and distribution of meaning also has the power to represent—and fashion—our perception of a specific reality according to a protocol of linguistic and political splitting and projection that is neither primary, natural, nor inescapable. And that purposefully divided representation of reality will work, by enlisting the unwitting participation in that version of all those denied or abused by it, to secure and protect and foster the representing group in its privileged and entitled position. Although human consciousness depends on the splitting and projective mechanism, it does not depend—totally—on the particularly split and projected version of reality operative in a given historical situation or period. In this theoretically posited discontinuity between the individual process and the political process resides the possibility for individual agency in history. Purposeful language analysis and use are crucial to both the recognition and realization of such possibility.

For a critique of the U.S. cold war uniquely split and divided version of reality that still governs more of our perceptions, talk, work, and social, political, and economic relationships than we can know, postmodernism may be more politically useful at this historical moment than some of its political critics have thought. Formally postmodernism—regardless of its content—is performing and teaching the functions necessary to a perhaps timely "gather[ing] of the splits." In purely formalist exercises in fracturing and interrogating coherent meaning systems of language and gestural communication, postmodernism is demonstrating an analytic technique for bringing perception to crisis, uncovering and admitting what has been occluded and excluded, split and projected. In more self-consciously and specifically political, social, and critical postmodernism, the split-off and projected—the politically repressed—is being named and returned for a new consideration of the chaotic and irrepressible, unplotted jumble. If postmodernism is, as I believe it to be, a motivated critical moment rather than a downward spiral into nihilism, then both as technique and activity it is making possible a reintroduction into political consciousness of those phenomena, groups, and interests that have been split off and projectively denied or occluded.

> Existentially, projective identification is that state of mind (or mindlessness) in which we conduct much of our lives—for we are all "sleepwalkers" more than we realize, and, in the act of trying to be our separate individual selves, we forget how much we walk in the shadow or even in the substance of others. Ultimately, it becomes the task of the [person's] understanding of his [this "his" is a split] experience of projective identification to resolve his battle with persecutors so that he may truly know his friends and be able to espy his *true* enemies. The confusion between persecutor and enemy may be one of the deepest causes of emotional [and political] impotence. [additions mine][1]

This gathering activity may be occurring as we are witnessing, experiencing, and performing the breakdown of exhausted political categories and perfecting myths and the new orderings of reality occasioned by feminism, environmentalism, multiculturalism, poststructuralism, the so-called end of the cold war, democratic national revolutions, an increasingly pervasive critique of individualism and absolute rights, and a renewed interest in local and communitarian politics. These new ways of perceiving social reality, and new kinds of linguistic, psychological, cultural, economic, and political gatherings of formerly disparate or invisible elements of that reality, are indeed allowing and forcing clearer recognitions of a more complex and conflictual "we" in a country that would be democratic and socially just. The responses evoked by every articulation of these new perceptions show us once again that language use is dangerous. These new kinds of perception also help us, as Grotstein suggests, to know friends from enemies—to distinguish between those with whom we legitimately differ within the context of any concept of a just world, and those individuals, groups, institutions, and nations that work to construct and maintain specific categories of difference that support a systematically unjust world under the rubric of freedom and democracy.

The linguistic interrogation of justifying myths, the metonymic, material unpacking of dominion-keeping metaphors, and the split-gathering activity of newly claimed political standpoints appear to hold political promise for the left. But, again, language use is dangerous. Even with conscious and critical determination to resist the linguistic temptations of obfuscating mythification, counterproductive exclusionary framing, and premature narrative closure, these inevitable tendencies of the linguistic process itself are counterproductive to any just social order. But the greatest threat to effective work for positive change will inhere in the degree to which an identification of the opposition allows us, through splitting and projection, to remain voluntarily blind to our own daily dependency on the order we would change.

Notes

PROLOGUE: MOTIVES OF NARRATIVE

1. See review of Joseph Sharlitt's *Fatal Error: The Miscarriage of Justice That Sealed the Rosenbergs' Fate* (New York: Scribner, 1989) by *New York Times* correspondent for the Supreme Court, Linda Greenhouse, "Guilt or Innocence Aside," *New York Times Book Review*, August 6, 1989, 1.

2. The trial record reveals the extent to which both Julius and Ethel were tried, convicted, and sentenced for treason despite the absence of any documentary evidence of any atomic secrets having been transmitted to the Soviet Union by or under the direction of any U.S. citizens. If such evidence existed, the Rosenbergs were executed without the constitutionally guaranteed privilege of seeing the evidence against them. At issue here is not guilt or innocence, but the narrative and representational strategies of the U.S. government in constructing guilt without making public any corroborative testimony or documentary evidence. In the fall of 1990 tapes said to have been made by Khrushchev but not verifiable by voice-print were abridged, edited, and published by Little, Brown under the title *Khrushchev Remembers: The Glasnost Tapes* (trans. and ed. Jerrold L. Schecter, with Vyacheslav V. Luchkov). The editors assembled a statement by Khrushchev indirectly quoting both Stalin and Molotov acknowledging the generosity of the Rosenbergs in helping the Soviet Union to produce its first atomic bomb. Reading Khrushchev's statement as evidence is problematic at best. More recently, a Soviet KGB officer, Colonel Vladimir Matveyevich Chikov, has written an article for the Soviet weekly *New Times* quoting the wartime head of the Soviet atomic project, Igor Kurchatov, as crediting Soviet espionage with "50% of the project's success." Chikov identifies Morris and Lona Cohen as U.S. communist espionage recruits for the Soviet Union. (The Cohens disappeared from the United States at the time of Klaus Fuchs's confession, as did several other members of the American Communist party, and were traded in 1967 to the Russians by the British for a British agent.) Neither Khrushchev's statement nor Kurchatov's acknowledgment in any way mitigates the story of U.S. institutional cynicism, manipulation, abuse, and illegalities in the staging of the Rosenberg story for purposes of ideological control and political power. See Walter Schneir's review of *Khrushchev Remembers*, "Time Bomb" (*Nation*, December 3, 1990, 682–88); and Ronald Radosh and Eric Breindel's "Bombshell" (*New Republic*, June 10, 1991, 10–12).

Notes to Prologue

3. See Victor Turner, *Dramas, Fields, and Metaphors: Symbolic Action in Human Society* (Ithaca, N.Y.: Cornell University Press, 1974).

4. Ibid., 13.

5. Working definitions of and distinctions between culture and history are essential to the argument of this book. *History* is the temporal succession or process of inorganic and organic matter—material reality knowable only through the mediation of human consciousness and representation. There is, for example, a natural history of Mars, which twentieth-century scientists are attempting to discover, but what those observers (*cyborgs,* in Donna Haraway's lexicon, who observe and function through interacting technological extensions) will construct of that history will be partial historiography, not history. That historiography—or the political historiographies of the 1991 Iraqi war, for another example—will become, willy-nilly, part of culture. *Culture,* in the sense intended here, is the total field of symbolic activity through time. Culture is knowable through its expressions and artifacts—performances, posters, newspapers, rap music, history books, the Torah, the Methodist hymnal, Doonesbury, Mappelthorpe photographs, the Constitution, and so on. Historiography is a part of culture; culture is a part of history; history is only knowable, beyond its partial and immediate experience, through culture (symbolic representations), and even immediate experience is mediated by previous symbolic organizations of meaning and value. But culture is not reducible to a result or a secondary product of history; it also has an undelimitable power to make history happen in certain ways. Culture in the total sense works on its own to make history, but not all by itself. Human beings can and do mobilize, construct, and use cultural methods to make history happen in accord with specific agendas. Thus, access to and control of the means of cultural production are crucial forms of political empowerment. For Haraway's definition of the cyborg, see "A Cyborg Manifesto," in *Simians, Cyborgs, and Women: The Reinvention of Nature* (New York: Routledge, 1991), 149–81.

6. See Bibliographical Note for Rosenberg historiography. It is impossible to assert that even a full release of all pertinent documents would provide the basis for certitude about the real Rosenberg story. "The difficulty, of course, is that in matters of espionage, information is always released selectively, is frequently at three removes, and involves anonymous informants, double agents, the dead, the defected, the disappeared, the disinformed. In such circumstances there may be no single heart of the matter, certainly no discoverable heart, other than the credibility of the principals" (Victor Navasky, "Weinstein, Hiss, and the Transformation of Historical Ambiguity into Cold War Verity," in *Beyond the Hiss Case: The FBI, Congress, and the Cold War,* ed. Athan G. Theoharis [Philadelphia: Temple University Press, 1982], 224).

7. From J. Edgar Hoover memo, quoted in Department of Justice memo "Hall to Tomkins," November 11, 1956. See Walter Schneir and Miriam Schneir, *Invitation to an Inquest* (New York: Pantheon, 1983), 478.

8. Structuralism, as a methodology of meaning analysis and social understanding developed primarily by the anthropologist Lévi-Strauss, extended into psychoanalysis by Jacques Lacan and into textual analysis in the early work of Roland Barthes, holds that events of social meaning, including meaning itself, are dependent upon a central organizing principle or phenomenon that itself

224

escapes or is transcendent to that which is organized into meaning. (New Criticism, dominant in academic literary studies from the 1930s until the 1980s, holds that literature is literary by virtue of its saturated coherence around such a transcendent central meaning.) Poststructuralism (as demonstrated in the work of philosopher Jacques Derrida, historian Michel Foucault, and literary critic Paul de Man, among others) demonstrates that no event or meaning ever stands apart from structuration, or construction, and that the originary construction is one of difference, not identity, unity, presence, or transcendence. This philosophical argument and demonstration effectively does away with the transcendent potentiality or noncontingency of any meaning, including truth claims. Carried to its logical extreme it does away with meaning, a critical activity that has its own strategic usefulness as well as absurdities.

9. See Vladimir Propp, *Morphology of the Folk Tale,* trans. Laurence Scott (Austin: University of Texas Press, 1975); and A. J. Greimas, *Structural Semantics: An Attempt at a Method,* trans. Daniele McDowell, Ronald Schleifer, and Alan Velie (Lincoln: University of Nebraska Press, 1983).

10. See n. 8 for the relation of structuralism to poststructuralism. The logical extreme of the poststructuralist argument is pantextualism: a textual demonstration that the only knowable reality is textual, with the resulting critique of the concept of metaphysical foundations for meaning or truth claims. A materialist critical point of view or methodology holds that individual experience and material history are the partially knowable products of partially knowable and analyzable material and cultural conditions, relationships, and forces produced by ensembles or complexes larger than the individual; that meaning and truth claims are socially produced, purposeful historical constructs; and that the individual in turn has a limited but real potential for affecting—defining, analyzing, shaping, changing—those relationships.

11. See Bibliographical Note for a discussion of methodological sources and models for this study of the Rosenberg stories. See also Barbara Herrnstein Smith on bypassing the "language problematic" (both the dualism of mimetic narrative theory and the endless chain-of-signifiers textuality of radical poststructuralism). Smith, like Kenneth Burke, prefers a construal of narrative as *"verbal responses—* that is as *acts* which, like any acts, are *performed in response to various sets of conditions,"* interests, and motivations ("Narrative Versions, Narrative Theories," in *On Narrative,* ed. W. J. T. Mitchell [Chicago: University of Chicago Press, 1981], 221–22). See Fredric Jameson on multiple methodologies and the dangers of pluralism: "Such pluralism is at best a refusal to go about the principal critical business of our time, which is to forge a kind of methodological synthesis from the multiplicity of critical codes; at worst, it is just one more veiled assault on the nonpluralistic (read 'totalitarian') critical systems—Marxism, for example" ("The Ideology of the Text," in *The Ideologies of Theory: Essays 1971–1986,* vol. 1 of *Situations of Theory* [Minneapolis: University of Minnesota Press, 1988], 59).

12. I use *rhetorical* in both of its classic senses: linguistic and persuasive. Rhetorical analysis in the service of cultural criticism would consider motives, sources, and strategies for the achievement of meaning and the ways in which any specific meaning achieves relative authority and power over what and whom, and for what purposes.

13. This kind of cultural analysis is necessarily a partial and speculative—that is, nonscientific—demonstration of the possible conditions of production and the political work of language in use. It requires a purposeful reading to discover the unarticulated assumptions and material interests underlying positive statments and narratives, especially the inexplicit linguistic classification of human beings into categories that operate with specific values and in specific configurations to structure and maintain specific power relations and resource distributions. In the late twentieth century such analysis has benefited from a complication of the Marxist concern exclusively with the category of class by the work of ethnic groups and feminists using race and gender also as primary categories of analysis. While these three categories have become rigidified into what Catherine Stimpson calls the "iron triangle," often reducing analysis to an ideological repetitiveness, as categories reemergent and functioning materially in the postwar period they are historically apt for an analysis of the cold war era. In what some political theorists see as a breaking up of traditional left-right affiliations into local and multiple interest formations, it is important to continue interrogating cultural texts (historiography, the media, art, sociology, government documents, etc.) for other categories that dispose of people and resources elliptically, bypassing a representative or democratic political process of deliberation and consent. In their varying perceptions of actual historical white men as privileged—not absolutely and universally, but rather in a relative and contingent manner in the twentieth-century political economy—materialist-feminist and cultural critical analyses often coincide; in this they both differ from more radical, separatist, and essentialist kinds of feminist analysis.

14. David Riesman and Nathan Glazer, "The Intellectuals and the Discontented Classes," *Partisan Review* 22, no. 1 (Winter 1955): 64; published also in Daniel Bell, ed., *The New American Right* (New York: Criterion, 1955), 56–90.

15. See "Our Country and Our Culture: A Symposium," *Partisan Review* 19, no. 3 (May–June 1952): 282–326; no. 4 (July–August 1952): 420–50; no. 5 (September–October 1952): 562–97.

16. In March 1991, in a review article for the film he directed about the House Un-American Activities Committee (HUAC) Hollywood hearings, *Guilty by Suspicion,* Irwin Winkler explains why he ultimately rejected Abraham Lincoln Polonsky's screenplay calling for the protagonist to have been a former member of the Communist party: "If it was about a Communist, the end result would be perceived as a defense of Communism. . . . You don't vitiate 70 years of anti-Communism with a Ronald Reagan visit to Red Square" (*New York Times,* March 31, 1991).

17. See Leslie Fiedler, "A Postscript to the Rosenberg Case," published initially in the first issue of *Encounter* in October 1953, the journal of the American Committe for Cultural Freedom, later revealed as CIA funded; published also as "Afterthoughts on the Rosenbergs" (*Collected Essays of Leslie Fiedler,* vol. 1 [New York: Stein, 1971], 45). See also Robert Warshow, "The Idealism of Julius and Ethel Rosenberg," originally published in *Commentary* 16, no. 5 (November 1953): 413–18; published also in Warshow, *The Immediate Experience: Movies, Comics, Theatre, and Other Aspects of Modern Culture* (Garden City, N.Y.: Doubleday, 1964), 33–43. The British spelling of *theatre* in such a title marks the high-culture bias of the author.

18. See Andrew Ross, "Intellectuals and Ordinary People: Reading the Rosenberg Letters," *Cultural Critique* 9 (Spring 1988): 55–86, quote on 73; published also in Ross, ed., *No Respect: Intellectuals and Pop Culture* (New York: Routledge & Kegan Paul, 1989), 15–41; and "Containing Culture in the Cold War," *Cultural Studies* 1, no. 3 (Winter 1987): 328–48.

19. See Morris Dickstein, "Cold War Blues: Politics and Culture in the Fifties," in *Gates of Eden: American Culture in the 60s* (New York: Basic, 1977), 25–50.

20. See Jock O'Connell, "Crewcuts, Carhops, and the Cold War," *New York Times,* August 2, 1989.

21. *New York Times,* September 16, 1989.

22. *Postmodernism* is a term impossible to define to the satisfaction of all. It is a name used by academic and public critics to characterize—prematurely and incorrectly, many say—late twentieth-century history and culture. It has been used to refer to such disparate and inclusive phenomena that it verges on meaning anything or everything to its users. I find it to be useful and even necessary to refer to a cultural practice of the last half of the twentieth century, although its formal precursors can be found as early as writing itself, in the work of narrators, image makers, and performers who in the act of performing their work also perform a self-aware skepticism toward the manifest achievements of the work. A postmodern cultural practice is one of undoing coherent and explanatory narratives or images or social roles in a self-conscious way, using any tactics that work, and attacking variously language itself or the social meanings and values established by a historically specific organization of language. I am convinced that as a cultural practice, postmodernism is a reponse to the experienced hypocrisies and more or less brutal oppressions, injustices, and terrors practiced in the twentieth century in the name of rationality and justified by explanatory narratives, such as those of the cold war, racial and sexual stereotypes, or the so-called free market.

23. See the Introduction, n. 5, for working definitions of history and culture.

24. Anders Stephanson, "Regarding Postmodernism—A Conversation with Fredric Jameson," in *Universal Abandon? The Politics of Postmodernism,* ed. Andrew Ross (Minneapolis: University of Minnesota Press, 1988), 20.

25. Ibid., 14.

26. Since words like *use* and *excess* evoke for any student of Marx concepts of use- and exchange-value, I am indebted to Gayatri Spivak for having already textualized this difference. Her analysis allows me to bypass that problematic, as interpreted from Marx, in favor of a reading that shows any communicable use-value to be already a motivated and elaborated excess in the form of social value. See Gayatri Spivak, "Scattered Speculations on the Question of Value," in *In Other Worlds: Essays in Cultural Politics* (New York: Methuen, 1987), 154–75.

27. John Dos Passos, *Boston Herald,* April 27, 1927. Quoted in G. Louis Joughin and Edmund M. Morgan, *The Legacy of Sacco and Vanzetti* (New York: Harcourt, Brace 1948), 244.

28. This communication among texts from different or similar fields, discoverable by reading for historical and cultural patterns larger than the formal borders and semantic jurisdictions of any one text or discipline, and attributable to larger

ensembles than are scientifically knowable, is called *intertextuality* in the post-structuralist lexicon.

CHAPTER 1. COLD WAR FRAME NARRATIVE

1. Kenneth Burke, *The Rhetoric of Religion: Studies in Logology* (Boston: Beacon, 1961), 240–41, 170. Logology, words about words—philological and rhetorical analysis—is the method Burke uses to critique coherent systems of meaning.

2. Louis Althusser, "Ideology and Ideological State Apparatuses (Notes Toward an Investigation)," in *Essays on Ideology* (London: Verso Editions, 1984), 36.

3. Being American apparently is more than an accident of birth, or of marriage, or of a naturalization procedure. Being American, in the second half of the twentieth century, has meant thinking, giving voice to, and working for the material fulfillment of the prevailing masculist-capitalist ideology. To express and work for ideas that differ from this order—to be "un-American"—has been costly in social, political, and economic terms.

4. E. L. Doctorow, *The Book of Daniel* (New York: Ballantine, 1971), 311–12.

5. "Frame-up" in the sense of a collectively and incrementally narrated enclosure delimiting meaning and determining specific events; see Dos Passos's working definition in the Introduction. For a provocative and compelling fictional analysis of the "world within worlds" aspect of the unconscious and collective playing out of a specific history through individual actions, see Don DeLillo's 1988 *Libra* (New York: Penguin Books, 1988), in which the Rosenbergs also play a thematic role.

6. Formalism as a critical school of interpretation in the arts discovers a formal coherence that both establishes the object under consideration as art and at the same time removes it from the contingencies of the everyday world. In the larger sense, as a rhetorical concept, formalism refers to the fundamentally and inescapably *constructed* achievement of any meaning. Language operates, from its most basic level of organization in terms of single sounds and letters through its most complex combinations, as an arbitrary rather than natural arrangement of sounds, letters, gestures, and symbols to conjure up a specific reality or an attitude toward a specific reality. Fundamental operations of differentiation—inclusion and exclusion—establish meanings of relative coherence, and these meanings are performative in the sense that they constitute one version of reality instead of another. The formal accomplishments of language, then—meanings—are always vulnerable to a formal analysis that would discover the operative systems of difference and similarity in a given text, combined with a historical analysis that would critique form and content in terms of interest: for whom and for what purposes does this text work? A linguistic ordering of reality, as Plato warned, is always potentially the construction of a false reality. The critical reader asks, for what purposes, then, is a given linguistic order rendered?

7. Hayden White notes that "the perception of the 'Same in the Different' and the 'Different in the Same' is the origin of all hierarchy in social practice, as it is the origin of syntax in grammar and logic in thought" (Hayden White, *Content of the Form: Narrative Discourse and Historical Representation* [Baltimore: Johns Hopkins University Press, 1987], 117). This interlocking splitting

and projective mechanism, following the principles of displacement (distinctions, difference) and condensation (generalization, similarity), allows good/bad discriminations and suspension of emotion in order to form judgments; it allows analysis of an event in the service of thinking and maturity (see James S. Grotstein, *Splitting and Projective Identification* [New York: Aronson, 1981], 15). As a common denominator also in all psychological defense mechanisms, it tends in extreme situations toward a disavowal of past and future and supports organismic (totalizing) anxiety at the expense of signal (specific, local) anxiety (ibid., 4–8). Splitting, with its "auxiliary" projective [dis]identification (ibid., 11), is a defense that wishes to "postpone confrontation with some experience that cannot be tolerated; but it also . . . can negate, destroy, and literally obliterate the sense of reality" (ibid., 131). It involves alienation of one's own experience into a "mystification, mythification, and re-personification" (ibid., 11), thus resulting in a transformation of both self and object, "assigning the split off percept to a container for a postponement or for eradication" (ibid., 131). Since this is a mental process, however, the projected object or qualities are also internalized, exhibiting all the characteristics of the return of the repressed. Melanie Klein saw projective identification as one of the "fundamental defenses against persecutory anxiety," accompanied by "idealization, denial, and omnipotent control of internal and external objects. It implies a combination of splitting off parts of the self and projecting them on to (or rather into) another person. These processes have many ramifications and fundamentally influence object relations" (ibid., 129); Freud saw splitting and projective identification, in its neurotic and pathological defensive form, as a costly response to conflicts between desire and reality (ibid., 25–29).

8. The atomic age produced a new level of universal terror in the face of history. "Even for Hegel the sublimity of the spectacle of history had to be transcended if it was to serve as an object of knowledge and deprived of the terror it induced as a 'panorama of sin and suffering'" (White, *Content of the Form,* 70, quoting Georg Wilhelm Friedrich Hegel, *Lectures on the Philosophy of History,* trans. J. Sibree [New York: Willey, 1944], 20–22). Ideology and perfecting myths as attempts to transcend irrational, impalatable, or unbearable social and historical realities must be critiqued for the political exclusions and repressions they inevitably enact in the process of making the (sublime) world cognitively apprehensible in bearable terms.

9. Myth is to be understood here in its Lévi-Straussian structural definition as a unified narrative that functions culturally to reconcile irreconcilable or antagonistic historical phenomena. "Since the purpose of myth is to provide a logical model capable of overcoming a contradiction (an impossible achievement if, as it happens, the contradiction is real), a theoretically infinite number of slates will be generated, each one slightly different from the others. Thus, myth grows spiral-wise until the intellectual impulse which has produced it is exhausted. Its *growth* is a continuous process, whereas its structure remains discontinuous" (Claude Lévi-Strauss, "The Structural Study of Myth," in *Structural Anthropology* [New York: Basic, 1963], 229).

10. Burke, *Rhetoric of Religion,* 230, passim.

11. See Burke, ibid., and Theodore Draper, "American Hubris: From Truman to the Persian Gulf," *New York Review of Books,* July 16, 1987, 40–48.

12. See the Introduction, n. 22, for a working definition of postmodernism.

13. Jameson, "Marxism and Postmodernism," *New Left Review* 176 (July–August 1989): 41.

14. Devastation from the two world wars was the immediate cause of the British relinquishment of its empire and world power. The extensive V-2 rocket and bombing attacks from Germany and the loss of lives during World War II (following the losses in the trenches of World War I) left Britain in a severely crippled and diminished state. The war as it was waged by the Allies, requiring unconditional surrender of the Axis powers, took severe population, economic, and industrial tolls of all participating countries except the United States. Britain, with a population of 46,000,000, lost 335,000 soldiers and sailors, 62,000 civilians (*The World Almanac and Book of Facts for 1945* [New York: New York World Telegram, 1945], 289; and *Louis L. Snyder's Historical Guide to WWII,* ed. Louis L. Snyder [Westport, CT: Greenwood, 1982], 125–26).

15. In 1989 alone the U.S. government, according to its own records, produced 6,796,501 new secrets (George Will, "Wrong Man Is Leaving Government," *The Missoulian,* June 30, 1991).

16. During the depression 50% of people in the United States lived below the poverty line. By 1945, although the gross national product had doubled during the war, a third of the population still resided within the poverty category (Susan M. Hartmann, *The Home Front and Beyond: American Women in the 1940s* [Boston: Twayne, 1982], 4). "Even had all of the Fair Deal been enacted, liberal reform would have left many millions beyond the benefits of government." The Fair Deal appears, despite its rhetoric, to have been designed to prevent extensions of benefits to the poor, while granting enough concessions to organized male workers to ensure their allegiance. "The very poor, the marginal men, those neglected but acknowleged by the New Deal, went ultimately unnoticed by the Fair Deal" (Barton J. Bernstein, "America in War and Peace: The Test of Liberalism," in *Twentieth-Century America: Recent Intepretations,* ed. Barton J. Bernstein and Allen J. Matusow [New York: Harcourt Brace & World, 1969], 364).

17. Organized labor in its postwar activism displayed a number of fatal contradictions. Not least of these was its determinedly masculist practice of racism and sexism toward blacks and women. It had already rejected an alliance with farmers in the 1890s.

18. Jameson, "Marxism and Postmodernism," 41.

19. *Naturalized* refers to a process by which a specific material or symbolic complex becomes so integrated into conventional wisdom, common sense, or tradition that it is assumed or taken for granted by a group in ways that overlook the historical specificities, complexities, and contradictions of its formation.

20. Pluralism as it operates in the United States pretends to a political dynamic of general consensus while it operates to exclude and disempower majority and minority interests, to discredit socialism of any form, democratic or state, and rhetorically to occlude hierarchical and elitist socioeconomic and political relations. See Ellen Rooney, *Seductive Reasoning: Pluralism as the Problematic of Contemporary Literary Theory* (Ithaca, N.Y.: Cornell University Press, 1985).

21. Howard Zinn, *Postwar America: 1945–1971* (New York: Bobbs-Merrill, 1973), 31. The Chamber of Commerce in its assessment of the postwar status of business and industry noted that "we have lost virtually all oil wells and refineries in the Balkans, as well as giant industrial plants in Germany and Hungary" (David Caute, *The Great Fear: The Anti-Communist Purge under Truman and Eisenhower* [New York: Simon & Schuster, 1978], 349). This loss was somewhat balanced by the fact that in 1945 corporate profits were at an all-time high. At $26 billion from 1936 to 1939, they rose to $117 billion from 1940 to 1945 and rose 30% more in 1946 (Lawrence Lader, *Power on the Left: American Radical Movements Since 1946* [New York: Norton, 1979], 4).

22. See Michael Parenti, *Inventing Reality: The Politics of the Mass Media* (New York: St. Martin's, 1986), 118–19; and James Aronson, *The Press and the Cold War* (Boston: Beacon, 1970), 35.

23. The United States repeated under Roosevelt its assumption of the separation and chronological priority of military over political objectives, as well as its construal of war as ending only in unconditional surrender by the defeated. As Secretary of the Navy and soon-to-be Secretary of Defense James Forrestal wrote in his diary on April 25, 1947, "[Our] diplomatic planning of the peace was far below the quality of planning that went into the conduct of the war. We regarded the war, broadly speaking, as a ball game which we had to finish as quickly as possible, but in doing so there was comparatively little thought as to the relationships between nations which would exist after Germany and Japan were destroyed" (James Forrestal, *The Forrestal Diaries*, ed. Walter Millis [New York: Viking, 1951], 53). This unrealistic separation of political from military goals made it possible to remove the material basis for postwar negotiating strength—military presence in crucial areas—when negotiations and implementation of postwar policies had hardly begun. The editor of Forrestal's diaries, Walter Millis, wrote, "Forrestal's subsequent career was to revolve around the anguished problem of how to deal with an ominous world-power situation when one's own power had been laid aside" (ibid., 81). While it is always risky to draw implications from history for history in the making, it appears that Bush's 1991 rapid withdrawal of forces from the war with Iraq (a war metaphorically indistinguishable in U.S. military and media commentary from a Superbowl game, just as World War II had been regarded, according to Forrestal, as a ball game) before certain necessary postwar agreements had been reached was to give up the political bargaining strength gained by the war. This was to repeat once again a pattern of foreign intervention that only exacerbates civil war and genocidal strife without effectively negotiating long-term agreements necessary to the protection of national interests and stability in a multinational political economy.

24. "Massive retaliation" was adopted as policy in part to reduce the defense budget under Eisenhower. The United States would depend on nuclear weapons to deter aggression rather than on conventional ground forces and weapons. When the fallacy of this approach became clear—massive retaliation was global overkill for local nationalist civil wars, even if they were also supported by Soviet aid—the government simply added conventional military resources back into its budget and arsenal and retained massive retaliation capability.

25. Read any of the political memoirs of the immediate postwar period to understand the degree to which international communism and Soviet national interests were at first argued as separate phenomena, even with certain acknowledged legitimacies, requiring careful and specific responses or initiatives on the part of the United States—actions that could take into account national interests of both countries while remaining sensitive to complex realities and changing circumstances. See, among others, the writings of George Kennan, Henry Stimson, James Forrestal, Dean Acheson, Paul Nitze, McGeorge Bundy, and journalist Walter Lippmann. Specifically, see Forrestal, *Forrestal Diaries*, 72, 139–40.

26. See Athan Theoharis and John Stuart Cox, *The Boss: J. Edgar Hoover and the Great American Inquisition* (Philadelphia: Temple University Press, 1988), 169; and Richard Gid Powers, *Secrecy and Power: The Life of J. Edgar Hoover* (New York: Free Press, 1987). See also William W. Keller, *The Liberals and J. Edgar Hoover: The Rise and Fall of a Domestic Intelligence State* (Princeton, N.J.: Princeton University Press, 1989).

27. Powers, *Secrecy and Power*, 228–31.

28. Howard Zinn, *Declarations of Independence: Cross-Examining American Ideology* (New York: HarperCollins, 1990), 264.

29. From 1945 to 1960 advertising increased 400%, to three times the nation's annual investment in higher education (William H. Chafe, *The Unfinished Journey: America Since World War II* [New York: Oxford University Press, 1986], 119).

30. Aronson, *Press and Cold War*, 25.

31. Even in 1952, when the extent of anti-Communist irrationality was widely apparent, Peter Kihss justified press reporting of news releases as factual by saying: "For the newspapers Fort Monmouth has been a lesson that will not be quickly forgotten, but the reading public should understand that it is difficult if not impossible to ignore charges by Senator McCarthy just because they are usually proved exaggerated or false. The remedy lies with the reader" (quoted in Michael Paul Rogin, *The Intellectuals and McCarthy: The Radical Specter* [Cambridge, Mass.: MIT Press, 1967], 255). See also Caute, *Great Fear;* Aronson, *Press and Cold War;* Parenti, *Inventing Reality;* Powers, *Secrecy and Power;* and Theoharis and Cox, *The Boss.*

32. Zinn, *Postwar America*, 9–13; see also Bernstein, "America in War and Peace," 362.

33. *Declaratory* as opposed to *action* policy is a necessary and strategically manipulative governmental distinction between words and perceived or intended reality. Credibility gaps and international cynicism are the most obvious worldwide responses in the twentieth century to the gap between U.S. words and actions. But the self-defeating effects of such a gap in the relatively young and ideologically idealistic United States reside in the gullible willingness of the populace and its representatives to give interpretive priority to the words, understanding the actions in terms of the (usually moral) declaratory policy, or fiction. This tendency, or peculiarity, of subjects of the United States made possible for forty years a largely nonskeptical acceptance of the declaratory policy of cold war. It allowed an ongoing misinterpretation of events, actions, and alternatives in accord with the rationale that justified the cold war, and a relative blindness

to the political, business, and military interests being served by that rationale. Paul Nitze warns: "To be clear as to the wisdom of a declaratory policy, one must be sure first that the action policy it suggests is one which is, and will continue to be, in conformity with our interests and with basic realities, and second that the political and psychological consequences of the declaration will be favorable." I would revise his warning by asking, In conformity with whose interests does a given declaratory policy also work, and for whom will its political and psychological consequences be favorable? See Nitze, with Ann M. Smith and Steven L. Rearden, *From Hiroshima to Glasnost: At the Center of Decision, A Memoir* (New York: Grove Weidenfeld, 1989), 152.

34. Quoted in Schneir and Schneir, *Invitation to an Inquest*, 30.

35. *Liberalism,* a word that originated in a class distinction setting off free from nonfree men, suffers from and practices, in the twentieth-century United States especially, semantic and material contradictions and political co-optation. For a history of the word, see Raymond Williams, *Keywords: A Vocabulary of Culture and Society,* rev. ed. (New York: Oxford University Press, 1983), 179–81. Conventionally and rhetorically opposed to *conservatism* In the United States, the word serves the domestic strategic political function of defining diverse groups of disempowered others and their advocates for government protection and services in an individualist capitalist society. Liberalism's philosophical and historical, rather than strategic, counterengagement is with socialism, not conservatism. In the United States both liberalism and conservatism are belief systems based on an individualist theory of the relationship of the individual to society and are "thus in fundamental conflict not only with 'socialist' but with most strictly 'social' theories" (ibid., 181). George Bush, an almost perfect embodiment of the elitist or privileged possessive individualist doctrine of U.S. liberalism, was able, because of the tradition of cold war rhetorical abuse of *liberal* and of liberals, to use the label against his presidential opponent to signify its opposite, socialist, with its domestic taint of communism.

The poststructuralist Jacques Lacan imagines disposing of by using up a word that no longer serves a useful purpose, or that is only too useful in constructing an oppressive symbolic order. Referring to his use of *essence,* Lacan claims, "One must make use, but really use them up, really wear out these old words, wear them threadbare, use them until they're thoroughly hackneyed!" (*Le Séminaire livre XX: Encore* [Paris: Éditions du Seuil, 1975], 56). Jane Gallop suggests that perhaps Lacan is attempting just that with *phallus* and *castration* but maintains the view that a word upon which a given order depends cannot be voluntarily and completely used up from within that order (*The Daughter's Seduction: Feminism and Psychoanalysis* [Ithaca, N.Y.: Cornell University Press, 1982], 55). *Liberal* works conceptually in complex and multiple ways to maintain a certain order in the twentieth-century United States. If *liberal* can even be imagined as used up and disposed of, its opposite in the United States, *conservative,* would lose much of its rhetorical function and effectivity, perhaps opening the way toward a more complex and realistic politics. Perhaps that disposal process is under way in the late twentieth century, with the proliferation and vocalization of multiple, regional, and local interest formations that confound the use of such a mystifying and false distinction. See Chantal Mouffe, "Radical Democracy:

Modern or Postmodern," Stanley Aronowitz, "Postmodernism and Politics," and Ernesto Laclau, "Politics and the Limits of Modernity," in *Universal Abandon? The Politics of Postmodernism,* ed. Andrew Ross (Minneapolis: University of Minnesota Press, 1988), 31–45, 46–62, 63–82. See also Aronowitz, *Crisis in Historical Materialism: Class, Politics, and Culture in Marxist Theory,* 2d ed. (Minneapolis: University of Minnesota Press, 1990).

36. *Masculist* is my arbitrarily defined and constructed, empirically descriptive—not essential or normative—term for the twentieth-century political status quo: an order favoring men and characterized by values conventionally associated with stereotypical U.S. masculinity: individualism, elitism, competitivism, expansionism, aggression, militarism. Although it can be argued that there is no necessary relation between capitalism and a sociopolitical elitism, there is a functional relationship observably—behaviorally and statistically—at work in the modern U.S. and world political economy. The two have become symbolically and institutionally implicated and naturalized to the extent that any analysis must take both into account as mutually dependent organizing systems of power, people, and resources. The self-sustaining and progressive reciprocity between the two systems of selection—capitalism and an elitism of the historically empowered—paradoxically threatens the imagined order the relationship is theorized and rationalized as sustaining: free enterprise democracy.

The differences between rich and poor, educated and miseducated, old and young, healthy and sick, attractive and ugly, insider and outsider (or member and nonmember), Christian and non-Christian, men and women, abled and differently abled, strong and weak, mentally well and mentally ill, citizens and criminals, lighter and darker, and owners and workers, and between other less obvious interpreted and constructed and *at the same time* objectively observable categories of differentiation cluster in various configurations to make possible a spectrum of individual experiences of relative power or powerlessness in daily life. The general and measurable allocations of political, economic, and social power during the modern period, from a close historical perspective, have favored white men with money. That is, the actual historical practice of twentieth-century global politics (in the broadest, most inclusive sense) has been governed by an elitist and masculist capitalism, not by the democratic free enterprise articulated by liberal theory and ideology. Those who would argue the inevitability and even necessity of social and political hierarchies (including the present writer) remain relatively blinded to or seriously concerned about their implications for the realization—or nonrealization—of an envisioned and much-invoked free or freer society. The critical and most disturbing question, especially to relatively empowered and articulate critics of the status quo (including the present writer), asks to what degree hierarchical categories are constructed at the service of maintaining a specific power configuration in which all the empowered are complicit at the expense of and maintained by the labor, disaffection, or both of all the others.

For the purposes of considering the ways in which language and narrative derive from, depart from, and direct material history, it appears to be empirically valid to describe the twentieth-century U.S. political order as characterized generally by relative white male individualist entitlement in what has effectively been a zero-sum competitive economy based on hierarchical exclusions to and exploitations of certain categories of people with observable differences from and defined by the entitled. This particular historical order, which I reductively but aptly and provisionally name *masculist-capitalist,* is rehearsed and reproduced throughout society in traditional hierarchical families and in churches, schools, businesses, political organizations, and administrative bureaucracies (see Heidi Hartmann, "The Unhappy Marriage of Marxism and Feminism: Towards a More Progressive Union," in *Women and Revolution: A Discussion of the Unhappy Marriage of Marxism and Feminism,* ed. Lydia Sargent [Boston: South End, 1981], 1–41). *Patriarchy* historically has both a more rigidly hierarchical and a more narrow connotation and is thus limited in describing the implicated relationships of twentieth-century U.S. society. In Hartmann's definition, *patriarchy* refers to "relations between men, which have a material base, and which, though hierarchical, establish or create interdependence and solidarity among men that enable them to dominate women" (ibid., 14). See also Gayle Rubin, "The Traffic in Women: Notes on the 'Political Economy' of Sex," in *Toward an Anthropology of Women,* ed. Rayna R. Reiter (New York: Monthly Review Press, 1975), 157–210; and R. W. Connell, *Gender and Power: Society, the Person, and Sexual Politics* (Cambridge: Polity, 1987).

37. See George Lipsitz, *Class and Culture in Cold War America: "A Rainbow at Midnight"* (South Hadley, Mass.: Bergin, 1981); see also Thomas Geoghegan, *Which Side Are You On? Trying to Be for Labor When It's Flat on Its Back* (New York: Farrar, Straus & Giroux, 1991).

38. The American Labor party, under the leadership of Congressman Vito Marcantonio, was a primarily New York City coalition of political, ethnic, social, and economic interests (workers and union members, ethnic minorities, Communists, New Dealers, teachers, professionals, intellectuals, socialists, and liberals) working pragmatically through neighborhood organizations and on specific local issues. It was one of the most effective left organizations in the country.

39. Michael Rogin notes that any group that is labeled radical (and most often this means anti-industrial, according to Rogin) is per se defined as a mass movement, allegedly characterized by irrationality and tendencies to totalitarianism or anarchy (*Intellectuals and McCarthy,* 27).

40. Maurice Isserman, *If I Had a Hammer: The Death of the Old Left and the Birth of the New Left* (New York: Basic, 1987), 48.

41. There were never more than 100,000 U.S. Communists at any one time, yet labor unions, youth groups, peace organizations, civil rights groups, and a host of miscellaneous clubs, gatherings, and assemblies were influenced by members of the CPUSA (Harvey Klehr, *The Heyday of American Communism* [New York: Basic, 1984], 373). "Between mid-1944 and the beginning of 1946, 50,000 members had left the CPUSA" (Ilene Philipson, *Ethel Rosenberg: Beyond the Myths* [New York: Franklin Watts, 1988], 175).

42. The historical accident of postwar party control by a zealous hardliner like Foster and its implications for American anticommunism are emphasized by a comparison with the more open working of Western European Communist parties in their national political forums, rendering them positive voices somewhat

more informed by and subject to their own specific national circumstances and less vulnerable to domestic movements of reactionary political repression.

43. Howard Zinn contrasts 1950s and 1960s defense strategies used by those accused by the government of Communist sympathies or affiliations. The earlier resort to the Fifth, suggesting something to hide, was a defense for an already weakened and even guilty position, or for one constructed as such. Later First Amendment defenses, despite requiring judicial ruling as to applicability of that amendment as protection against the allegedly illegal behavior, were more successful. But in the 1960s, defendants accused of seditious behavior used the hearing or trial as a forum for the kind of constitutional political dissent for which they were being investigated. When a member of HUAC asked Tom Hayden if his present aim was "to seek the destruction of the present American democratic system," Hayden replied, "Well, I don't believe the present American democratic system exists. That is why we can't get together to straighten things out. You have destroyed the American democratic system by the existence of a committee of this kind" (Zinn, *Declarations of Independence*, 265).

44. Joseph McCarthy biographer Allen J. Matusow quoted in Dickstein, "Cold War Blues," 41.

45. The gradual resolution of policy-level arguments over the nature of the Communist threat in favor of a reductive and overstated analysis and description was disproportionate to the realities of a Soviet Union exhausted and depleted by two wars and Moscow's capacity for developing, sustaining, and controlling a global communism. This description—backed by statistics and estimates of numbers and strenth—to a significant degree constituted the threat it seemed to be describing. It became a kind of ahistorical reality to which U.S. leaders took a reactive position with policy, resources, and actions. For the next forty-five years, it served as a self-fulfilling prophecy and interpretation for global political events, a too-ready interpretation that foreclosed the necessity for pragmatic, local, and historically specific considerations of the inconsistent complexities of daily international political operations.

A conceptual international communism was real; a material and full-blown international Moscow-controlled communism was not then nor has it ever been real. Nor has the Soviet Union ever had the military capacity for world conquest (it has had the capacity for world *destruction* since 1949) or the capacity for ideological-political global domination. But the warnings by U.S. policymakers and politicians of a realizable global international communism, even when offered in good faith, also served the political ambitions of Republicans and conservatives, as well as the economic/political agenda of business and the military. The universal nature of the perceived and publicized threat of international communism served to exclude from consideration all the middle terms and options under consideration for international relations: negotiated, shared, and interrelated political and economic autonomies; arms control negotiation; active initiatives for regular communications among powers on all issues; and domestic socioeconomic reforms, empowerments, and alternative relationships. "At no time did Russsia constitute a military threat to the United States. 'Economically,' U.S. Naval Intelligence reported in 1946, 'the Soviet Union is exhausted. . . . The U.S.S.R. is not expected to take any action in the next five years which might develop into hostility with Anglo Americans'" (Chafe, *Unfinished Journey*, 73). For a fuller analysis, see George Kennan, *Russia and the West under Lenin and Stalin* (New York: New American Library, 1961). The first Soviet atomic test took place in 1949; by then the cold war had already been rhetorically, politically, and economically launched.

A working definition of international communism as a material force has always been elusive in U.S. policy advisers' attempts to use it as justification for military and political interventions in other countries. In 1957, during the Senate hearings on the Eisenhower Doctrine (the presidential right to use the armed forces to protect any Middle Eastern nation or nations against overt aggression from another nation controlled by international communism), Secretary of State John Foster Dulles was questioned repeatedly about the nature of international communism. He finally responded to Senator Henry Jackson: "Well, international communism is a conspiracy composed of a certain number of people, all of whose names I do not know, and many of whom I suppose are secret. They have gotten control of one government after another. They first got control of Russia after the First World War. They have gone on getting control of one country after another until finally they were stopped. But they have not gone out of existence. International communism is still a group which is seeking to control the world, in my opinion. . . . I do not believe that the kind of internal security forces we are trying to build up here [in Middle Eastern countries] would be used against the general will of the people unless it is stirred up and organized by international communism. That is the great danger, and if that is the purpose of it, then we want to have forces to resist them." In this tautology can be noted the crucial slippage between overt aggression from another nation "controlled by international communism," and internal nationalist politics *perceived* by U.S. business, media, and political leaders as "controlled by international communism" (Lloyd C. Gardner, ed., *American Foreign Policy, Present to Past: A Narrative with Readings and Documents* [New York: Free Press, 1974], 194).

46. Postwar literary modernism and formalism (attention to the formal qualities and coherence of a work of art to the relative exclusion of any considerations of purpose, context, conditions of production, or sociopolitical meanings and/ or effects—see n. 6) emerged from the more complex and socially implicated critical practices of I. A. Richards and William Empson in England in the 1920s. T. S. Eliot used some of the assumptions of their work to shape an influential formalist aesthetics. In the 1930s the southern Fugitives and Agrarians, led by John Crowe Ransom and Allen Tate, developed a theory and practice based on such an aesthetics, laying the foundations for a formalist New Critical orthodoxy for literary criticism and pedagogy that prevailed in secondary and higher education from the 1940s to the 1980s. New York intellectuals Hilton Kramer, Clement Greenberg, and Harold Rosenberg provided the same theoretical and prescriptive function for formalism in the visual arts, and specifically for the emerging New York school of abstract expressionism, occluding and taming through a formalist grid its original impetus as an unco-optable political outcry against the horrors of twentieth-century Western liberal civilization.

47. By 1950 this number would be reduced to less than 15% of the total U.S. population (Rogin, *Intellectuals and McCarthy*, 189–90).

48. Ibid., 191.

49. From 1940 to 1945 the female labor force grew by more than 50%, with a 6,500,000 increase during the war of jobs held by women. In 1944 nearly 50% of all women were employed at some time during the year. The gap between men's and women's earnings was 62% in 1939, and 53% in 1950. See S. Hartmann, *The Home Front and Beyond,* 20, 77, 93.

50. Chafe, *Unfinished Journey,* 97.

51. Althusser, "Ideology and Ideological State Apparatuses," 36.

52. Zinn, *Postwar America,* 29–30.

53. Herbert Marcuse, "Affirmative Character of Culture," in *Negations: Essays in Critical Theory* (Boston: Beacon, 1968), 88–133. Marcuse defines affirmative culture as "that culture of the bourgeois epoch which led in the course of its own development to the segregation from civilization of the mental and spiritual world as an independent realm of value that is also considered superior to civilization. Its decisive characteristic is the assertion of a universally obligatory, eternally better and more valuable world that must be unconditionally affirmed: a world essentially different from the factual world of the daily struggle for existence, yet realizable by every individual for himself 'from within,' without any transformation of the state of fact" (ibid., 95). Marcuse's definition of affirmative culture is also an altogether accurate description of the traditional women's sphere in nineteenth- and twentieth-century U.S. gender ideology and practice. Affirmative culture not only requires no transformation of the state of fact; it also fosters a voluntary blindness to the state of fact.

54. See Bernstein, "America in War and Peace," 369; Lipsitz, *Class and Culture,* 17, 239–40. See also Aldon Morris, *The Origins of the Civil Rights Movement: Black Communities Organizing for Change* (New York: Free Press, 1984).

55. Again, Althusser's formulation of the function of ideology in producing compliant subjectivities capable of residing within a given field of social relationships which they imagine to be other than they actually are: "All ideology represents in its necessarily imaginary distortion not the existing relations of production (and the other relations that derive from them), but above all the (imaginary) relationship of individuals to the relations of production and the relations that derive from them" (Althusser, "Ideology and State Apparatuses," 38–39).

56. Bernard Bailyn, David Brion Davis, David Herbert Donald, John L. Thomas, Robert H. Wiebe, and Gordon Wood, *The Great Republic: A History of the American People,* 3d ed. (Lexington, Mass.: Heath, 1985), 642.

57. Powers, *Secrecy and Power,* 94.

58. During the German Army siege of Leningrad, more than 600,000 Russians died of starvation. Soviet Union wartime casualties were 18–20 million; U.S. casualties totaled 300,000. The Soviet Union had been engaged with an invading German army on the eastern front from 1941 until 1944 when the Allied landing at Normandy initiated the western front (Bailyn, et al., *Great Republic,* 760; and Chafe, *Unfinished Journey,* 36).

59. John Sharnik, *Inside the Cold War: An Oral History* (New York: Arbor House, 1987), 27–28.

60. When Truman was told at the Potsdam Conference of the successful atomic test explosion on July 16, 1945, he responded with a joke about the girl who swore to drown herself if pregnant, to which her boyfriend replied, "It has taken a great load off my mind." Truman's main objective at Potsdam had been to secure a Russian agreement to invade Japan, but the atomic bomb obviated that need, as well as making it unnecessary for the Russians, as Secretary of State James Byrnes said, to "get in so much on the kill" (Yergin, *Shattered Peace,* 115, 116).

61. Sharnik, *Inside the Cold War,* 27–28; and Yergin, *Shattered Peace,* 93.

62. Secretary of State James Byrnes declared that "the interest of every Church in the U.S., the economic and strategic interests of the U.S. dictate the U.S. policy in China [as a client state]" (Yergin, *Shattered Peace,* 150).

63. Yergin, *Shattered Peace,* 161–62.

64. See chap. 2, "Ownership and Secrecy."

65. Some key excerpts from Kennan's 5,500 word telegram: "We have here a political force committed fanatically to the belief that with the U.S. there can be no permanent *modus vivendi,* that it is desirable and necessary that the internal harmony of our society be disrupted, our traditional way of life be destroyed, the international authority of our state be broken, if Soviet power is to be secure. This political force has complete power of disposition over the energies of one of the world's greatest peoples and the resources of the world's richest national territory. . . . In addition, it has an elaborate and far-flung apparatus for the exertion of its influence in other countries. . . . Finally, it is seemingly inaccessible to considerations of reality in its basic reactions. For it, the vast fund of objective fact about human society is not, as with us, the measure against which outlook is constantly being tested and reformed, but a great grab bag from which individual items are selected arbitrarily and tendentiously to bolster an outlook already preconceived. This is admittedly not a pleasant picture. The problem of how to cope with this force is undoubtedly the greatest task our diplomacy has ever faced and probably the greatest it will ever have to face.

"Gauged against the Western world as a whole, the Soviets are still by far the weaker force. Thus their success will really depend on the degree of cohesion, firmness and vigor which the Western world can muster. . . . [The first step is to study and recognize the Soviet force for] what it is; [the second is to tell the American public the truth:] we must see that our public is educated to the realities of the Russian situation. I cannot overemphasize the importance of this. . . . I am convinced that there would be far less hysterical anti-Sovietism in our country today if realities of this situation were better understood by our people. There is nothing as dangerous or as terrifying as the unknown. It may also be argued that to reveal more information on our difficulties with Russia would reflect unfavorably on Russian-American relations. I feel that if there is any real risk here involved, it is one which we should have the courage to face, and the sooner the better. . . . [I suggest] courage and self-confidence, [for the greatest possible improvement in the] health and vigor of our own society, [and for putting before the peoples of the world a] much more positive and constructive picture of the sort of world we would like to see than we have put forward in the past" (Forrestal, *Forrestal Diaries,* 138–40; bracketed passages from editorial commentary by editor Walter Millis).

Kennan's analysis remained blinded to its own "ideology." Kennan perceived a nonideological, "objective," and empirical decision-making capability on the part of U.S. political leaders, opposed by an ideologically driven procrustean and selective distortion of that same world by Soviet leaders. Despite what have proven to be Kennan's realistic, flexible, and often accurate assessments of the Soviet Union, his consistent attribution to the United States of epistemological superiority and material entitlement are common, to varying degrees, to all the policy analyses and recommendations of the postwar period. The consensus historiography of the 1950s depends upon the same undergirding assumptions.

66. "From Stettin in the Baltic to Trieste in the Adriatic, an Iron Curtain has descended across the Continent" (Sharnik, *Inside the Cold War,* 25–26). In the summer of 1991 Secretary of State James Baker semantically echoed Churchill when he posited a new world order of East-West cooperation "from Vancouver to Vladivastok." His assertion lacked, however, the compelling metaphorical representation of the future established by Churchill's "iron curtain" and was an example of individual agency at work with neither the language nor the material circumstances sufficient to an effective intervention in history. Churchill had both at his disposal.

67. Yergin, *Shattered Peace,* 267–68.

68. Sharnik, *Inside the Cold War,* 241–44.

69. A socially divisive and destructive, but politically successful, strategy employed by Republicans after the 1946 success of "Republicanism vs. Communism" began with Nixon in his first successful presidential campaign. It was the contribution of Democratic Alabama governor George Wallace when he opposed Lyndon Johnson and his civil rights legislation: the mobilization of the racist fears of white voters. Thomas and Mary Edsall credit racism with being the "most important and the most powerful" contributor to Republican electoral victories since 1964. In that year, when Wallace articulated white fears of potential losses resulting from black gains, and when Barry Goldwater and George Bush came out against the Civil Rights Act, the implicit and explicit racism of their positions seemed at best sincere and principled. It was Richard Nixon and then George Bush who recognized and consciously utilized the *instrumental* value of mobilizing latent racism as a means to election. Two months before the 1988 Republican National Convention, at a planning meeting in Kennebunkport, Bush authorized the use of whatever racial strategies southerner Lee Atwater and his other campaign managers chose; the Willie Horton ads were only the least subtle product of those strategies. Jefferson Morley finds that Patrick Buchanan and David Duke best articulate the dominant Republican racial politics of the past twenty-five years, that "the aspirations and behavior of blacks are a threat to the well-being of the rest of the country." Morley credits Senator John Danforth and Secretary of Housing Jack Kemp with continuing a tradition of Republican racial moderation practiced by Bush's father, Prescott Bush, among others, in arguing that "policies successfully incorporating blacks into the American mainstream will help the country and the Republican Party." See Thomas Edsall and Mary Edsall, *Chain Reaction* (New York: Norton, 1991); and Jefferson Morley, "Bush and the Blacks: An Unknown Story," *New York Review of Books,* January 16, 1992, 26.

70. Lenin's 1904 pamphlet attacking rivals in the Russian revolution was called "One Step Forward, Two Steps Back" (Yergin, *Shattered Peace,* 263).

71. Ibid., 281.

72. Draper, "American Hubris," 40–48. Presidential adviser Clark Clifford thought Truman, in his speech to Congress to secure financial aid for Greece and Turkey, should refer to the threat to vital U.S. interests, specifically "the great natural resources of the Middle East" (Zinn, *Postwar America,* 46). Truman later described an early draft of this speech as sounding like an "investment prospectus" (Draper, "American Hubris," 41). After Acheson's preliminary success in appealing to Congress for foreign aid by comparing the postwar world to "apples in a barrel infected by one rotten one," and by describing the issue in terms of the greatest "polarization of power on this earth . . . since Rome and Carthage" (Chafe, *Unfinished Journey,* 66–67), Truman rewrote his congressional address to convey the high-toned moral principles that became known as the Truman Doctrine: "I believe that it must be the policy of the United States to support free peoples who are resisting attempted subjugation by armed minorities or by outside pressures" (Gardner, *American Foreign Policy,* 329). This abstract formulation already occluded crucial contradictions: the totalitarian kind of regime Truman wanted to protect the world against described the Greek rightwing government for which he was asking support; and the armed rebellion Truman attributed to Communists was internal and Greek, with support from Yugoslavian Communists, whom Stalin in 1948 urged not to interfere in the affairs of a country that lay within the Western sphere of influence (Zinn, *Postwar America,* 45; Sharnik, *Inside the Cold War,* 33). See also Edmund Keeley, *The Salonika Bay Murder* (Princeton, N.J.: Princeton University Press, 1989); and Kati Marton, *The Polk Conspiracy: Murder and Cover-Up in the Case of CBS News Correspondent George Polk* (New York: Farrar, Straus & Giroux, 1990).

The Truman Doctrine, supported by the Monroe Doctrine and the Eisenhower Doctrine, justified for the rest of the century various kinds of U.S. interventions in nationalist civil wars involving perceived Communist party participation or Soviet aid. It served ultimately to extend ideological justification to the U.S. version of the Communist party's practices of internal subversion in other countries, beginning with Iran in 1953 and including Guatemala, Panama, Cuba, the Belgian Congo, Vietnam, Angola, Chile, and Nicaragua. The premier of the Iranian nationalist government, Muhammad Mossadegh, was overthrown after he nationalized the Anglo-Iranian Oil Company when British producers continued to refuse Iranians an equal share in the profits from the production of Iranian oil. After the CIA-planned coup and the restoration of the Shah, American oil interests (Gulf, Texaco, and Standard Oil of New Jersey) joined the British in a Western monopoly of Iranian oil. See John Patrick Diggins, *The Proud Decades: America in War and Peace, 1941–1960* (New York: Norton, 1988), 141–42.

73. Sharnik, *Inside the Cold War,* 6; Chafe, *Unfinished Journey,* 71.

74. For Kennan's article outlining what became—beyond his intentions—a global cold war foreign policy under the rubric of containment of Soviet aggression, see Kennan [Mr. X], "The Sources of Soviet Conduct," *Foreign Affairs* 25, no. 4 (July 1947): 566–82. The cold war containment policy is a telling example of the ways in which the gap between words, especially relatively

abstract words, and their referents allows a manipulation of words toward arbitrary but specific ends. The policy of U.S. intervention in other nations' internal affairs inaugurated by the Truman Doctrine and justified by Kennan's metaphor of containment had hardly begun when Kennan began a lifelong informed critique of the costly and ultimately self-destructive effects—politically, militarily, and economically—of such an interpretive overreach of his word. Kennan's identification as the author of containment *as practiced by the government* denies the realistic complexity of perception and interpretation, open to revision over time, actually practiced by Kennan. He was and is one of the best critics of the cold war practices for which he unwittingly supplied, in a specific and valuable historical and political analysis of postwar power relationships, a crucial metaphor.

75. In his 1947 response to Kennan's analysis, journalist Walter Lippmann had the historical imagination necessary to critique containment, when Kennan first recommended it, for its abstract tendency toward a practicably and materially impossible universal application: "Now the strength of the western world is great, and we may assume that its resourcefulness is considerable. Nevertheless there are weighty reasons for thinking that the kind of strength we have and the kind of resourcefulness we are capable of showing are peculiarly unsuited to operating a policy of containment.

"How, for example, under the Constitution of the United States is Mr. X going to work out an arrangement by which the Department of State has the money and the military power always available in sufficient amounts to apply 'counterforce' at constantly shifting points all over the world? Is he going to ask Congress for a blank check on the Treasury and for a blank authorization to use the armed forces? Not if the American constitutional system is to be maintained.

"Having omitted from his analysis the fact that we are dealing with a victorious Russia—having become exclusively preoccupied with the Marxian ideology, and with the communist revolution—it is no wonder that the outcome of Mr. X's analysis is nothing more definite, concrete, and practical than that the Soviets will encroach and expand 'at a series of constantly shifting geographical and political points'" (*The Cold War: A Study in U.S. Foreign Policy* [New York: Harper, 1947], 15, 31).

For contemporary reassessments of that policy as implemented, including George Kennan's, see Terry L. Deibel and John Lewis Gaddis, eds., *Containing the Soviet Union: A Critique of U.S. Policy* (Washington, D.C.: Pergamon-Brassey's International Defense Publishers, 1987).

76. Quoted in Parenti, *Inventing Reality,* 118–19.

77. At the beginning of World War II, Secretary of State Cordell Hull's staff numbered twenty-one (Draper, "American Hubris," 40). The tendency and even conscious strategy of U.S. politicians to project all self-serving behavior, opportunism, deceit, repression, illegality, corruption, and immorality onto an other interpreted and perceived as aggressively world hungry, a projection received by an audience only too vulnerable to a moral narrative of national purpose, established the long term and primary postwar importance of foreign over domestic policy and actions. Such a priority of foreign over domestic interests established a hierarchy for political analysis, with the result that domestic concerns could be defined in terms of their relationship to foreign policies, producing

a short-sighted and self-defeating neglect of internal divisions and contradictions that would come into play with increasing dissonance in the following years. As Michael Rogin notes, "In foreign policy, the nation as a whole and its interests are at stake; hence foreign policy may be included in the 'nongroup' sphere of politics," lending itself to moralistic formulations and supporting the silencing of conflicting views and alternative policies. Only in a misadventure or action of questionable legality does foreign policy come under any kind of public scrutiny and reality check, and the effects of this kind of challenge are prolonged and dispersed into tedium by hearings and legal procedures that last years. See Rogin, *Intellectuals and McCarthy,* 21, 223, 266.

The postatomic national security state effectively promotes and protects a gap between declaratory policy—public rationales—and the articulation of national interests, which are too often construed as requiring secrecy for security purposes in a democratic state. This gap not only removes the determination of such interests from democratically essential public scrutiny and participation; it also allows dominant interests and political parties to co-opt national interests under the cover of the declaratory policy, or justifying myth.

78. George Kennan, Top Secret State Department internal document, 1948, quoted in Harold Pinter, "Language and Lies," *Index on Censorship* 17, no. 6 (June–July 1988), 2.

79. By 1952, 87% of black women and 65% of black men in the South had never voted (Hartmann, *Home Front,* 136).

80. As the congressional doorkeeper William ("Fishbait") Miller recounted in his memoirs concerning the staged discovery of the "pumpkin papers," "[Nixon] was so delighted with something that he had to share it. He said, 'I'm going to get on a steamship and you will be reading about it. I am going out to sea and they are going to send for me. You will understand when I get back, Fishbait!' He looked very elated and keyed up, as if he were dancing on wires. Even his eyes were dancing" (quoted in Athan Theoharis, "Unanswered Questions: Chambers, Nixon, the FBI, and the Hiss Case," in *Beyond the Hiss Case: The FBI, Congress, and the Cold War,* ed. Theoharis (Philadelphia: Temple University Press, 1982), 277.

81. Louis Budenz, an ex-Communist government witness, was given unusual latitude by the trial judge, Harold Medina, in the 1949 sedition trial of eleven Communist party leaders to establish the connection between domestic communism and revolutionary intent, including espionage. Budenz accomplished this identification not by testifying about illegal activities of contemporary party members, but by interpreting the *words* of theoretical Marxist and Leninist texts. He was supported in this interpretation by two other ex-Communists, Elizabeth Bentley, the Red Spy Queen, and Whittaker Chambers. The eleven Communist party leaders were convicted under the Smith Act for conspiracy and sent to prison for five years. Because of the "inflammatory nature of world conditions," the Supreme Court upheld this abrogation of its own distinction between speech protected by the First Amendment and speech identified as "clear and present danger." It was not until 1957, when California Communist leaders on trial hired a constitutional lawyer to represent them, that the Supreme Court reempowered the First Amendment distinctions between statements of belief and advocacy of

illegal action. A year's investigation of the several hundred other people named by the ex-Communist government witnesses produced no indictments, but by the mid-1950s some 150 other members of the Communist party had been arrested and another 150 non-native-born Communists deported under the Smith Act because of the Communist–treason equation. At the end of the 1949 trial, CPUSA leader William Z. Foster's decision for party leaders to go underground was the effective end of the Communist party in the United States (Lader, 71–76, 86; see also Powers, 294–96; and William Reuben, *The Atom Spy Hoax* [New York: Action Books, 1955], 120–99).

82. *Syllogism* connotes the sense of a "specious piece of reasoning," but in terms of logic, the word refers to a form of deductive reasoning consisting of a major premise, a minor premise, and a conclusion. Anti-Communists misused the form by not beginning with the most general term in the major premise: to say that all Communists are traitors is not the same thing as saying that all traitors (and eventually all dissenters) are Communists. But the illogical strategy worked anyway, with long-lasting material and psychological effects worldwide, as well as in the individual lives of U.S. citizens.

83. Kenneth Burke maintains that all forms of expression are either tautologies or non sequiturs. Astute reading of the political world would require vigilance for identifying both forms of meaning, which generally appear as logical articulations, and for attempting to uncover the differences they elide or occlude (Burke, *Rhetoric of Religion,* 128).

84. In the 1990s left academics found themselves, in their attempts to resist and refuse oppressive language terminology and constructions, incurring charges of "left fascism" and "totalitarianism." Indeed, any insistence on "pure" language or thought operates according to the same dynamic: the establishment of polarized systems of value and meaning that tend to override and silence the expression and critical examination of and arguments about complex, middle-ground, and socially situated understandings, beliefs, and practices. Many on the left recognized this tendency in any effort toward "political correctness" and found attacks from the right both ironic and indicative of the effectiveness of its work to make linguistic discriminatory differences explicit: differences lying within expressions of the commonsensical, the traditional, the humorous, and the stereotypical, expressions that have real cultural, social, political, and material effects.

85. Caute, *Great Fear,* 349–50. See also ibid., 26; "American Business and the Origins of McCarthyism: The Cold War Crusade of the US Chamber of Commerce," Robert Griffith and Athan Theoharis, eds., *The Specter: Original Essays on the Cold War and the Origins of McCarthyism* (New York: Franklin Watts, 1974), 72–89; Powers, *Secrecy and Power,* 285; and "The Nuclear Family: or, the Last Rosenberg Piece You'll Ever Have to Read," *Village Voice,* January 31, 1984.

86. Lader, *Power on the Left,* 24; Caute, *Great Fear,* 349.

87. Rogin, *Intellectuals and McCarthy,* 256.

88. Lader, *Power on the Left,* 76–77, 79. See also Caute.

89. Lader, *Power on the Left,* 56. See also Lipsitz, *Class and Culture,* for a more specific and local historiography of labor activities following World War II.

90. Lader, *Power on the Left,* 56–69; and conversation with Tom Geoghegan, *Which Side Are You On?* See also Charles P. Larrowe, *Harry Bridges: Rise and Fall of Radical Labor in the United States* (New York: Laurence Hill, 1972); and Ronald Radosh, *American Labor and U.S. Foreign Policy* (New York: Random House, 1969).

91. "Our Country and Our Culture."

92. Christopher Lasch, "The Cultural Cold War: A Short History of the Congress for Cultural Freedom," in *Towards a New Past: Dissenting Essays in American History,* ed. Barton J. Bernstein (New York: Random House, 1968), 322–59. At the first meeting of the Congress in 1950 the "end to ideology" was announced in the interests of opposing communism, socialism, and domestic liberal intellectualism as "ideology," while claiming a pure objectivity and rationality untainted by ideology for members themselves. Their rationality was expressed in the polarized and reductive diction of ex-communism, anticommunism, and demonized cold war politics. Lasch notes the "amazing tenacity of the Bolshevik habit of mind" among those who now rejected Bolshevism, as well as the elitist entrenchment of antibourgois polemic (ibid., 327).

93. See Isserman, "*Dissent,* Journal of Tired Heroism," in *If I Had a Hammer,* 79–123.

94. See Caute; see also Victor Navasky, *Naming Names* (New York: Viking, 1980); Lillian Hellman, *Scoundrel Time* (Boston: Little, Brown, 1976).

95. Richard H. Rovere, *Senator Joe McCarthy* (New York: Harcourt, Brace, 1959), 123–27.

96. Rogin, *Intellectuals and McCarthy,* 224–25. The first test explosion by the Soviet Union of an atomic bomb had taken place in September 1949. If by 1950 the people at large were not yet worried about Communists, there were enormous political pressures among those at the top levels of government to produce an explanation for the U.S. loss of its main weapon and guarantor of world supremacy. It is probably not carrying a psychological analogy too far to say that the United States suffered a narcissistic wound (an offense to one's overvalued attributes and achievements—or those of one's group—that are considered essential to one's self- or group definition), especially at official levels, from the Soviet test explosion of the atomic bomb. The wound was reopened by the successful Soviet launching of the first orbiting space capsule, *Sputnik,* in 1957 and by the Soviet and Eastern European victories at the 1958 Olympic Games. These events were a serious challenge to U.S. concepts of superiority to a presumably or allegedly backward Soviet Union.

97. Grotstein, *Splitting and Projective Identification,* 26–29.

CHAPTER 2. EMBEDDED STORY

1. The nature of the atomic bomb remained incomprehensible to most people, even or especially at the highest levels of government. The Schneir and Schneir history of the Rosenberg case reports two diary entries made in 1949 by David E. Lilienthal, who chaired the Atomic Energy Commission. Following a meeting with the Joint Chiefs of Staff he reported: "The view of some of the military is that war is inevitable. The top, however, do not go so far; they believe

it's 'likely' in a relatively short time, four to five years. After it comes we must use the atomic bomb, as we can't hold Europe without it. . . . [They] regard the next four to five years the most critical in the entire history of the country." From a diary entry a few days later following a discouraging conversation with Senator Brien McMahon, chair of Congress's Joint Committee on Atomic Energy: "What he is talking is the inevitability of war with the Russians, and what he says adds up to one thing: blow them off the face of the earth, quick, before they do the same to us—and we haven't much time" (*Invitation to an Inquest*, 432). Chief arms reduction negotiator Paul Nitze writes in his 1989 memoir that during the 1950s he was an early advocate of "limited" nuclear wars, and that in the instance of the Berlin blockade he argued for considering a preemptive strategic strike. "This, I believed, could assure us victory in at least a military sense in a series of nuclear exchanges" (*From Hiroshima to Glasnost*, 204).

2. Richard Rhodes, *The Making of the Atomic Bomb* (New York: Simon & Schuster, 1988), 534–35.

3. Ibid., 534.

4. Schneir and Schneir, *Invitation to an Inquest*, 33, 37.

5. Reuben, *Atom Spy Hoax*, 104–5. See also Godfrey Hodgson, *Biography of Henry Stimson* (New York: Viking, 1988).

6. Reuben, *Atom Spy Hoax*, 7–8.

7. Ibid., 14.

8. Ibid., 1. Until *Sputnik* in 1957, U.S. policymakers successfully maintained the illusion that the Soviet Union was a peasant economy without the theoretical, technological, or industrial resources to challenge the United States militarily.

9. John Wexley, *The Judgment of Julius and Ethel Rosenberg* (New York: Cameron & Kahn, 1955), 16.

10. Reuben, *Atom Spy Hoax*, 108.

11. Ibid., 104–7.

12. The 1946 McMahon-Douglas Atomic Energy Act established the Atomic Energy Commission to oversee atomic energy research and development and to enforce guidelines for the protection and monitored dissemination of information concerning domestic atomic energy developments. The crucial question before the Supreme Court the day of the Rosenberg executions was whether their charge, trial, conviction, and sentencing should have followed this law, tailored specifically for atomic energy espionage, or the 1917 Espionage Act. As it turned out the government was allowed to have the advantages of the earlier act; ironically, the application of the Atomic Energy Act of 1946 to the alleged atomic Rosenberg espionage would have made it more difficult, if not impossible, to prosecute and execute the Rosenbergs.

13. Edward U. Condon, quoted in Schneir and Schneir, *Invitation to an Inquest*, 40.

14. The "ideal reader" is a necessarily relative concept, since there is no way to delimit or control a text's meaning. In this case I mean the reader who is well enough prepared by the context and by community beliefs to accept as adequate and true the government's public version of the Rosenberg story. In this sense, most U.S. citizens were sufficiently prepared to be ideal readers for that story.

Notes to Chapter 1

See Stanley Fish, *Is There a Text in This Class? The Authority of Interpretive Communities* (Cambridge, Mass.: Harvard University Press, 1980).

15. See David Holloway, "Entering the Nuclear Arms Race: The Soviet Decision to Build the Atomic Bomb, 1939–45," *Social Studies of Science* 11, no. 2 (1981): 169. Holloway, of the University of Edinburgh and the Center for International Security and Arms Control at Stanford University in California, is engaged in an exhaustive study of the Soviet atomic project. See also Phillip Knightley, *The Second Oldest Profession: Spies and Spying in the Twentieth Century* (New York: Norton, 1986), 258–67; and Radosh and Breindel, "Bombshell," 10–12.

16. One of these six people was convicted on her admission of having discussed the Spanish civil war and the second front in Europe with a member of the Canadian Communist party in 1939 (Reuben, *Atom Spy Hoax,* 45–49).

17. Ibid., 25.

18. Ibid., 98.

19. Ibid., 18.

20. Ibid., 19.

21. Press release from J. Parnell Thomas in September 1948: "The silence [of the executive branch] up to now as to the existence of that conspiracy [to give away the secret of the atomic bomb] and what it sought to accomplish has been tantamount to a representation to the American people that espionage against the development of the atom bomb just did not exist. A representation such as this in a free country, where such representation is palpably at variance with the facts, is un-American" (quoted in Reuben, *Atom Spy Hoax,* 144). One major ramification of the concept of the spy ring was the emergence of the FBI as a policy-making branch of the U.S. government. See Reuben, ibid., 114.

22. See Reuben, ibid., chaps. 2–5, 16–118, for a detailed history of each of the abortive spy cases following the war; for an account of the Klaus Fuchs confession and trial, see chaps. 11–12, 203–45.

23. Quoted in Schneir and Schneir, *Invitation to an Inquest,* 478.

24. See Daniel Isaacson's comments on this same phenomenon, quoted in chap. 1 (Doctorow, *The Book of Daniel,* 311–12).

25. This and the three preceding quotes appeared in the *New York Times,* September 24, 1949. Quoted in Schneir and Schneir, *Invitation to an Inquest,* 52–54.

26. *New York Journal-American,* September 24, 1949.

27. Don Whitehead, *The FBI Story,* quoted in Schneir and Schneir, *Invitation to an Inquest,* 405.

28. Unknown Subject was the name given to the FBI Los Alamos investigation (Schneir and Schneir, *Invitation to an Inquest,* 436).

29. See chap. 1, n. 19.

30. White, *Content of the Form,* 13.

31. Schneir and Schneir, *Invitation to an Inquest,* 405.

32. Wexley's summaries are the basis for the chronology and charge given here (*Judgment,* x–xiv).

33. For a summary of pretrial irregularities or anomalies, see Schneir and Schneir, *Invitation to an Inquest,* 434–63; and Ronald Radosh and Joyce Milton,

The Rosenberg File: A Search for the Truth (New York: Holt, Rinehart & Winston, 1983), 20–169.

34. Schneir and Schneir, *Invitation to an Inquest*, 463.

35. Ibid., 478.

36. Stanley Fish, "The Law Wishes to Have a Formal Existence" (paper delivered at a Cardozo School of Law symposium, "Deconstruction and the Possibility of Justice," New York City, October 2–3, 1989), 25.

37. Louis Nizer's 1973 book, *The Implosion Conspiracy* (Garden City, N.Y.: Doubleday, 1973), which reached the best-seller lists, is one of two principal volumes Americans have read to learn about the Rosenberg case (the other is E. L. Doctorow's *Book of Daniel*). Nizer's naïveté is remarkable given his legal reputation. He assumes the Rosenbergs guilty as charged, considers Harry Gold a "disinterested witness," and charges himself with the moral and chivalrous task of revealing an unproblematic truth concerning the case: "The Rosenberg trial and subsequent events . . . involve a succession of unexpected climaxes of which only the truth could be the author. . . . I ventured forth to subdue the facts in writing" (4). Consider this passage on evidence and jury findings: "Jurors must decide on what is put before them. They cannot respond to stimuli which are not there" (110). The only stimuli to which they can respond that are not there are pervasive cultural ideologies or background beliefs. These background and shaping assumptions announce themselves in textual gaps, occlusions, and ambiguities, as well as in overdetermined or figurative language or both, constructions that the political literary theorist Pierre Macherey would have us read for their positive content. See Macherey, *A Theory of Literary Production,* trans. Geoffrey Wall (New York: Routledge & Kegan Paul, 1978).

38. See "The Kaufman Papers" (New York: National Committee to Reopen the Rosenberg Case, 1976).

39. *Grunewald v. United States,* 353 U.S. 391 (1957).

40. Philip Elman, "An Oral History," quoted in Sharlitt, *Fatal Error,* 73.

41. An April 1951 report by the Congress's Committee on Atomic Energy reflects government understanding of the extent of atomic espionage at the time of the Rosenberg sentencing. Four people were named and evaluated in order of importance of information conveyed: Klaus Fuchs (German-born British Los Alamos physicist), Bruno Pontecorvo (Italian-born British physicist who worked on the Manhattan Project in Canada), Allan Nunn May (British physicist, also on the Anglo-Canadian atomic research team), and David Greenglass (Los Alamos machinist). The report judged that the alleged Greenglass transmittal of information had to do with "mechanical details of bomb gadgetry and weaponeering that might have supplemented the data divulged by a theoretical physicist such as Klaus Fuchs." See U.S. Congress, Joint Committee on Atomic Energy, *Soviet Atomic Espionage* (Washington, D.C.: Government Printing Office, April 1951), 3. See also H. Montgomery Hyde, "Klaus Fuchs and Bruno Pontecorvo" and "On to the Rosenbergs," in *The Atom Bomb Spies* (New York: Atheneum, 1980), 130–200, 201–61; and Sharlitt, *Fatal Error,* 202–56.

42. Trial record (1951) available from U.S. District Court for the Southern District of New York, Foley Square Courthouse, New York, 1612–16. Also published by the Committee for the Defense of the Rosenbergs (New York, 1951);

available in microform, *U.S. v. Rosenberg* (1951–52), prep
the Republic (Wilmington: M. Glazier, 1978?), 1582. Referre
Record."

43. Correspondence from members of the Atomic Ene
from members of Congress discusses the value of the Fucl
bilizing domestic support for the development of the hyd ＿＿＿ ＿＿＿, and in
silencing advocacy for negotiations and arms control. Because the Rosenberg
case was at first construed as the Fuchs case, the Rosenberg case by extension
served the same ideological purposes. See Schneir and Schneir, *Invitation to an
Inquest,* 433.

44. Ibid., 288.

45. Ibid.

46. From FBI and Justice Department memoranda, quoted in Schneir and
Schneir, ibid., 455–59 and 456–57.

47. Ibid., 456.

48. Ibid., 459.

49. Ibid.

50. Quoted from "Proceedings from the Joint Committee on Atomic Energy,"
February 8, 1950, in Radosh and Milton, *Rosenberg File,* 146–47. Lane was, in
fact, adhering to a statutory requirement of the 1946 Atomic Energy Act in holding
this combined meeting before a prosecution for alleged atomic energy informaton
transmittal to a foreign country with the intent to injure the United States. The
purpose of the statutory requirement for such a meeting was that the Atomic
Energy Commission might determine, with the advice of scientific and military
consultants, the extent of damage to national defense resulting from the alleged
information transmittal. There were two twists to Lane's adherence to the letter
of the law in this case: (1) It was Lane who instructed the Atomic Energy
Commission, rather than soliciting its opinion, not on the damage worked by
the alleged Greenglass information transmittal but on the need to *claim* the
information as vital to secure a death penalty for Rosenberg that would then
make him "disgorge" the entire atomic spy ring. (2) The Rosenbergs were not
prosecuted under the 1946 statute, which was enacted solely to protect atomic
energy information and which would have required proof of "intent to injure"
the United States and a jury recommendation for a death sentence, but under
the earlier 1917 Espionage Act, which had nothing to do with atomic energy and
which required no jury recommendation for the death sentence, giving the judge
complete sentencing discretion.

51. Robert Coover's *The Universal Baseball Association, Inc., J. Henry
Waugh, Prop.* (New York: Random House, 1968) employs this kind of self-
generating dice-based game as a metaphor for the dual or simultaneous operations
of meaning making and meaning reduction.

52. Schneir and Schneir, *Invitation to an Inquest,* 102.

53. Ibid., 102, 363, 412–13, 112–13.

54. Ibid., 443, 364.

55. Ibid., 103, 413.

56. Ibid., 420.

57. Ibid., 365.

58. One of the Greenglasses' attorneys, John Rogge, had records of confidential conversations with the Greenglasses. These files, stolen from his office and published in an April 1953 issue of the French newspaper *Le Combat*, revealed some discrepancies between the Greenglasses' trial testimony and their conversations with their attorneys. See Radosh and Milton, *Rosenberg File*, 366–68.

59. Quoted from interviews by Radosh and Milton with John Rogge and Benjamin Pollack, *Rosenberg File*, 349. David Greenglass was an army machinist with a high school education who had failed the several college courses he had attempted. After his assignment doing tooling work on implosion lens molds at Los Alamos during the Manhattan Project, he had come to the FBI's attention for having possibly engaged in black market trading in parts stolen from the Los Alamos project.

60. Schneir and Schneir, *Invitation to an Inquest*, 311.

61. Ibid., 312–13.

62. Dwight D. Eisenhower, *The White House Years: Mandate for Change 1953–1956* (Garden City, N.Y.: Doubleday, 1963), 223–24.

63. Ibid., 439–41.

64. Schneir and Schneir, *Invitation to an Inquest*, 423. Weldon Bruce Dayton, whose personality was significantly more stable than Gold's, was questioned by the FBI and before the grand jury a number of times, beginning a few weeks after the Rosenberg trial, in an attempt to identify the "second echelon of the Rosenberg spy ring." Dayton recalled, "I had the helpless feeling that I really might be indicted for telling the truth." And, "I have been told . . . so many things by so many FBI agents . . . and they have all gotten kind of melded together and congealed [so] that it is awfully hard for me to know now what I knew in the first instance" (quoted in Schneir and Schneir, ibid., 306).

65. Ibid., 443.

66. Quoted in Schneir and Schneir, ibid., 444–45.

67. Ibid., 444–50.

68. Ibid., 451–52.

69. Radosh and Milton, *Rosenberg File*, 366, 368.

70. Schneir and Schneir, *Invitation to an Inquest*, 456–57; Wexley, *Judgment*, 138.

71. Schneir and Schneir, *Invitation to an Inquest*, 453.

72. Ibid., 459–60.

73. Quoted in Schneir and Schneir, ibid., 462.

74. Ibid.

75. Quoted in John Anthony Scott, "Greetings from Julius" (New York: Fund for Open Information and Accountability, 1978), 5.

76. "Trial Record," 1521.

77. Reprinted by the Senate Internal Security Subcommittee, "Hearings— Scope of Soviet Activity in the United States," quoted in Schneir and Schneir, *Invitation to an Inquest,* 370.

78. Quoted in Radosh and Milton, *Rosenberg File*, 171.

79. Wexley, *Judgment*, 487.

80. See Harvey Matusow, *False Witness* (New York: Cameron and Kahn, 1955).

81. *Rosenberg et al. v. United States*, CA2 195 F. 2d 583 (1952).

82. Robert Mccropol and Michael Meeropol, *We Are Your Sons: The Legacy of Ethel and Julius Rosenberg*, 2d ed., rev. (Urbana: University of Illinois Press, 1986), 187.

83. "Trial Record," 183.

84. Harold Urey and J. Robert Oppenheimer have volunteered that the government never contacted them concerning the Rosenberg trial (Elinor Langer, "The Case of Morton Sobell: New Queries from the Defense," *Science: American Association for the Advancement of Science* 153, no. 3743 [September 23, 1966], 1504).

85. "Trial Record," 479.

86. Ibid., 912. Philip Morrison, a senior nuclear physicist working on the bomb, testified in 1967, "If, in truth, Major Derry had occasion to see the actual bomb under development at Los Alamos 'many times,' as he stated, he ought to have added, 'and it did not look like that'" (from Morrison's affidavit to the Supreme Court, 1967, quoted in Sharlitt, *Fatal Error*, 235).

87. Philip Morrison comments on the bomb as an industry in a television documentary, "The Unquiet Death of Julius and Ethel Rosenberg," produced by Alvin Goldstein in 1974 and revised in 1985. Available from Impact Video, New York, and Icarus Films, Chicago.

88. Quoted in Schneir and Schneir, *Invitation to an Inquest*, 276. Scientists' comments were in affidavits evaluating Greenglass's sketch by atomic scientists Philip Morrison and Henry Linschitz, both involved in high level development of the implosion bomb at Los Alamos (quoted in Schneir and Schneir, ibid., 464).

89. Revealed in a memorandum from Hoover to Attorney General Brownell in 1954 and quoted in Schneir and Schneir, ibid., 466.

90. Wexley, *Judgment*, 132. The Korean War had begun on June 25, 1950, several weeks before Ethel Rosenberg's arrest on August 11.

91. *Delaney v. United States*, 199 F. 2d 107 (1952), quoted in Wexley, *Judgment*, 132.

92. *Rosenberg et al. v. United States*, 200 F. 2d 666, 670 (1952).

93. Meeropol and Mecropol, *We Are Your Sons*, 187.

94. Judge Hand's courtroom comment quoted in Wexley, *Judgment*, 494.

95. Quoted in Meeropol and Meeropol, *We Are Your Sons*, 193.

96. Ibid.

97. In the 1988 video collection of art about the Rosenbergs, "Unknown Secrets," Margia Kramer alternated film clips of the Army-McCarthy hearings and Iran/contra hearings to dramatize the uses of the Fifth Amendment for opposite and contradictory purposes, depending on the prevalent ideology and political hegemony.

98. "Trial Record," 1372–1402.

99. "Trial Record," 1385.

100. *Grunewald v. United States*, 353 U.S. 391 (1957), cited in Radosh and Milton, *Rosenberg File*, 528–29, n. 263.

101. *Sobell v. United States*, 314 F. 2d 314 (1963), cited in Meeropol and Meeropol, *We Are Your Sons*, 376. Marshall's question and the U.S. attorney's answer are recorded in two FBI internal memoranda, quoted and cited in Radosh and Milton, *Rosenberg File*, 429; and also in the *National Guardian*, December

13, 1962, 12. Morton Sobell was named as the Rosenberg codefendant and linked to Julius Rosenberg's alleged conspiracy by the testimony of Max Elitcher and by Sobell's erratic behavior during a trip to Mexico with his family in the summer of 1950, following the Rosenberg arrests. He was illegally kidnapped and turned over to U.S. authorities in order to be charged and tried as a codefendant with the Rosenbergs and David Greenglass. Although he was not linked to any aspect of the alleged atomic espionage, nor did anyone indicate that he had any knowledge of such activity, and he was accused only by Elitcher of having been involved in naval espionage for the Soviet Union, he was sentenced to thirty years in prison by Judge Kaufman, who considered his alleged espionage as only one arm of the larger Rosenberg espionage conspiracy. Sobell served eighteen years of his sentence—several years in Alcatraz with hard-core criminals—before being paroled on June 14, 1969. Hoover's 1951 message to the attorney general explaining the need for a death penalty for Sobell uses the same reasoning as that justifying the plan for a Rosenberg death penalty: "He has not cooperated with the Government and has undoubtedly furnished highly classified information to the Russians although we cannot prove it. . . . If he agreed to talk after he was given the death sentence, it is possible he might be a good witness in other cases" (see Schneir and Schneir, *Invitation to an Inquest,* 479; see also Morton Sobell, *On Doing Time* [New York: Scribner's, 1974]). Sobell said in 1983, "Even though Julius was my friend, all I can tell you is that I don't know if there was anything else. I would not take the position that they were absolutely innocent." In that same year, Robert Meeropol, one of the Rosenberg sons, said he was still searching. "It's something I have to live with every day. . . . A number of people said 'You might uncover something you might not want to find out.' I would rather know the truth. I wish I could get into a time machine and know it all" (Sam Roberts, "The Rosenbergs: New Evidence, Old Passions," *New York Times,* September 23, 1983).

102. Maurice Berger, "Of Cold Wars and Curators," *Artforum,* February 1989, 86–87.

103. Radosh and Milton, *Rosenberg File,* 450.

104. Ibid., 451.

105. In the early 1940s, just at the time that women were being called upon to enter the workplace for the duration for patriotic purposes, and still within the context of traditional domesticity and dependency for women, alternative visions for women's lives were expressed and celebrated in comic strips, films, and women's magazines. "Wonder Woman" appeared in the comics in 1941 as the first powerful and independent (black-haired) woman superhero. Her creator, psychologist William Marston, began the strip to illustrate his theories of male-female relationships. See "Wonder Woman," unpublished cartoon by William Marston (194?) in the Cartoon, Graphic, and Photographic Arts Research Library, Ohio State University, Columbus. For the differing functions of dark and fair women in U.S. literature, see Leslie Fiedler, *Love and Death in the American Novel* (New York: New American Library, 1962). By 1947, when millions of women were being returned to their rightful places following the war, Wonder Woman became more dependent upon men. See S. Hartmann, *Home Front and Beyond,* 188–91, 202.

106. From a letter from Ethel to Julius in prison, April 17, 1951, quoted in Meeropol and Meeropol, *We Are Your Sons*, 40.

107. The collected letters (selected and edited) were published in 1953 as *Death House Letters* (New York: Jero) and *The Rosenberg Letters* (London: Dennis Dobson); in 1954 as *The Testament of Ethel and Julius Rosenberg* (New York: Cameron and Kahn). Meeropol and Meeropol, ibid., reproduces many previously unpublished letters. Various letters appeared in the *National Guardian* and the *Daily Worker* from 1951 to the time of the executions in June 1953.

108. A few years later, however, after McCarthy's censure by the Senate, and with more sophistication on the part of the defense, members of the Communist party charged with conspiracy were successfully able to use the First Amendment instead of the Fifth, admitting party membership and challenging the state to prove illegal actions or clear and present danger. This would probably have been a more powerful stance for the Rosenbergs but still might not have prevailed against a relatively easy-to-prove conspiracy charge requiring only one uncorroborated witness.

109. Schneir and Schneir, *Invitation to an Inquest*, 458, 459.

110. Quoted in Reuben, *Atom Spy Hoax*, 423.

111. Eisenhower, *White House Years*, 225.

112. Radosh and Milton, *Rosenberg File*, 146.

113. "Trial Record," 1523. Italics added.

114. Wexley, *Judgment*, 418–19.

115. "Trial Record," 1615.

116. Hoover's development of domestic intelligence, under the terms of an informal, secret, and unconstitutional agreement with Roosevelt in the 1930s, laid the groundwork for the national security state formally inaugurated in the postwar period, as it did for the anticommunism of that period. The major biographies of Hoover invariably turn to psychoanalytic explanations for the obsessional nature of his institution and administration of the FBI as an extralegal guardian of domestic ideological purity. Hoover's private secret files gave him enormous extralegal political power and leverage, and his access to a national network of information endowed his public pronouncements with great authority. See Powers, *Secrecy and Power*, 228–31; see also Theoharis and Cox, *The Boss*.

117. Radosh and Milton, *Rosenberg File*, 376.

118. Ibid., 358, 379. An example of the report's continuing influence is the 1989 explanation by Maurice Berger of Ethel as "perhaps . . . the driving force behind her mild-mannered husband" quoted at the head of this section. This is intertextuality at work: a communication and repetition among texts that has the effect over time of achieving cultural—and thus political—adherence to a specific version of reality not necessarily based in material history. Intertextuality in this sense combines the conscious or unconscious manipulation of language for material political and economic purposes with the relatively mindless reproduction of such linguistic constructs—ideas, categories, explanations—from text to text and across fields. Intertextuality, as I demonstrate in this section, pervades and organizes both the frame narrative of the cold war and its embedded Rosenberg story. See Introduction, n. 28.

119. These documents have been withheld because the identity of an "informant . . . of unimpeachable reliability [the person who allegedly convinced Hoover of the existence of a large atomic spy ring in which Julius played a key role] . . . is not available under any circumstances" (Schneir and Schneir, *Invitation to an Inquest,* 478).

120. Eisenhower, *White House Years,* 225. Eisenhower wrote to a friend concerning the Rosenberg case, "That their crime is a very real one and that its potential results are as definitive as I have just stated, are facts that seem to me to be above contention" (ibid.). In 1986 Richard Nixon was quoted in the *New York Times:* "In the case of Communist couples . . . the wife is often more extremist than the husband" (David Bonetti, "Rosenbergs Remembered," *Image, San Francisco Sunday Examiner,* February 25, 1990, 24).

121. Bob Considine, *It's All News to Me: A Reporter's Deposition* (New York: Meredith, 1967), 170–72. Considine had portrayed the Rosenbergs guilty as charged in his syndicated reporting of their case. He was the only one of the three witnesses able to describe the executions to the world media; the two other media representatives at the execution were emotionally overwhelmed and allowed Considine to speak for all three to the waiting reporters. Considine's highly interpretive and projective comments thus appeared in newspapers and on radio both nationwide and globally as the definitive story of the Rosenberg deaths.

122. For feminist discussions of the phallic mother (the mother who, according to Freud, is to the child still imaginatively "complete," endowed with a penis and omnipotent) see Dorothy Dinnerstein, *The Mermaid and the Minotaur: Sexual Arrangements and Human Malaise* (New York: Harper & Row, 1976); Nancy Chodorow, *Reproducing Motherhood: Psychoanalysis and the Sociology of Gender* (Berkeley: University of California Press, 1978); and Julia Kristeva, *The Powers of Horror: An Essay on Abjection,* trans. Leon S. Roudiez (New York: Columbia University Press, 1982).

123. This shift in discourse level from public, institutional, and instrumental rational to private, personal, and primitive rational requires a shift in analytic perspective from political to psychological. While this shift may seem disjunctive, my argument and demonstration depend on my perception of a homology between the psychological and the political explained by the same dynamics of splitting, projection, and inclusion and exclusion that structure language. For all three in modern masculist capitalist global society—language, psychology, and politics—the driving forces for expression, behavior, and administration tend to be the desire for mastery and power and the fear of the absence of mastery or power.

124. For a discussion of splitting and projection as the two fundamental cognitive mechanisms, see chap. 1, n. 7.

125. Alice Jardine analyzes historically and philosophically this kind of textual disruption gendered as feminine, which she calls "gynesis," in *Gynesis: Configurations of Woman and Modernity* (Ithaca, N.Y.: Cornell University Press, 1985).

126. Throughout I have ignored the separate issues surrounding the naming of Morton Sobell as a codefendant in the Rosenberg-Greenglass-Sobell trial. I perceive Sobell's alleged role, as described and asserted by Max Elitcher, as that

of participant in a completely separate conspiracy, with no evidence connecting him with the alleged conspiracy to gather and transmit atomic bomb information to the Soviet Union. With no evidence presented to the contrary, the linking of the two conspiracies was presumably an arbitrary yet purposeful rhetorical government strategy to prosecute the Rosenbergs and Sobell together under the 1917 Espionage Act, the terms of which were most likely to allow the conviction and stiff sentences needed to force the exposure of the entire alleged atomic espionage network. Judge Frank stated in his majority opinion for the Second Circuit Court of Appeals that the question of one or two conspiracies should have been submitted by the judge to the jury, and that because it was not, he considered error to have been committed. His colleagues, however, did not agree with him, preferring the trial judge's version of one giant conspiracy (*Rosenberg et al. v. United States,* CA2 195 F. 2d 583, 600–602 [1952]).

127. Ibid., 592.

128. A complex of nonverbal semiotics—audible, gestural, material, visual, and affective—is invisible in a literal verbal transcript of a social interaction.

129. The conversation between Brownell and Eisenhower concerning unavailable evidence proving Rosenberg guilt occurred at a cabinet meeting the morning of June 19, the day of the executions. It was recorded by a presidential speech writer, Emmet John Hughes, who was present at the meeting. In response to an inquiry by the Schneirs Brownell's secretary replied that he had no such evidence and no memory of having said anything to Eisenhower about its existence. See "Kaufman Papers" and Schneir and Schneir, *Invitation to an Inquest,* 245.

130. *Rosenberg et al. v. United States,* CA2 195 F. 2d 583, 594 (1952), quoting in part *Simon v. US,* CA4 123 F. 2d, 80 (1941).

131. See "Kaufman Papers." *Ex parte communications* are communications held privately and apart from other interested parties between members of different hierarchical levels or constitutionally separated institutions holding jurisdiction over or interests in the outcome of the adversarial procedure under discussion.

132. The afternoon of the Rosenberg executions, June 19, immediately following the Supreme Court denial of a stay granted by Justice Douglas for what he considered the substantive issue of applicability to the Rosenberg case of the 1946 Atomic Energy Act, attorneys for the defense attempted to persuade the circuit court to convene to grant a stay on the same issue, following a denial by Judge Kaufman. Judge Thomas W. Swan agreed to convene a panel if they could find two other judges, but the attorneys were unable to do so. While they were attempting to persuade Judge Frank—the author of the first, comprehensive opinion for the circuit court in February 1952—to hear their point, Frank agreed with them that the 1946 act did indeed apply, and that their point was not only substantial, but correct. But when Frank was asked to grant a stay, "he broke down. He sobbed audibly and shook his head. He said, 'I know you are right, but when the bosses have acted, what can you do?' Frank then added, through a voice choked with sobs, that the 'bosses' were more than just the Supreme Court— there were other elements involved in controlling this tragic situation. He said,

'There has been such touch and go; perhaps it would be better to get it over with'" (Sharlitt, *Fatal Error,* 134).

133. *Rosenberg et al. v. United States,* CA2 195 F. 2d 583, 596 (1952).

134. Judge Frank noted that 28 U.S.C.A. Sec. 2106, dating back to the Judiciary Act of 1789, grants a sentence-modifying authority to federal courts and the Supreme Court—the power to "affirm, modify, or reverse judgments on appeal"—but that sixty years of precedent denied the use of such authority. "No decision by the Supreme Court or any federal court of appeals seems to have cited or considered this statute in passing on the question of the power to reduce a sentence when a conviction is affirmed. Were this question *res nova,* this court should give that section serious consideration. . . . Because, however, for six decades federal decisions . . . have denied the existence of such authority, it is clear that the Supreme Court alone is in a position to hold that Sec. 2106 confers authority to reduce a sentence which is not outside the bounds set by a valid statute. As matters now stand, this court properly regards itself as powerless to exercise its own judgment concerning the alleged severity of the defendants' sentences." He mentions that this reluctance may also have to do with the existence of the executive's pardoning power, as well as with a desire not to engage in a most difficult undertaking [sentencing] that "calls for training and specialized knowledge of a kind which the education of few judges provides." Then he adds the qualification to the court's dismissal of the Rosenbergs' and Martin Sobell's appeal: "It has been held that, [where upper court modification authority does exist], the upper court may consider, for such purposes, the quality of the evidence on which the verdict rests. . . . So here, had this court such power, it might take into consideration the fact that the evidence of the Rosenbergs' activities after Germany's defeat (as well as of their earliest espionage activities) came almost entirely from accomplices" (*Rosenberg et al. v. United States,* CA2 195 F. 2d 583, 604–7 [1952]).

135. Ibid., 611.

136. *Rosenberg et al. v. United States,* CA2 200 F. 2d 666, 670 (1952).

137. Quoted in Wexley, *Judgment,* 494.

138. *Rosenberg et al. v. United States,* 345 U.S. 965 (1953).

139. There were twenty-three appellate considerations of the case, involving the trial judge Irving Kaufman, the various three-judge panels of the Second Circuit Court of Appeals, and the nine Supreme Court justices (*Implosion Conspiracy,* 493–95).

140. Finerty had represented labor leader Tom Mooney, taking his case to the Supreme Court to demonstrate California use of perjured testimony to secure Mooney's conviction; Finerty also contributed to the defense of Sacco and Vanzetti.

141. Felix Frankfurter, quoted in Sharlitt, *Fatal Error,* 71.

142. Ibid., 183.

143. See Sharlitt, ibid., 30–35.

144. FBI memorandum, June 17, 1953, cited in Sharlitt, ibid., 66.

145. American Bar Association's Canons of Judicial Conduct 17 and 4. See Sharlitt, ibid., 4, 67, 187.

146. Brownell claimed in his Supreme Court application for a special Court term to review and vacate Douglas's stay, "It is important in the interests of the administration of criminal justice and in the national interests that this case be brought to a final determination as expeditiously as possible" (Schneir and Schneir, *Invitation to an Inquest*, 243).

147. In vacating the stay the majority cited two cases that even to the lay person seem irrelevant. In his dissent, Justice Black cited *Lambert v. Barrett* (157 U.S. 697), decided "in 1895 and never overruled, [in which] this Court held that it has no jurisdiction over an appeal from a habeas corpus order of a circuit judge entered in chambers. The stay order in this case derived from petitions for habeas corpus and was entered by Mr. Justice Douglas in chambers." See Sharlitt, *Fatal Error*, 147–50 (Black quotation from *Rosenberg v. United States*, 346 U.S. 273, 298 (1953), 149).

148. See Michael E. Parrish, "The Supreme Court and the Rosenbergs," *American Historical Review* 82, no. 4 (October 1977): 805–41; see also Sharlitt, *Fatal Error*.

149. Quoted in Parrish, "Supreme Court," 823.

150. Quoted in Sharlitt, *Fatal Error*, 56; quoted in Parrish, "Supreme Court," 823.

151. Parrish, "Supreme Court," 827.

152. *Rosenberg v. United States*, 346 U.S. 273, 292–93 (1953). Justice Jackson had received a memorandum in 1953 from his law clerk, William Rehnquist, now chief justice of the Supreme Court. Rehnquist wrote that Julius and Ethel Rosenberg were "fitting candidates" for execution, adding, "It is too bad that drawing and quartering has been abolished" (quoted in Sharlitt, *Fatal Error*, 131). The justices' individual opinions (except for Frankfurter's dissent, which was published three days after the executions) were printed in the *New York Times* June 20, 1953, the day after the executions.

153. *Rosenberg v. United States*, 322 U.S. 273, 322–23 (1953). The executions, instead of being delayed for clemency consideration by the president as Frankfurter had expected, were moved up by Attorney General Brownell to 8:00 P.M. that same evening, in order to avoid executing Jews on the sabbath. The rescheduling also obviated any possibility of Eisenhower's hearing defense arguments for clemency or reading the majority and dissenting opinions for the Court's vacating of Douglas's stay, opinions that would have called into serious question some of the president's certainties concerning the justice of the Rosenbergs' conviction and sentence.

154. *Rosenberg v. United States*, 346 U.S. 273, 296–301 (1953).

155. Fish, "Law Wishes," 25.

156. Quoted in Schneir and Schneir, *Invitation to an Inquest*, 248–49.

157. The only available legal commentary on the issues and problems established by the 1946 Atomic Energy Act was an article by James Newman who was special counsel to the Senate Special Committee on Atomic Energy while that act was being argued and written. Newman's article, which also took into consideration the relationship of the 1946 act to the 1917 act, appeared in the *Yale Law Journal* in 1947. Whereas Newman interpreted Section 10(b)(6) of the 1946 act as protecting against omissions rather than as giving a prosecutor the option of using

the 1917 act for offenses that fell within the definitions of the 1946 act, the Supreme Court majority in vacating Douglas's stay cited Newman's article in support of its holding that the 1917 act was applicable in the Rosenberg case. See James Newman, "Control of Information," *Yale Law Journal* 56 (May 1947): 798. Quoted in Sharlitt, *Fatal Error,* 174.

158. See Sharlitt, ibid., 163–67.

159. For a 1949 *New York Times* editorial asserting the impossibility of national ownership of atomic weaponry, see chap. 2.

160. Quoted in Schneir and Schneir, *Invitation to an Inquest,* 425.

161. Gore Vidal, *Myra Breckinridge* (New York: Little, Brown, 1968), 94.

CHAPTER 3. CULTURE AS CRITIQUE IN THE POST-ROSENBERG ERA

1. I identify the U.S. cold war period as extending from 1945, when the Truman administration began establishing the cold war as national policy, to 1990, when the Soviet Union under Mikhail Gorbachev abandoned its statist economy in favor of a free market, reduced military spending, began democratization of its political system, allowed democratic revolutions in the Eastern bloc countries, and allowed liberation movements in its own republics. The United States was faced then with a reworking of policy and of its justifying rhetoric in response to the resignation of its superpower antagonist, the Soviet Union, from its partially real, partially projective cold war role.

2. Here I use Terry Eagleton's Althusserian definition of ideology, extending his class standpoint to allow a more complex interplay of gender, race, and class: ideology is "that complex structure of social perception which ensures that situation in which [power relationships] are either seen by most members of the society as 'natural,' or not seen at all." According to Eagleton, following Althusser, ideology has a relative power and life of its own. "Not always a direct expression of ruling class interests, it even may be in contradiction with them at moments. Ideology, then, is not a set of deliberate distortions imposed on us from above, but a complex and contradictory system of representations (discourses, images, myths) through which we experience ourselves in relation to each other and to the social structures in which we live. . . . The work of ideology is also to construct coherent subjects: the individual thus lives his [or her] subjection to social structures as a consistent subjectivity, an imaginary wholeness" (*Marxism and Literary Criticism* [Berkeley: University of California Press, 1976], 5–7).

3. Vidal, *Myra Breckinridge,* 94.

4. Fredric Jameson, "Postmodernism, or the Cultural Logic of Late Capitalism," *New Left Review* 146 (July–August 1984): 53–92.

5. See *U.S. News and World Report,* August 12, 1991.

6. The fracturing of U.S. academic humanities departments in the 1980s and 1990s over these issues has been pervasive and bitter. During 1990 and 1991 almost every major newspaper and weekly news and commentary magazine carried significant articles and even cover stories on the division in the humanities occasioned by poststructuralism and multiculturalism—both of which work to break down unified and universal explanatory narratives, with various outcomes,

depending on the critical orientation. William Bennett as Secretary of Education and Republican senator Jesse Helms of North Carolina as ranking minority member of the Appropriations Committee were only two of the most vocal and effective institutional defenders of the traditional Enlightenment narrative of Western civilization in its white masculist and moralist version, to the contradictory extent of overriding and corrupting values central to any ethical version of Enlightenment rationality.

7. Quoted in Eagleton, "Aesthetics and Politics," *New Left Review* 107 (January–February 1978): 30.

CHAPTER 4. *THE BOOK OF DANIEL*

1. Stanley Kauffmann, "Wrestling Society for a Soul," *New Republic,* June 5, 1971, 25.

2. See the Introduction, n. 22, for a working definition of postmodernism.

3. John Dos Passos is Doctorow's most direct predecessor; both writers work in the tradition of Daniel Defoe (*Journal of the Plague Year, Moll Flanders*), using fiction and fact interchangeably to write critical and provocative social fiction. Dos Passos is usually classified as a realist/naturalist writer, but he formally anticipates or initiates postmodern forms of historiographic metafiction (Linda Hutcheon's term), interspersing fictional segments with documentary texts, headlines, newsreels, impressionistic biographical fragments, and a stream-of-consciousness commentary he calls "Camera Eye." His work is more naturalistic than Doctorow's in that the fictions are always subordinate to and finally foreclosed by the forces of a coherent and antagonistic history. Doctorow reverses this balance, using fictions to interrogate a motivated but often incoherent history, as well as to challenge readers' preconceived historical assumptions. He calls his writing "false documents," as opposed to true documents like the Gulf of Tonkin Resolution or the Watergate tapes. See Barbara Foley, "From USA to Ragtime: Notes on the Form of Historical Consciousness in Modern Fiction," in *E. L. Doctorow: Essays and Conversations,* ed. Richard Trenner (Princeton, N.J.: Ontario Review Press, 1983). See also Linda Hutcheon, "Historiographic Metafiction: The Pastime of Past Time," in *A Poetics of Postmodernism: History, Theory, Fiction* (New York: Routledge, Chapman and Hale, 1988).

4. Tom LeClair and Larry McCafferty, eds., "An Interview with E. L. Doctorow," in *Anything Can Happen: Interviews with Contemporary American Novelists* (Urbana: Illinois University Press, 1983), 98, 104.

5. Irving Howe, "Radical Criticism and the American Intellectuals," in *Steady Work* (New York: Harcourt Brace & World, 1966), 324–25.

6. Jerry Rubin, *Do It!* (New York: Simon & Schuster, 1979), 90–91.

7. The old left, before its split by Stalinism, was characterized by a liberal faith in and commitment to the progress of history toward a just world, recognizing the necessity for state protection from and amelioration of the inequalities, injustices, and self-defeating deprivations established and promoted by a national free-market economy. The Marxist version of the inevitability of this historical progress toward freedom and justice through the agency of the working class was predominant among various theories of socialism and its

practice, ranging from democratic to statist forms and combinations. The American old left tended not to see the contradictions between Enlightenment individualist liberal theory as interpreted in the twentieth century and the possiblity of a collectively just world. When confronted with the extreme oppressions practiced in the Soviet Union, in the Eastern bloc countries following the war, and in China, many old left intellectuals abandoned socialist theory in favor of liberal democratic capitalism. Some old left stalwarts remained faithful to the dream of Marxism and the Russian revolution despite the realities of Stalinism; some attempted the difficult work of rethinking socialism for the postwar twentieth century. In this fractured and antagonistic state of disarray, the old left was rejected and scorned by the emergent New Left in the late 1950s and early 1960s.

8. Quoted in William O'Neill, *Coming Apart* (New York: Quadrangle, 1971), 279.

9. See Henry Adams, *The Education of Henry Adams: An Autobiography* (Boston: Houghton Mifflin, 1918 [first published privately in 1906]).

10. As a "criminal of perception," Daniel performs the role of the cultural critic, able to transgress the rules and assumed legal structures that make possible a coherent narrative rationale for a given material reality. "We cannot but be struck by the frequency with which narrativity, whether of the fictional or the factual sort, presupposes the existence of a legal system against which or on behalf of which the typical agents of a narrative account militate. And this raises the suspicion that narrative in general, from the annals to the fully realized 'history,' has to do with the topics of law, legality, legitimacy, or, more generally, authority" (White, *Content of the Form,* 12–13).

11. See Haraway, "A Cyborg Manifesto."

12. Richard Trenner, "Politics and the Mode of Fiction," in *E. L. Doctorow: Essays and Conversations,* ed. Trenner (Princeton, N.J.: Ontario Review Press, 1983), 50.

13. Ibid., 52, 54.

14. Jochen Barkhausen, "Determining the True Color of the Chameleon: The Confusing Recovery of History in E. L. Doctorow's *Loon Lake,*" in *E. L. Doctorow: A Democracy of Perception: A Symposium with and on E. L. Doctorow,* ed. Herwig Friedl and Dieter Schulz (Essen: Verlag Die Blaue Eule, 1988), 183, 130.

15. Epigraph in Richard King, "Between Simultaneity and Sequence," in *E. L. Doctorow,* ed. Friedl and Schulz, 45.

16. Trenner, "Politics and the Mode of Fiction," 50.

17. "There is no document of civilization which is not at the same time a document of barbarism" (Walter Benjamin, "Theses on the Philosophy of History," in *Illuminations,* ed. Hannah Arendt [New York: Harcourt Brace & World, 1968], 256).

18. E. L. Doctorow, "Living in the House of Fiction," *Nation,* April 22, 1978, 459.

19. This symbolic conversion is what Hegel considered necessary to a comprehension of the terrors of human history. No wonder the messenger (with the more realistic, more terrifying story) is never welcome, often not heard, and as often ostracized or killed. See chap. 1, n. 8.

20. In an interview with Arthur Bell, Lumet said, "I set out to make a movie about parents and children." Bell responds, "We don't know as much about their politics as we do about their characters. When they're finally electrocuted we've become so fond of them we don't care—or really want to know what their politics are." "Dead on," Lumet replies (Arthur Bell, "Not the Rosenbergs' Story," *Village Voice,* September 6, 1983, 42).

21. "The family I was born into gave me love and caring, and the family which adopted me continued the love, caring and values that my first parents began. In my case, resistance and family and community worked together" (Robert Meeropol, quoted in Carolyn Toll Oppenheim's review of the "Unknown Secrets" exhibit in "Spirit of Rosenbergs' Resistance," *Jewish Advocate,* November 17, 1988).

22. Myra Jehlen, "Archimedes and the Paradox of Feminist Criticism," in *Feminist Theory: A Critique of Ideology,* ed. Nannerl O. Keohane, Michelle Z. Rosaldo, and Barbara C. Gelpi (Chicago: University of Chicago Press, 1982), 209–11.

23. See Friedrich Engels, *The Origin of the Family, Private Property, and the State* (New York: International Publishers, 1972). See also Karl Marx and Friedrich Engels, *The German Ideology,* part 1, ed. C. J. Arthur (New York: International Publishers, 1981), 44, 52, passim.

24. The extent to which a theorized twentieth-century U.S. capitalism was defined by its Manichaean other—communism or socialism—began to become evident in the years following *perestroika, glasnost,* and the democratization of formerly statist socialist states. We in the United States have not fully analyzed or understood the dependence of the particularly corrupt form of capitalism practiced in the United States on the function of the Communist Soviet union and its satellites as a worse alternative. Nor do current government officials seem to realize or acknowledge the ways in which the practice of U.S. capitalism will change now that its defining other is radically changing. Its own failures and corruptions will undoubtedly be foregrounded by the collapse of the Communist threat. It may be difficult to further postpone examining the manner in which the United States uses socialist fiscal and monetary strategies to support the nonpoor, the military-government-industrial complex, and capital accumulation (85% of domestic social outlays support the nonpoor, while tax expenditures in the form of credits, deductions, and depreciation allowances effectively and significantly subsidize capital). See Michael Harrington, *The Next Left: The History of a Future* (New York: Holt, 1986), 51, passim.

25. Michael Dukakis inadvertently served such a sacrificial function in the 1988 presidential sound-bite campaign. Michael Aronson and Christopher J. Georges have shown, point for point, how quickly Bush adopted many of Dukakis's major policies: fiscal policy, housing reform, gun control legislation, health care program revisions, and environmental policies, among others. ("Dukakis Triumphs," *New York Times,* June 7, 1990).

26. E. L. Doctorow, "The State of Mind of the Union," *Nation,* March 22, 1986: 327–32, 328.

CHAPTER 5. *THE PUBLIC BURNING.*

1. LeClair and McCaffery, *Anything Can Happen,* 77.

2. Donald Hall, "Three Million Toothpicks," *National Review,* September 30, 1977, 1118; Robert Tower, "Nixon's Seventh Crisis," *New York Review of Books,* September 29, 1977, 8; Norman Podhoretz, "Uncle Sam and the Phantom," *Saturday Review,* September 9, 1977, 27–28, 34; Tom LeClair, "The Public Burning by Robert Coover," *New Republic,* September 17, 1977, 38.

3. LeClair and McCaffery, *Anything Can Happen,* 75–76.

4. Bertolt Brecht, paraphrased by Eagleton, "Aesthetics and Politics," 21–37.

5. Burke, *Rhetoric of Religion,* 305.

6. Ibid., 240–41. Myth is to be understood in this section in its Levi-Straussian structural definition as a unified narrative that functions culturally to reconcile irreconcilable or antagonistic historical phenomena. See chap. 1, n. 9.

7. Kenneth Burke, *Permanence and Change: An Anatomy of Purpose,* 3d ed. (Berkeley: University of California Press, 1984), 89–90. As Paul Jay points out, Burke prefigured poststructuralist practice, but always with political and ethical positionality. Both Burke and Jacques Derrida construe language as instrumentality, and interrogate texts on the basis of the relationships that inhere between metaphor and knowledge; both use stylistic interventions to unsettle assumed categories and oppositions, and both "aim neither at recovery or death, but at sustaining the dis-ease that constitutes the critical condition." This is precisely Coover's project and achievement in *Public Burning.* See Paul Jay, "Modernism, Postmodernism, and Critical Style: The Case of Burke and Derrida," *Genre* 21, no. 3 (Fall 1988): 356.

8. Jay, "Modernism," 351, 353.

9. Doctorow, *Daniel,* 37.

10. See Ernst Bloch et al., *Aesthetics and Politics* (London: New Left Books, 1978). Two radical postmodernist fiction writers, Christine Brooke-Rose and Raymond Federman, whose work is considered antirealist, both insist that "the novel cannot escape realism" (Christine Brooke-Rose, "Eximplosions," and Raymond Federman, "What Are Experimental Novels and Why Are There So Many Left Unread?" *Genre* 14, no. 1 [Spring 1981]: 9–22, 23–31).

11. Burke, *Permanence and Change,* 107; Jay, "Modernism," 353.

12. Jay, "Modernism," 356. *Sacrificial fiction* refers to writing that accomplishes its critical and political objectives by unsettling generic expectations and assumptions, as well as cultural notions of literary decorum, to the extent that it fails to satisfy or actively offends a general audience. *Ulysses* and *Gravity's Rainbow* are sacrificial in this sense, but they are also elitist, excluding a general audience in their erudition and highly allusive style. Much postmodern fiction is popular in its images, allusions, and humor but frustrates its audience because of the antinarrative, antirealist, antiindividualist standpoint from which it is generated. Discovering how all this comes together in some postmodern literary and visual arts to sustain "the dis-ease that constitutes the critical condition" is a challenge for artist, critic, and audience in the late twentieth century.

13. Frank Gado, "Robert Coover," in *First Person: Conversations on Writers and Writing* (Schenectady, N.Y.: Union College Press, 1973), 149–50.

14. See Bibliographical Note for selected criticism of literary postmodernism.

15. Gado, "Robert Coover," 142–43.

16. See Richard Rorty, *Contingency, Irony, and Solidarity* (Cambridge: Cambridge University Press, 1989), for a philosophical, historical, and political exploration of the implications of the priority of language systems in shaping what is perceived as reality and truth in any given period. While acknowledging that no one person can "manage" or "develop" a more adequate language, he insists on individual agency in imagining and using new and "better" language as incrementally significant in working toward a better world.

17. LeClair and McCaffery, *Anything Can Happen*, 69; see also Georg Lukács, *History and Class Consciousness: Studies in Marxist Dialectics* (Cambridge, Mass.: MIT Press, 1968), 83–110; and Carolyn Porter, *Seeing and Being: The Plight of the Participant Observer in Emerson, James, Adams, and Faulkner* (Middletown, Conn.: Wesleyan University Press, 1981), 23–30, passim.

18. Gado, "Robert Coover," 148.

19. LeClair and McCaffery, *Anything Can Happen*, 72.

20. The Greek word *histor* refers to "not a recorder or recounter but an [inquirer or] investigator [who] examines the past with an eye toward separating out actuality from myth." The histor's authority comes from a critical spirit and methodology, not from the authority of his sources (Robert Scholes and Robert Kellog, *The Nature of Narrative* [New York: Oxford University Press, 1966], 58, 242–43).

21. There are also specific echoes of another grand epic, Milton's *Paradise Lost*. Nixon, after his marriage and after his return from the war, feels "the whole world before him" as did Adam and Eve when they were sent from the garden after the Fall. But as expected in a parodic epic inversion, Nixon resolves his post-Fall dilemma of freedom by a problematic choice of allegiance to Mammon, in the form of Uncle Sam, whose actions are not that different in effect from those attributed to the evil Phantom, the Soviet Union.

22. Leo J. Hertzel, "Interview with Robert Coover," *Critique* 11, no. 3 (1969): 28.

23. The August 12, 1950, *New York Times* headline the day after Ethel Rosenberg's arrest, "Atomic Spy Plot Laid to Woman," is an example, I would suggest, of the largely unperceived continuum of rhetoricity that is culturally operative—in excess of any individual intention—in shaping and interpreting material history.

24. LeClair and McCaffery, *Anything Can Happen*, 74.

25. See chap. 1, n. 71.

26. Schneir and Schneir, *Invitation to an Inquest*, 52–53.

27. LeClair and McCaffery, *Anything Can Happen*, 75. See also Burke, *Rhetoric of Religion:* "There is a sense in which the principle of personality does sum up or implicitly contain, the kind of social and political order in which it participates. We could even say, without straining a point, that *every* member of a given order in his way 'represents' that order" (310).

28. Peter Nelson, "An Interview with Robert Coover," *Telescope* 4, no. 1 (1985): 24–25.

29. Theodor Adorno, "Commitment," *New Left Review* 87–88 (September-December 1974): 87.

30. See Fiedler, *Love and Death*. Fiedler notes a general failure of U.S. fictionists to deal with adult heterosexual love and an obsession with death, incest, and innocent homosexuality. He insists, correctly, on the cultural influence of such representations, that these "are not merely matters of historical interest or literary relevance. They affect the lives we lead from day to day." And he notes the possibility that the nation's fictionists are operating under the cultural constraints of a "pattern imposed by the conditions of life in the United States that no writer can escape no matter what philosophy he consciously adopts or what theme he thinks he pursues" (Fiedler, *Love and Death*, xi). This view is consistent with feminist materialist analyses of the reciprocal effects of cultural texts and artifacts with social conditions and material history in a twentieth-century masculist capitalist society.

31. Katharine Wallingford points out the similarity of Nixon's image of Ethel as a little girl pulling up her underpants to Benjy's remembered image of Caddy's muddy underpants in William Faulkner's *The Sound and the Fury*. This intertextual image recalls Fiedler's thesis concerning the immaturity and limitations of U.S. fiction's representation of men's perceptions of female sexuality (conversation with Wallingford; Fiedler, *Love and Death*).

32. Eve Sedgewick, noting that the relation of sexual desire to political power and of sexual alienation to political repression is an actual but unstable relationship hard to articulate, values literature for its access to "oblique paths of meaning" in "panic-inducing images of real violence, especially the violence of, around, and to sexuality." Sexuality can act as signifier for various and more or less specific practices of power and subjugation among races, classes, and genders (Eve Kosofsky Sedgwick, *Between Men: English Literature and Male Homosocial Desire* [New York: Columbia University Press, 1985], 10–11).

CHAPTER 6. CLOSURE

1. Stephanson, "Regarding Postmodernism," 54.

2. Much of the language if not the practice of psychoanalytic theory, especially in the United States, tenaciously holds to ahistorical and essentialist categories. But "development of ways of knowing" here refers to the formal cognitive skills of splitting and projective identification, the fundamental differentiating mechanisms—establishing difference and similarity—of language and cognition. If these mechanisms are historically determined, then the poststructuralist critique of language and meaning could indeed lead to a new epistemology. In this case, is the anal stage itself a product of binary logic, rather than a producer of it? I think not. As an apparently necessary bodily developmental stage involved with learning to hold and let go, it can only lead to a binary logic. But it is an immature and preliminary stage in psychogenic development; further development produces the ability for a situational and purposeful complicating and undoing of such logic. Apparently, anal logic must be learned and mastered before it can be critiqued, mitigated, and resisted for its costly simplifications. See chap. 1, n. 7.

3. Leonard Shengold, *Halo in the Sky: Observations on Anality and Defense* (New York: Guilford, 1988), 11, 19.

4. Jacques Derrida, *The Margins of Philosophy*, quoted in Jardine, *Gynesis*, 132.

5. Shengold, *Halo in the Sky*, 20.

6. Ibid., 37.

7. "There is a certain pederasty implicit in pedagogy. A greater man penetrates a lesser man with his knowledge. The *homo*sexuality means that both are measurable by the same standards, by which measure one is greater than the other. Irigaray uncovers a sublimated male homosexuality stucturing all our institutions: pedagogy, marriage, commerce, even Freud's theory of so-called heterosexuality. These structures necessarily exclude women, but are unquestioned because sublimated—raised from suspect homosexuality to secure homology, to the sexually indifferent logos, science, logic. . . . Once [heterosexuality] is exposed as an exchange of women between men, [it] reveals itself as a mediated form of homosexuality. All penetration, considered to be sadistic penetration of the body's defensive envelope, is thought according to the model of anal penetration. . . . The penetrated is a humiliated man." Once this penetration is conceived as also psychic and rhetorical, then the analogy between anal aggression and the reproduction of ideology in a masculist society is complete. See Gallop, *Daughter's Seduction*, 63–64, 84.

CHAPTER 7. FRAMED ARTS

1. Consider the arguments—won by the formalists—over the meaning of abstract expressionism or, more recently, over Pop art. Pop art is a perfect example of an art that wished to be deeply critical of contemporary society, through an ironizing intensification of the consumer-produced image, but failed to establish its own ironizing context. Not that the critical apparatus for Pop art has failed to provide that necessary context, but in the meantime, the art itself has been co-opted through elite consumption and trivialization.

2. Arthur C. Danto, "Art for Activism's Sake: The 1991 Whitney Biennial," *Nation*, June 3, 1991, 743–47. "Art, as it had been historically understood, came to an end in that strange and tumultuous decade [the 1960s]. . . . we have with Postmodernism in fact entered the Posthistorical phase of the history of art. It is a difficult but wonderful time to be alive" (Danto, "Introduction: Artphilohistocritisophory Today," in *Encounters and Reflections: Art in the Historical Present* [New York: Farrar Straus & Giroux, 1990], 6, 8).

3. Danto, "Art for Activism's Sake," 746.

4. Ibid., 747.

5. "Bad Aesthetic Times," in *Encounters and Reflections*, 299.

6. Donald Freed, *Inquest* (New York: Hill and Wang, 1969).

7. Clive Barnes, "Theater: 'Inquest' Opens," *New York Times*, April 4, 1970; and Walter Kerr, "'Inquest': Kerr Votes Against It," *New York Times Sunday Magazine*, May 3, 1970.

8. Quoted from FBI memoranda, Rob Okun, ed., *The Rosenbergs: Collected Visions of Artists and Writers* (New York: Universe, 1988), 100.

9. Donald Freed, interviewed by Beatrice Berg, "'Inquest': Its Author Speaks For It," *New York Times Sunday Magazine*, May 3, 1970.

10. Kenneth Burke, in his study of the psychology of form, criticizes the substitute of information for form: "Thus, the great influx of information has led the artist to lay his emphasis on the giving of information—with the result that art tends more and more to substitute the psychology of the hero (subject) for the psychology of the audience" ("Psychology and Form," *Counter-Statement* [Berkeley: University of California Press, 1968], 32).

11. See *The Rosenbergs: Collected Visions of Artists and Writers,* ed. Rob A. Okun (New York: Universe, 1988). By the end of 1991 "Unknown Secrets" had been exhibited at the Hillwood Museum at Long Island University in Brookville, the North Gallery at the Massachusetts College of the Arts in Boston, the Olin Gallery at Kenyon College, the Palmer Museum at Pennsylvania State University, the University of Colorado in Boulder, San Diego State University, Otis-Parsons Institute in Los Angeles, the San Francisco Jewish Museum, the Spertus Museum in Chicago, the Charlotte, N.C., Spirit Square Center for the Arts, a double exhibit at the Brody and Addison-Ripley galleries in Washington, D.C., and the Vermont College Art Center in Montpelier.

12. Kramer and Will quoted by John Strand, "Unquiet Ghosts," *Museum & Arts Washington,* January/February 1991, 25; for Kramer see also Leo Seligsohn, "Renewed Fervor Over the Rosenbergs," *Weekend, New York Newsday,* September 30, 1988, 11. Lippard quoted in *Publishers Weekly,* November 11, 1988, 30. George Will's strategy of identifying specific and particularly imaginative left cultural and political critical work as disloyal and treacherous bespeaks self-limiting blindness in an analyst whose own specific criticisms of the United States are often astute. He denounced as a "bad influence" Don DeLillo's *Libra* (1988) that analyzes the events of history—the Kennedy assassination, in this case—as collective enterprises larger than but fueled by the disparate expressions of individual (U.S.) desires. DeLillo himself, according to Will, is a "literary vandal and bad citizen." See Frank Lentricchia, "The American Writer as Bad Citizen— Introducing Don DeLillo," *South Atlantic Quarterly* 89, no. 2 (Spring 1990): 241.

13. See Martha Rosler, "In, Around, and Afterthoughts," *3 Works* (Halifax, Nova Scotia: Nova Scotia College of Art and Design Press, 1981), 59–86; and Martha Gever, "An Interview with Martha Rosler," *Afterimage* 9 (October 1981): 10–17.

14. Martha Rosler, "Notes on Quotes," *Wedge* 2 (Fall 1982): 72.

15. Murray Chotiner was Nixon's Lee Atwater. Managing Nixon's 1950 California senatorial race, he devised the "pink lady" anticommunist campaign against Nixon's opponent, Helen Gahagan Douglas. He also coached Nixon for his Checkers and cloth coat speech, which returned him to Eisenhower's good graces.

16. Benjamin H. D. Buchloh, "Allegorical Procedures: Appropriation and Montage in Contemporary Art," *Artforum* 21, no. 1 (September 1982): 50.

17. Robert L. Pincus, "Perspectives on an Era Painted Red," *San Diego Union,* September 17, 1989.

18. See Robert Storr, "Peter Saul: The Uses of Disenchantment," Catalogue for the exhibit "Peter Saul" (Aspen, Colo.: Aspen Art Museum, 1989), p. 4 of Storr essay; see also "Peter Saul: Radical Distaste," *Art in America* 73, no. 1 (January 1985): 92.

19. See Peter Saul, "Artist's Statement," catalogue for the exhibit "Peter Saul" (Aspen, Colo.: Aspen Art Museum, 1989); see also Katherine Gregor, "An Interview with Peter Saul," available from Laguna Gloria Art Museum, Austin, Texas.

20. Laura Caruso, "Remembering the Rosenbergs," *Sunday Camera,* June 18, 1989.

EPILOGUE

1. Grotstein, *Splitting and Projective Identification* (New York: Aronson, 1981), 214.

Bibliographical Note

The most substantive historiographies of the Rosenberg story are William A. Reuben, *The Atom Spy Hoax* (New York: Action Books, 1955); John Wexley, *The Judgment of Julius and Ethel Rosenberg,* originally published in 1955 and revised in 1977 after release of FBI documents (New York: Cameron & Kahn, 1955); Walter Schneir and Miriam Schneir, *Invitation to an Inquest,* originally published in 1965, reprinted in 1967, 1968, 1973 and revised (New York: Pantheon, 1983); Ronald Radosh and Joyce Milton, *The Rosenberg File: A Search for the Truth* (New York: Holt, Rinehart & Winston, 1983); Robert Meeropol and Michael Meeropol, *We Are Your Sons: The Legacy of Julius and Ethel Rosenberg,* 2d ed., rev. (Urbana: University of Illinois Press, 1986); and Joseph H. Sharlitt, *Fatal Error: The Miscarriage of Justice that Sealed the Rosenbergs' Fate* (New York: Scribner, 1989). See also "Bibliographical Note" in Radosh and Milton.

There is a spectrum of critical theory and practice concerning the relationship of culture to history that bears on my project: that of Kenneth Burke, Mikhail Bakhtin, Walter Benjamin, Roland Barthes, Michel Foucault, Raymond Williams, Fredric Jameson, Frank Lentricchia, Hayden White, Dominique LaCapra, Robin Wagner-Pacifici, and Theodore Draper. Burke is always concerned with the motivations and real effects of the use of words, as well as with the shaping power of a binary language in the exercise of dominion. Bakhtin considered discursive signification "translinguistically," partaking of its concrete historical situation but never in a simply reiterative way. Benjamin in his "Theses on the Philosophy of History" notes the extent to which there is a continuity of dominant power within history and accordingly within the symbolic realm of art and culture, a continuity one must stand apart from to resist replicating that power through a naive historicism. Barthes, Foucault, LaCapra, and White, concerned with the ideological and material effects of discourse and oriented either toward language or toward history, call into question the distinctions between historical and fictional discourse without conflating them; Barthes focuses on rhetoric and semiotics, Foucault on the collective and cultural dispersals and reproductions of power differentials, LaCapra on the intertextuality of historiography and literature, and White on tropology and narrativity. Williams, Jameson, and Lentricchia privilege history and analyze the communications and reciprocal effects between cultural artifacts and material, processual history to better apprehend a given historical period and its prevalent socioeconomic relationships. Both Draper and Wagner-Pacifici perform a kind of cultural/historical analysis that I take as my methodological model.

Absent in most cases from these forms of theoretical work and cultural criticism are concepts and analyses of gender and race as primary categories structuring power relations. To the extent that gender and race are occluded, the work of these scholars remains inadequate and distorting to their object of study. Materialist-feminist critics, while never achieving an impossibly complete theory or practice, by privileging gender and race as well as class in varying and always problematic combinations as categories of analysis, have the potential for a cultural criticism that is more fully adequate to its object. The purpose of my analysis of the Rosenberg story is to explore the narrative structures and political operations of language as variously deriving from, discontinuous with, and productive, reproductive, or critical of historical circumstances. Since gender and race are throughout unavoidable critical analytic categories for the cold war period, I closely identify this project with the practice of materialist-feminist criticism.

See Burke's *The Rhetoric of Religion: Studies in Logology* (Boston: Beacon, 1961), *Permanence and Change: An Anatomy of Purpose,* 3d ed. (Berkeley: University of California Press, 1984), *Attitudes Toward History,* 3d ed. (Berkeley: University of

California Press, 1984), and *Counter-Statement,* originally published in 1931 (Berkeley: University of California Press, 1968). See also Tzvetan Todorov, *Mikhail Bakhtin: The Dialogical Principle,* trans. Wlad Godzich (Minneapolis: University of Minnesota Press, 1984), 24–27; Walter Benjamin, "Theses on the Philosophy of History," *Illuminations,* ed. Hannah Arendt (New York: Harcourt Brace & World, 1968), 253–64; Roland Barthes, *A Barthes Reader,* ed. Susan Sontag (New York: Hill and Wang, 1982); Theodore Draper, *A Present of Things Past: Selected Essays* (New York: Hill & Wang, 1990); Michel Foucault, *The Foucault Reader,* ed. Paul Rabinow (New York: Pantheon, 1984); Raymond Williams, *Marxism and Literature* (Oxford: Oxford University Press, 1977) and *Keywords: A Vocabulary of Culture and Society,* rev. ed. (New York: Oxford University Press, 1983); Fredric Jameson, *Marxism and Form: Twentieth-Century Dialectical Theories of Literature* (Princeton, N.J.: Princeton University Press, 1971) and *The Political Unconscious: Narrative as a Socially Symbolic Act* (Ithaca, N.Y.: Cornell University Press, 1981); Robin Erica Wagner-Pacifici, *The Moro Morality Play: Terrorism as Social Drama* (Chicago: University of Chicago Press, 1986); Frank Lentricchia, *Criticism and Social Change* (Chicago: University of Chicago Press, 1983); Hayden White, *Content of the Form: Narrative Discourse and Historical Representation* (Baltimore: Johns Hopkins University Press, 1987); Dominique LaCapra, *History and Criticism* (Ithaca, N.Y.: Cornell University Press, 1985); and Judith Newton and Deborah Rosenfelt, "Introduction: Toward a Materialist-Feminist Criticism," in *Feminist Criticism and Social Change: Sex, Class, and Race in Literature and Culture,* ed. Judith Newton and Deborah Rosenfelt (New York: Methuen, 1985), xv–xxxix.

For U.S. historiographical resources I have used Dean Acheson, *The Pattern of Responsibility,* ed. McGeorge Bundy (Boston: Houghton Mifflin, 1952), and *Present at the Creation: My Years in the State Department* (New York: Norton, 1969); Lloyd C. Gardner, ed., *American Foreign Policy, Present to Past: A Narrative with Readings and Documents.* (New York: Free Press, 1974); James Aronson, *The Press and the Cold War* (Boston: Beacon, 1970); Barton J. Bernstein and Allen J. Matusow, eds.,

Twentieth-Century America: Recent Interpretations (New York: Harcourt Brace & World, 1969); David Caute, *The Great Fear: The Anti-Communist Purge Under Truman and Eisenhower* (New York: Simon & Schuster, 1978); William H. Chafe, *The Unfinished Journey: America Since World War II* (New York: Oxford University Press, 1986); Terry L. Deibel and John Lewis Gaddis, eds., *Containing the Soviet Union: A Critique of US Policy* (Washington, D.C.: Pergamon-Brassey's International Defense Publishers, 1987); Morris Dickstein, *Gates of Eden: American Culture in the 60s* (New York: Basic, 1977); John Patrick Diggins, *The Proud Decades: America in War and Peace, 1941– 1960* (New York: Norton, 1989); Theodore Draper, *A Present of Things Past: Selected Essays* (New York: Hill and Wang, 1990); James Forrestal, *The Forrestal Diaries,* ed. Walter Millis (New York: Viking, 1951); Robert Griffith and Athan Theoharis, eds., *The Specter: Original Essays on the Cold War and the Origins of McCarthyism* (New York: Franklin Watts, 1974); Michael Harrington, *The New American Poverty* (New York: Penguin, 1984) and *The Next Left: The History of a Future* (New York: Holt, 1986); Susan M. Hartmann, *The Home Front and Beyond: American Women in the 1940s* (Boston: Twayne, 1982); Lillian Hellman, *Scoundrel Time* (Boston: Little, Brown, 1976); Irving Howe and Lewis Coser, *The American Communist Party: A Critical History* (New York: Praeger, 1962); Maurice Isserman, *If I Had a Hammer: The Death of the Old Left and the Birth of the New Left* (New York: Basic, 1987); George F. Kennan, *Memoirs, 1925– 1950* (Boston: Little, Brown, 1967) and *Russia and the West under Lenin and Stalin* (New York: New American Library, 1961); Phillip Knightley, *The Second Oldest Profession: Spies and Spying in the Twentieth Century* (New York: Norton, 1986); Lawrence Lader, *Power on the Left: American Radical Movements Since 1946* (New York: Norton, 1979); Walter Lippmann, *The Cold War: A Study in U.S. Foreign Policy* (New York: Harper Bros., 1947); George Lipsitz, *Class and Culture in Cold War America: "A Rainbow at Midnight"* (South Hadley, Mass.: Bergin, 1981); Aldon Morris, *The Origins of the Civil Rights Movement: Black Communities Organizing for Change* (New York: Free Press, 1984); Paul Nitze, with Ann M. Smith and Steven L.

Rearden, *From Hiroshima to Glasnost: At the Center of Decision, A Memoir* (New York: Grove Weidenfeld, 1989); Michael Parenti, *Inventing Reality: The Politics of the Mass Media* (New York: St. Martin's, 1986); Richard Gid Powers, *Secrecy and Power: The Life of J. Edgar Hoover* (New York: Free Press, 1987); Richard Rhodes, *The Making of the Atomic Bomb* (New York: Simon & Schuster, 1988); Michael Paul Rogin, *The Intellectuals and McCarthy: The Radical Specter* (Cambridge, Mass.: MIT Press, 1967); John Sharnik, *Inside the Cold War: An Oral History* (New York: Arbor House, 1987); Henry L. Stimson and McGeorge Bundy, *On Active Service in Peace and War* (New York: Harper Bros., 1947); Athan Theoharis, ed., *Beyond the Hiss Case: The FBI, Congress, and the Cold War* (Philadelphia: Temple University Press, 1982); Athan Theoharis and John Stuart Cox, *The Boss: J. Edgar Hoover and the Great American Inquisition* (Philadelphia: Temple University Press, 1982); Howard Zinn, *Postwar America: 1945–1971* (New York: Bobbs-Merrill, 1973) and *Declarations of Independence: Cross-Examining American Ideology* (New York: Harper Collins, 1990).

I have relied on the following articles and books to introduce me to critical issues of literary postmodernism: John Barth, "A Literature of Exhaustion" and "A Literature of Replenishment," *The Friday Book: Essays and Other Nonfiction* (New York: Putnam, 1985), 62–206. See also Linda Hutcheon, *A Poetics of Postmodernism: History, Theory, Fiction* (New York: Routledge, Chapman and Hale, 1988); Ihab Hassan, *The Postmodern Turn: Essays in Postmodern Theory and Culture* (Columbus: Ohio State University Press, 1987); Ronald Sukenick, *Death of the Novel and Other Stories* (New York: Dial, 1969), "The New Tradition," in *Postmodernism in American Literature: A Critical Anthology,* ed. Manfred Putz and Peter Freese (Darmstadt: Thesen-Verlag, 1984), 117–23, and *In Form: Digressions on the Act of Fiction* (Carbondale: Southern Illinois University Press, 1985); Raymond Federman, ed., *Surfiction: Fiction Now . . . and Tomorrow* (Chicago: Swallow, 1981), and Raymond Federman, "Self/Voice/Performance in Contemporary Writing," in *Coherence,* ed. Don Wellman (Cambridge, Mass.: O ARS Books, 1981), 195–99;

Bibliographical Note

Christine Brooke-Rose, *A Rhetoric of the Unreal: Studies in Narrative and Structure, Especially of the Fantastic* (Cambridge: Cambridge University Press, 1981); Douwe Fokkema, *Literary History, Modernism, and Postmodernism* (Amsterdam: John Benjamins, 1984); Douwe Fokkema and Hans Bertens, eds., *Approaching Postmodernism* (Amsterdam: John Benjamins, 1986); Hal Foster, ed., *The Anti-Aesthetic: Essays on Postmodern Culture* (Port Townsend, Wash.: Bay Press, 1983); Jerome Klinkowitz, *Literary Disruptions: The Making of a Post-Contemporary American Fiction* (Urbana: University of Illinois Press, 1980); Tom LeClair, *The Art of Excess: Mastery in Contemporary American Fiction* (Urbana: University of Illinois Press, 1989). For a counterview, see Gerald Graff, *Literature Against Itself* (Chicago: University of Chicago Press, 1979), and Charles Newman, *The Postmodern Aura: The Act of Fiction in an Age of Inflation* (Evanston, Ill.: Northwestern University Press, 1985). Feminist critiques fault male postmodern fiction for its repetitive and formal gestures of linguistic undoing with no imaginative envisioning of a better order. Female postmodern fiction writers tend more toward the positing of and engagement in alternative worlds, a recombinatory fiction that imagines a new social political order—as in the work of Joanna Russ, Toni Morrison, and Octavia Butler, among others.

Bibliography

Acheson, Dean. *The Pattern of Responsibility.* Edited by McGeorge Bundy. Boston: Houghton Mifflin, 1952.

———. *Present at the Creation: My Years in the State Department.* New York: Norton, 1969.

Adams, Henry. *The Education of Henry Adams: An Autobiography.* Boston: Houghton Mifflin, 1918.

Adorno, Theodor. "Commitment." *New Left Review* 87-88 (September-December 1974): 75-89.

Althusser, Louis. "Ideology and Ideological State Apparatuses (Notes Toward an Investigation)." In *Essays on Ideology,* 1–60. London: Verso, 1984.

Aronowitz, Stanley. *Crisis in Historical Materialism: Class, Politics, and Culture in Marxist Theory.* 2d ed. Minneapolis: University of Minnesota Press, 1990.

———. "Postmodernism and Politics." In *Universal Abandon? The Politics of Postmodernism,* ed. Andrew Ross, 46-62. Minneapolis: University of Minnesota Press, 1988.

Aronson, James. *The Press and the Cold War.* Boston: Beacon, 1970.

Bailyn, Bernard, and David Brion Davis, David Herbert Donald, John L. Thomas, Robert H. Wiebe, and Gordon S. Wood. *The Great Republic: A History of the American People.* 3rd ed. Lexington, Mass.: Heath, 1985.

Bakhtin, M. M. *The Dialogic Imagination.* Translated by Caryl Emerson and Michael Holquist. Austin: University of Texas Press, 1981.

Barkhausen, Jochen. "Determining the True Color of the Chameleon: The Confusing Recovery of History in E. L. Doctorow's *Loon Lake.*" In *E. L. Doctorow: A Democracy of Perception: A Symposium with and on E. L. Doctorow,* ed. Herwig Friedl and Dieter Schulz, 125-47. Essen: Verlag Die Blaue Eule, 1988.

Barth, John. "A Literature of Exhaustion" and "A Literature of Replenishment." In *The Friday Book: Essays and Other Nonfiction,* 62-206. New York: Putnam, 1985.

Barthes, Roland. "The Discourse of History." Translated by Stephen Bann. In *Comparative Criticism: A Yearbook,* vol. 3, ed. E. S. Schaffer, 3–20. Cambridge: Cambridge University Press, 1981.

Benjamin, Walter. "Theses on the Philosophy of History." In *Illuminations,* ed. Hannah Arendt, 253-64. New York: Harcourt Brace & World, 1968.

Berger, Maurice. "Of Cold Wars and Curators." *Artforum* 27, no. 6 (February 1989): 86-92.

Bibliography

Bernstein, Barton J., ed. *Towards a New Past: Dissenting Essays in American History*. New York: Random House, 1968.

Bernstein, Barton J. and Allen J. Matusow, eds. *Twentieth-Century America: Recent Interpretations*. New York: Harcourt Brace & World, 1969.

Bloch, Ernst, and Georg Lukács, Bertolt Brecht, Walter Benjamin, and Theodor Adorno. *Aesthetics and Politics*. London: New Left, 1978.

Brooke-Rose, Christine. "Eximplosions." *Genre* 14, no. 1 (Spring 1981): 9-22.

———. *A Rhetoric of the Unreal: Studies in Narrative and Structure, Especially of the Fantastic*. Cambridge: Cambridge University Press, 1981.

Buchloh, Benjamin H. D. "Allegorical Procedures: Appropriation and Montage in Contemporary Art. *Artforum* 21, no. 1 (September 1982): 43-56.

Burke, Kenneth. *Attitudes Toward History*. 3d ed. Berkeley: University of California Press, 1984.

———. *Counter-Statement*. Berkeley: University of California Press, 1968.

———. *Language as Symbolic Action: Essays on Life, Literature, and Method*. Berkeley: University of California Press, 1968.

———. *Permanence and Change: An Anatomy of Purpose*. 3d ed. Berkeley: University of California Press, 1984.

———. *The Philosophy of Literary Form: Studies in Symbolic Action*. Berkeley: University of California Press, 1967.

———. *The Rhetoric of Religion: Studies in Logology*. Boston: Beacon, 1961.

Caute, David. *The Great Fear: The Anti-Communist Purge under Truman and Eisenhower*. New York: Simon & Schuster, 1978.

Chafe, William H. *The Unfinished Journey: America Since World War II*. New York: Oxford University Press, 1986.

Chodorow, Nancy. *Reproducing Motherhood: Psychoanalysis and the Sociology of Gender*. Berkeley: University of California Press, 1978.

Connell, R. W. *Gender and Power: Society, the Person, and Sexual Politics*. Cambridge: Polity, 1987.

Considine, Bob. *It's All News to Me: A Reporter's Deposition*. New York: Meredith, 1967.

Coover, Robert. *The Public Burning*. New York: Viking, 1977.

———. *The Universal Baseball Association, Inc., J. Henry Waugh, Prop.* New York: Random House, 1968.

Danto, Arthur C. "Art for Activism's Sake: The 1991 Whitney Biennial." *Nation*, June 3, 1991, 743-47.

———. *Encounters and Reflections: Art in the Historical Present*. New York: Farrar Straus & Giroux, 1990.

Deibel, Terry L., and John Lewis Gaddis, eds. *Containing the Soviet Union: A Critique of US Policy*. Washington, D.C.: Pergamon-Brassey's International Defense Publishers, 1987.

DeLillo, Don. *Libra*. New York: Penguin Books, 1988.

de Man, Paul. "Literary History and Literary Modernity." In *Blindness and Insight: Essays in the Rhetoric of Contemporary Criticism*. 2d ed., rev., 142-65. Minneapolis: University of Minnesota Press, 1983.

Derrida, Jacques. *The Margins of Philosophy*. Translated by Alan Bass. Brighton, England: Harvester, 1982.

Bibliography

Dickstein, Morris. "Cold War Blues: Politics and Culture in the Fifties." In *Gates of Eden: American Culture in the 60s*, 25-50. New York: Basic, 1977.

Diggins, John Patrick. *The Proud Decades: America in War and Peace, 1941-60*. New York: Norton, 1988.

Dinnerstein, Dorothy. *The Mermaid and the Minotaur: Sexual Arrangements and Human Malaise*. New York: Harper & Row, 1976.

Doctorow, E. L. *The Book of Daniel*. New York: Ballantine, 1971.

———. "Living in the House of Fiction." *Nation*, April 22, 1978, 459-62.

———. "United States: The State of Mind of the Union," *Nation*, March 22, 1986, 360–64.

Draper, Theodore. "American Hubris: From Truman to the Persian Gulf." *New York Review of Books*, July 16, 1987, 40-48.

———. *A Present of Things Past: Selected Essays*. New York: Hill and Wang, 1990.

Eagleton, Terry. "Aesthetics and Politics." *New Left Review* 107 (January-February 1978): 21-34.

———. *Marxism and Literary Criticism*. Berkeley: University of California Press, 1976.

Edsall, Thomas, and Mary Edsall. *Chain Reaction: The Impact of Race, Rights, and Taxes on American Politics*. New York: Norton, 1991.

Eisenhower, Dwight David. *The White House Years: Mandate for Change 1953–1956*. Garden City, N.Y.: Doubleday, 1963.

Engels, Friedrich. *The Origin of the Family, Private Property, and the State*. New York: International Publishers, 1972.

Federman, Raymond. "Self/Voice/Performance in Contemporary Writing." In *Coherence*, ed. Don Wellman, 195-99. Cambridge, Mass.: O ARS Books, 1981.

———, ed. *Surfiction: Fiction Now . . . and Tomorrow*. Chicago: Swallow, 1981.

———. "What Are Experimental Novels and Why Are There So Many Left Unread?" *Genre* 14, no. 1 (Spring 1981): 23–31.

Fiedler, Leslie. "A Postscript to the Rosenberg Case." *Encounter*, October, 1953, 12–21 (published also as "Afterthoughts on the Rosenbergs." In *Collected Essays of Leslie Fiedler*, 1:25–45. New York: Stein, 1971).

———. *Love and Death in the American Novel*. New York: New American Library, 1962.

Fish, Stanley. *Is There a Text in This Class? The Authority of Interpretive Communities*. Cambridge, Mass.: Harvard University Press, 1980.

———. "The Law Wishes to Have a Formal Existence." Paper presented at symposium, "Law, Deconstruction, and the Possibility of Justice," Cardozo School of Law, New York City, October 2-3, 1989.

Fokkema, Douwe. *Literary History, Modernism, and Postmodernism*. Amsterdam: John Benjamins, 1984.

Fokkema, Douwe, and Hans Bertens, eds. *Approaching Postmodernism*. Amsterdam: John Benjamins, 1986.

Foley, Barbara. "From USA to Ragtime: Notes on the Form of Historical Consciousness in Modern Fiction." In *E. L. Doctorow: Essays and Conversations*, ed. Richard Trenner, 158–78. Princeton, N.J.: Ontario Review Press, 1983.

Bibliography

Forrestal, James. *The Forrestal Diaries*. Edited by Walter Millis. New York: Viking, 1951.

Foster Hal, ed. *The Anti-Aesthetic: Essays on Postmodern Culture*. Port Townsend, Wash.: Bay Press, 1983.

Frankfurter, Felix. Frankfurter Papers. Cambridge, Mass.: Harvard Law School Library.

Freed, Donald. *Inquest*. New York: Hill and Wang, 1969.

Gado, Frank. "Robert Coover." In *First Person: Conversations on Writers and Writing,* 142–59. Schenectady, N.Y.: Union College Press, 1973.

Gallop, Jane. *The Daughter's Seduction: Feminism and Psychoanalysis*. Ithaca, N.Y.: Cornell University Press, 1982.

Gardner, Lloyd C., ed. *American Foreign Policy, Present to Past: A Narrative with Readings and Documents*. New York: Free Press, 1974.

Geoghegan, Thomas. *Which Side Are You On? Trying to Be for Labor When It's Flat on Its Back*. New York: Farrar, Straus & Giroux, 1991.

Gever, Martha. "An Interview with Martha Rosler." *Afterimage* (October 1981): 10–17.

Goldberg, Jonathan. "The Politics of Renaissance Literature: a Review Essay." *ELH* 49, no. 2 (Summer 1982): 514–42.

Goldstein, Alvin (producer). *The Unquiet Death of Julius and Ethel Rosenberg*. Rev. New York: Impact Video; Chicago: Icarus Films, 1985.

Graff, Gerald. *Literature Against Itself*. Chicago: University of Chicago Press, 1979.

Greenblatt, Stephen. "Introduction." *The Forms of Power and The Power of Forms in the Renaissance,* ed. Stephen Greenblatt, 3–6. *Genre* 15, nos. 1–2 (Spring-Summer 1982).

———. "Invisible Bullets: Renaissance Authority and Its Subversion." In *Glyph* 8, ed. Walter Benn Michaels, 40–61. Baltimore: Johns Hopkins University Press, 1981.

Greenhouse, Linda. "Guilt or Innocence Aside." *New York Times Book Review,* August 6, 1989, 1.

Gregar, Katherine. "An Interview with Peter Saul." Laguna Gloria Art Museum Archives, Austin, Tex.

Greimas, A. J. *Structural Semantics: An Attempt at a Method*. Translated by Daniele McDowell, Ronald Schleifer, and Alan Velie. Lincoln: University of Nebraska Press, 1983.

Griffith, Robert. *The Specter: Original Essays on the Cold War and the Origins of McCarthyism,* ed. Robert Griffith and Athan Theoharis. New York: Franklin Watts, 1974.

Grotstein, James S. *Splitting and Projective Identification*. New York: Aronson, 1981.

Hall, Donald. "Three Million Toothpicks." *National Review,* September 30, 1977, 1118–20.

Haraway, Donna J. "A Cyborg Manifesto." In *Simians, Cyborgs, and Women: The Reinvention of Nature,* 149–81. New York: Routledge, 1991.

Harrington, Michael. *The New American Poverty*. New York: Penguin, 1984.

———. *The Next Left: The History of a Future*. New York: Holt, 1986.

Bibliography

Hartmann, Heidi. "The Unhappy Marriage of Marxism and Feminism: Towards a More Progressive Union." In *Women and Revolution: A Discussion of the Unhappy Marriage of Marxism and Feminism,* ed. Lydia Sargent, 1–41. Boston: South End, 1981.

Hartmann, Susan M. *The Home Front and Beyond: American Women in the 1940s.* Boston: Twayne, 1982.

Hassan, Ihab. *The Postmodern Turn: Essays in Postmodern Theory and Culture.* Columbus: Ohio State University Press, 1987.

Hegel, Georg Wilhelm Friedrich. *Lectures on the Philosophy of History.* Translated by J. Sibree. New York: Willey, 1944.

Hellman, Lillian. *Scoundrel Time.* Boston: Little, Brown, 1976.

Hertzel, Leo. "Interview with Robert Coover." *Critique* 11, no. 3 (1969): 25–29.

Hodgson, Godfrey. *Biography of Henry Stimson.* New York: Viking, 1988.

Holloway, David. "Entering the Nuclear Arms Race: The Soviet Decision to Build the Atomic Bomb, 1939–45." *Social Studies of Science* 11, no. 2 (1981): 159–97.

Hoover, J. Edgar. "To All His Law Enforcement Officials." *FBI Law Enforcement Bulletin* 30 (June 1961): 1, 2.

Howe, Irving, and Lewis Coser. *The American Communist Party: A Critical History.* New York: Praeger, 1962.

———. "Radical Criticism and the American Intellectuals." In *Steady Work,* 3–35. New York: Harcourt Brace & World, 1966.

Hutcheon, Linda. *A Poetics of Postmodernism: History, Theory, Fiction.* New York: Routledge, Chapman and Hale, 1988.

Hyde, H. Montgomery. *The Atom Bomb Spies.* New York: Atheneum, 1980.

Irons, Peter H. "American Business and the Origins of McCarthyism: The Cold War Crusade of the United States Chamber of Commerce." In *The Specter: Original Essays on the Cold War and the Origins of McCarthyism,* ed. Robert Griffith and Athan Theoharis, 72–89. New York: Franklin Watts, 1974.

Isserman, Maurice. *If I Had a Hammer: The Death of the Old Left and the Birth of the New Left.* New York: Basic, 1987.

Jackson, Robert. Jackson Papers. Washington, D.C.: Library of Congress.

Jameson, Fredric. "The Ideology of the Text." In *The Ideologies of Theory: Essays, 1971-1986,* 17–71. Vol. 1 of *Situations of Theory.* Minneapolis: University of Minnesota Press, 1988.

———. *Marxism and Form: Twentieth-Century Dialectical Theories of Literature.* Princeton, N.J.: Princeton University Press, 1971.

———. "Marxism and Postmodernism." *New Left Review* 176 (July–August 1989): 31–45.

———. "On Interpretation." In *The Political Unconscious: Narrative as a Socially Symbolic Act,* 17–102. Ithaca, N.Y.: Cornell University Press, 1981.

———. "Postmodernism, or the Cultural Logic of Late Capitalism." *New Left Review* 146 (July–August 1984): 53–92.

Jardine, Alice. *Gynesis: Configurations of Woman and Modernity.* Ithaca, N.Y.: Cornell University Press, 1985.

Jay, Paul. "Modernism, Postmodernism, and Critical Style: The Case of Burke and Derrida." *Genre* 21, no. 3 (Fall 1988): 339–58.

Bibliography

Jehlen, Myra. "Archimedes and the Paradox of Feminist Criticism." In *Feminist Theory: A Critique of Ideology,* ed. Nannerl O. Keohane, Michelle Z. Rosaldo, and Barbara C. Gelpi, 189–215. Chicago: University of Chicago Press, 1982.

Joughin, G. Louis, and Edmund M. Morgan. *The Legacy of Sacco and Vanzetti.* New York: Harcourt, Brace, 1948.

Kauffmann, Stanley. "Wrestling Society for a Soul." *New Republic,* June 5, 1971, 25–27.

"The Kaufman Papers." New York: National Committee to Reopen the Rosenberg Case, 1976. Pamphlet.

Keeley, Edmund. *The Salonika Bay Murder.* Princeton: Princeton University Press, 1989.

Keller, William W. *The Liberals and J. Edgar Hoover: The Rise and Fall of a Domestic Intelligence State.* Princeton, N.J.: Princeton University Press, 1989.

Kennan, George F. *Memoirs, 1925–1950.* Boston: Little, Brown, 1967.

———. *Russia and the West under Lenin and Stalin.* New York: New American Library, 1961.

——— [Mr. X]. "The Sources of Soviet Conduct." *Foreign Affairs* 25, no. 4 (July 1947): 566–82.

Khrushchev, Nikita. *Khrushchev Remembers: The Glasnost Tapes.* Translated and edited by Jerrold L. Schecter, with Vyacheslav V. Luchkov. New York: Little, Brown, 1990.

King, Richard. "Between Simultaneity and Sequence." In *E. L. Doctorow: A Democracy of Perception: A Symposium with and on E. L. Doctorow,* ed. Herwig Friedl and Dieter Schulz, 45–60. Essen: Verlag Die Blaue Eule, 1988.

Klehr, Harvey. *The Heyday of American Communism.* New York: Basic, 1984.

Klinkowitz, Jerome. *Literary Disruptions: The Making of a Post-Contemporary American Fiction.* Urbana: University of Illinois Press, 1980.

Knightley, Phillip. *The Second Oldest Profession: Spies and Spying in the Twentieth Century,* 258–67. New York: Norton, 1986.

Kristeva, Julia. *The Powers of Horror: An Essay on Abjection.* Translated by Leon S. Roudiez. New York: Columbia University Press, 1982.

Lacan, Jacques. *Le Séminaire livre XX: Encore.* Paris: Éditions du Seuil, 1975.

Laclau, Ernesto. "Metaphor and Social Antagonisms." In *Marxism and the Interpretation of Culture,* ed. Cary Nelson and Lawrence Grossberg, 249–57. Urbana: University of Illinois Press, 1988.

———. "Politics and the Limits of Modernity." In *Universal Abandon? The Politics of Postmodernism,* ed. Andrew Ross, 63-82. Minneapolis: University of Minnesota Press, 1989.

Lader, Lawrence. *Power on the Left: American Radical Movements Since 1946.* New York: Norton, 1979.

Langer, Elinor. "The Case of Morton Sobell: New Queries from the Defense." *Science: American Association for the Advancement of Science* 153, no. 3743 (September 23, 1966): 1501–5.

Larrowe, Charles P. *Harry Bridges: Rise and Fall of Radical Labor in the United States.* New York: Laurence Hill, 1972.

Lasch, Christopher. "The Cultural Cold War: A Short History of the Congress for Cultural Freedom." In *Towards a New Past: Dissenting Essays in American History,* ed. Barton J. Bernstein, 322–59. New York: Random House, 1968.

Bibliography

LeClair, Tom. *The Art of Excess: Mastery in Contemporary American Fiction.* Urbana: University of Illinois Press, 1989.

———. "*The Public Burning* by Robert Coover." *New Republic,* September 17, 1977, 37-38.

LeClair, Tom and Larry McCaffery, eds. *Anything Can Happen: Interviews with Contemporary American Novelists.* Urbana: University of Illinois Press, 1983.

Lentricchia, Frank. "The American Writer as Bad Citizen—Introducing Don DeLillo." *South Atlantic Quarterly* 89, no. 2 (Spring 1990): 239–44.

———. *Criticism and Social Change.* Chicago: University of Chicago Press, 1983.

Lévi-Strauss, Claude. "The Structural Study of Myth." In *Structural Anthropology.* New York: Basic, 1963, 206-31.

Levin, Murray. *The Alienated Voter.* New York: Holt, Rinehart and Winston, 1960.

Lippmann, Walter. *The Cold War: A Study in U.S. Foreign Policy.* New York: Harper Bros., 1947.

Lipsitz, George. *Class and Culture in Cold War America: "A Rainbow at Midnight."* South Hadley, Mass.: Bergin, 1981.

Lukács, Georg. *History and Class Consciousness: Studies in Marxist Dialectics.* Cambridge, Mass.: MIT Press, 1968.

Macherey, Pierre. *A Theory of Literary Production.* Translated by Geoffrey Wall. New York: Routledge & Kegan Paul, 1978.

MacKinnon, Catherine A. *Toward a Feminist Theory of the State.* Cambridge, Mass.: Harvard University Press, 1989.

Marcuse, Herbert. "Affirmative Character of Culture." In *Negations: Essays in Critical Theory,* 88–133. Boston: Beacon, 1968.

Marton, Kati. *The Polk Conspiracy: Murder and Cover Up in the Case of CBS News Correspondent George Polk.* New York: Farrar Straus & Giroux, 1990.

Marx, Karl, and Friedrich Engels. *The German Ideology,* ed. C. J. Arthur. New York: International Publishers, 1981.

Matusow, Allen J., ed. *Joseph R. McCarthy.* Englewood Cliffs, N.J.: Prentice-Hall, 1970.

Matusow, Harvey. *False Witness.* New York: Cameron and Kahn, 1955.

Meeropol, Robert, and Michael Meeropol. *We Are Your Sons: The Legacy of Ethel and Julius Rosenberg.* 2d ed., rev. Urbana: University of Illinois Press, 1986.

Mills, C. Wright. *The Power Elite.* New York: Oxford University Press, 1956.

Morley, Jefferson. "Bush and the Blacks: An Unknown Story." *New York Review of Books,* January 16, 1992, 16–26.

Morris, Aldon. *The Origins of the Civil Rights Movement: Black Communities Organizing for Change.* New York: Free Press, 1984.

Mouffe, Chantal. "Radical Democracy: Modern or Postmodern." In *Universal Abandon? The Politics of Postmodernism,* ed. Andrew Ross, 31–45. Minneapolis: University of Minnesota Press, 1989.

Navasky, Victor. *Naming Names.* New York: Viking, 1980.

———. "Of 'Atom Spies' and Ambiguities." *Nation,* October 22, 1983, 353, 375–80.

———. "Weinstein, Hiss, and the Transformation of Historical Ambiguity into Cold War Verity." In *Beyond the Hiss Case: The FBI, Congress, and the Cold*

Bibliography

War, ed. Athan G. Theoharis, 215–45. Philadelphia: Temple University Press, 1982.

Nelson, Peter. "An Interview with Robert Coover." *Telescope* 4, no. 1 (1985): 24–27.

Newman, Charles. *The Postmodern Aura: The Act of Fiction in an Age of Inflation.* Evanston, Ill.: Northwestern University Press, 1985.

Newman, James. "Control of Information." *Yale Journal of Law* 56 (May 1947): 769–802.

Newton, Judith, and Deborah Rosenfelt. "Introduction: Toward a Materialist-Feminist Criticism." In *Feminist Criticism and Social Change: Sex, Class, and Race in Literature and Culture,* ed. Judith Newton and Deborah Rosenfelt, xv-xxxix. New York: Methuen, 1985.

Nietzsche, Friedrich. "On the Uses and Disadvantages of History for Life." In *Untimely Meditations,* translated by R. J. Hollingdale, 57–123. Cambridge: Cambridge University Press, 1983.

Nitze, Paul, with Ann M. Smith and Steven L. Rearden. *From Hiroshima to Glasnost: At the Center of Decision, A Memoir.* New York: Grove Weidenfeld, 1989.

Nizer, Louis. *The Implosion Conspiracy.* Garden City, N.Y.: Doubleday, 1973.

Okun, Rob A., ed. *The Rosenbergs: Collected Visions of Artists and Writers.* New York: Universe, 1988.

O'Neill, William. *Coming Apart.* New York: Quadrangle, 1971.

"Our Country and Our Culture: A Symposium." *Partisan Review* 19, no. 3 (May-June 1952): 282–326; no. 4 (July-August 1952): 420–50; no. 5 (September-October 1952): 562–97.

Parenti, Michael. *Inventing Reality: The Politics of the Mass Media.* New York: St. Martin's, 1986.

Parrish, Michael E. "The Supreme Court and the Rosenbergs." *American Historical Review* 82, no. 4 (October 1977): 805–41.

Philipson, Ilene. *Ethel Rosenberg: Beyond the Myths.* New York: Franklin Watts, 1988.

Pinter, Harold. "Language and Lies." *Index on Censorship* 17, no. 6 (June-July 1988): 2.

Podhoretz, Norman. "Uncle Sam and the Phantom." *Saturday Review,* September 17, 1977, 27–28, 34.

Porter, Carolyn. "Are We Being Historical Yet?" *South Atlantic Quarterly* 87, no. 4 (Fall 1988): 743–86.

———. *Seeing and Being: The Plight of the Participant Observer in Emerson, James, Adams, and Faulkner.* Middletown, Conn.: Wesleyan University Press, 1981.

Powers, Richard Gid. *Secrecy and Power: The Life of J. Edgar Hoover.* New York: Free Press, 1987.

Propp, Vladimir. *Morphology of the Folk Tale.* Translated by Laurence Scott. Austin: University of Texas Press, 1975.

Putz, Manfred, and Peter Freese, eds. *Postmodernism in American Literature: A Critical Anthology.* Darmstadt: Thesen-Verlag, 1984.

Bibliography

Radosh, Ronald. *American Labor and U.S. Foreign Policy.* New York: Random House, 1969.

Radosh, Ronald, and Eric Breindel. "Bombshell: The KGB Fesses Up." *New Republic,* June 10, 1991, 10-12.

Radosh, Ronald, and Joyce Milton. *The Rosenberg File: A Search for The Truth.* New York: Holt, Rinehart & Winston, 1983.

Reuben, William A. *The Atom Spy Hoax.* New York: Action Books, 1955.

Rhodes, Richard. *The Making of the Atomic Bomb.* New York: Simon & Schuster, 1988.

Riesman, David, and Nathan Glazer. "The Intellectuals and the Discontented Classes." *Partisan Review* 22, no. 1 (Winter 1955): 47-72 (published also in *The New American Right,* ed. Daniel Bell, 56-90. New York: Criterion, 1955).

Rogin, Michael Paul. *The Intellectuals and McCarthy: The Radical Specter.* Cambridge, Mass.: MIT Press, 1967.

Rooney, Ellen. *Seductive Reasoning: Pluralism as the Problematic of Contemporary Literary Theory.* Ithaca, N.Y.: Cornell University Press, 1985.

Rorty, Richard. *Contingency, Irony, and Solidarity.* Cambridge: Cambridge University Press, 1989.

Rosenberg, Ethel, and Julius Rosenberg. *Death House Letters.* New York: Jero, 1953.

———. *The Rosenberg Letters.* London: Dennis Dobson, 1953.

———. *The Testament of Ethel and Julius Rosenberg.* New York: Cameron and Kahn, 1954.

Rosler, Martha. "In, Around, and Afterthoughts." In *3 Works,* 59-86. Halifax, Nova Scotia: Nova Scotia College of Art and Design Press, 1981.

———. "Notes on Quotes." *Wedge* 2 (Fall 1982): 68-73.

Ross, Andrew. "Containing Culture in the Cold War." *Cultural Studies* 1, no. 3 (Winter 1987): 328-48.

———. "Intellectuals and Ordinary People: Reading the Rosenberg Letters." *Cultural Critique* 9 (Spring 1988): 55-86 (published also in *No Respect: Intellectuals and Pop Culture,* ed. Andrew Ross, 15-41. New York: Routledge & Kegan Paul, 1989).

Rovere, Richard. *Senator Joe McCarthy.* New York: Harcourt Brace, 1959.

Rubin, Gayle. "The Traffic in Women: Notes on the 'Political Economy' of Sex." In *Toward an Anthropology of Women,* ed. Rayna R. Reiter, 157-210. New York: Monthly Review Press, 1975.

Rubin, Jerry. *Do It!* New York: Simon & Schuster, 1979.

Salinger, J. D. *Catcher in the Rye.* Boston: Little, Brown, 1945.

Saul, Peter. "Artist's Statement." Catalogue for the exhibit "Peter Saul." Aspen, Colo.: Aspen Art Museum, 1989.

Schneir, Walter. "Time Bomb." *Nation,* December 3, 1990, 682-88.

Schneir, Walter, and Miriam Schneir. *Invitation to an Inquest.* New York: Pantheon, 1983.

Scholes, Robert, and Robert Kellog. *The Nature of Narrative.* New York: Oxford University Press, 1966.

Scott, John Anthony. "Greetings from Julius." New York: Fund for Open Information and Accountability, 1978.

Bibliography

Sedgewick, Eve Kosofsky. *Between Men: English Literature and Male Homosocial Desire.* New York: Columbia University Press, 1985.

Sharlitt, Joseph. *Fatal Error: The Miscarriage of Justice that Sealed the Rosenbergs' Fate.* New York: Scribner, 1989.

Sharnik, John. *Inside the Cold War: An Oral History.* New York: Arbor House, 1987.

Shengold, Leonard. *Halo in the Sky: Observations on Anality and Defense.* New York: Guilford, 1988.

Smith, Barbara Herrnstein. "Narrative Versions, Narrative Theories." In *On Narrative,* ed. W. J. T. Mitchell, 209–32. Chicago: University of Chicago Press, 1981.

Snyder, Louis L., ed. *Louis L. Snyder's Historical Guide to WWII.* Westport, Conn.: Greenwood, 1982.

Sobell, Martin. *On Doing Time.* New York: Scribner, 1974.

Spivak, Gayatri Chakravorty. "Scattered Speculations on the Question of Value." In *In Other Worlds: Essays in Cultural Politics,* 154–75. New York: Methuen, 1987.

Stephanson, Anders. "Regarding Postmodernism—A Conversation with Fredric Jameson." In *Universal Abandon? The Politics of Postmodernism,* ed. Andrew Ross, 3–30. Minneapolis: University of Minnesota Press, 1988.

Stimson, Henry L., and McGeorge Bundy. *On Active Service in Peace and War.* New York: Harper Bros., 1947.

Storr, Robert. "Peter Saul: Radical Distaste." *Art in America* 73, no. 1 (January 1985): 92—101.

———. "Peter Saul: The Uses of Disenchantment." Catalogue for the exhibit "Peter Saul." Aspen, Colo.: Aspen Art Museum, 1989.

Strand, John. "Unquiet Ghosts." *Museum & Arts Washington,* January/February 1991, 22–25.

Sukenick, Ronald. *Death of the Novel and Other Stories.* New York: Dial, 1969.

———. *In Form: Digressions on the Act of Fiction.* Carbondale: Southern Illinois University Press, 1985.

———. "The New Tradition." In *Postmodernism in American Literature: A Critical Anthology,* ed. Manfred Putz and Peter Freese, 117–23. Darmstadt: Thesen-Verlag, 1984.

Theoharis, Athan. "Unanswered Questions: Chambers, Nixon, the FBI, and the Hiss Case." In *Beyond the Hiss Case: The FBI, Congress, and the Cold War,* ed. Athan Theoharis. Philadelphia: Temple University Press, 1982.

Theoharis, Athan, and John Stuart Cox. *The Boss: J. Edgar Hoover and the Great American Inquisition.* Philadelphia: Temple University Press, 1988.

Theoharis, Athan, and Robert Griffith, eds. *The Specter: Original Essays on the Cold War and the Origins of McCarthyism.* New York: Franklin Watts, 1974.

Todorov, Tzvetan. *Mikhail Bakhtin: The Dialogical Principle,* trans. Wlad Godzich. Minneapolis: University of Minnesota Press, 1984.

Tower, Robert. "Nixon's Seventh Crisis." *New York Review of Books,* September 29, 1977, 8–10.

Trenner, Richard. "Politics and the Mode of Fiction." In *E. L. Doctorow: Essays and Conversations,* ed. Richard Trenner, 48–56. Princeton, N.J.: Ontario Review Press, 1983.

Bibliography

Turner, Victor. *Dramas, Fields, and Metaphors: Symbolic Action in Human Society.* Ithaca, N.Y.: Cornell University Press, 1974.

U.S. Congress. Joint Committee on Atomic Energy. *Soviet Atomic Espionage.* 82d Cong., 1 sess., 1951. Washington, D.C.: Government Printing Office, April 1951.

————. Senate. Internal Security Subcommittee. *Hearings on the Scope of Soviet Activity in the United States.* 84th Cong., 2 sess., 1956. Washington, D.C.: Government Printing Office, 1956.

U.S. v. Rosenberg (1951–52). Prepared by the Fund for the Republic. Wilmington, Del.: M. Glazier, 1978(?). Microfilm.

Vidal, Gore. *Myra Breckinridge.* New York: Little, Brown, 1968.

Wagner-Pacifici, Robin Erica. *The Moro Morality Play: Terrorism as Social Drama.* Chicago: University of Chicago Press, 1986.

Warshow, Robert. "The Idealism of Julius and Ethel Rosenberg." *Commentary* 16, no. 5 (November 1953): 413–18 (published also in Warshow, *The Immediate Experience: Movies, Comics, Theatre, and Other Aspects of Modern Culture,* 33–43. Garden City, N.Y.: Doubleday, 1964).

Wexley, John. *The Judgment of Julius and Ethel Rosenberg.* New York: Cameron & Kahn, 1955.

White, Hayden. *The Content of the Form: Narrative Discourse and Historical Representation.* Baltimore, Md.: Johns Hopkins University Press, 1987.

Williams, Raymond. *Keywords: A Vocabulary of Culture and Society.* Rev. ed. New York: Oxford University Press, 1983.

————. *Marxism and Literature.* Oxford: Oxford University Press, 1977.

World Almanac and Book of Facts for 1945. New York: New York World Telegram, 1945.

Yergin, Daniel. *Shattered Peace: The Origins of the Cold War.* New York: Penguin, 1990.

Zinn, Howard. *Declarations of Independence: Cross-Examining American Ideology.* New York: HarperCollins, 1990.

————. *Postwar America: 1945–1971.* New York: Bobbs-Merrill, 1973.

Index

Index

Index

freedom: meaning of, 193; rhetoric
of, 144

Freedom of Information Act (FOIA),
xiv, 61, 66, 104

Freud, Sigmund, 48, 106, 203, 229 n.
7

Friendly, Fred, 16

Fuchs, Klaus: altered statements of,
65; confessed role of, 60–61, 62,
68–69; prison sentence of, 68,
100; spy ring of, 88; technical
report of, 86. *See also*, Gold,
Harry

gender: in *Book of Daniel*, 147–49;
in *Public Burning*, 159, 179, 181;
Ethel Rosenberg and, 181; in Rosler's art, 211. *See also* women

Ginsberg, Allen, 140, 141

Glazer, Nathan, xvi

Gold, Harry: altered statements of,
78–79; biography of, 74–76; government charges against, 65; as
government witness, 63, 79–82,
108; greeting code and, 73; memory discrepancies of, 79. *See also*
FBI; Fuchs, Klaus; Greenglass,
David

Golos, Jacob, 75, 108

Gottlieb, Robert, 158

government, U.S.: atomic spy ring
story and, xxiv; charges against
Rosenbergs, 64–65; Rosenberg
execution and, 98; Rosenberg
story and, 66–67, 71–73, 78–82,
98, 120. *See also* atomic spy ring
story

Gramsci, Antonio, 139

grand jury: failing to indict spies, 58;
Ruth Greenglass and, 89

Grass, Günter, 154

Greenglass, David: background of,
76–77, 250 n. 59; FBI dictates to,
76, 80; role in Rosenberg case,
64–66, 107–8; as "unknown subject," 79, 81. *See also* FBI; Gold,
Harry

Greenglasses, David and Ruth: attor-

ney for, 72, 77; charges and sentences against, 63, 65;
comparative stability of, 77; FBI
and, 72; grand jury and, 89; prosecution roles of, 63–66, 81; recalling Rosenbergs, 66, 100–101;
testimony of, 108. *See also* FBI;
Gold, Harry; Rogge, John; Sobell,
Morton

Groves, Gen. Leslie, 52, 85, 88

Grunewald v. United States, 95. *See
also* Fifth Amendment

guilt: as factor of class, 177–78; and
Fifth Amendment, 91–95. *See also*
FBI; Justice Department;
prosecution

Guilty by Suspicion, 226 n. 16

gynesis, 254 n. 125

Hamilton, Alexander, 13

Hand, Judge Learned, 90, 112

Hayden, Tom, 136, 236 n. 43

headlines: Rosenbergs and, 88, 99.
See also media; Rosenbergs

Hecht, Selig, 52

Hegel, Georg Wilhelm Friedrich, 229
n. 8; 260 n. 19

Hiroshima. *See* Japan.

Hiss, Alger, 39, 82, 101, 172

Hiss, Priscilla, 101

history: addressed in drama, 203;
Book of Daniel's portrayal of,
151–52; cause–effect constructions of, 137; defined, 224 n. 5;
end of, 140, 196; impact of language on, xvi; individual participation in, 191, 195–96, 220;
oversaturation with, 131; symbolism in, 4, 143

homosexuality, 185, 188, 264 n. 32,
265 n. 7. *See also* Fiedler, Leslie

Hoover, J. Edgar: atomic spy ring
story and, 57, 60, 100; disappoint-
ments of, 96, 100; doctored press
release and, 61, 88; domestic files
of, 16, 42, 57; executing women
and, 102–3; HUAC, 16, 60;
Inquest and, 202; a "loony," 193;

Index

Index

Nixon *(continued)*
and, 210; sexual assault on, 184–85; as symbol, 175; women and, 179–82. *See also Public Burning;* Uncle Sam
Nizer, Louis, 145, 248 n. 37
No Stomach (art exhibit), 212

Oaths. *See* loyalty
Okun, Rob, 206
old left: communitarian, 146–47; versus new left, 134–36, 259 n. 7; viewed by Daniel Isaacson, 144; *See also* Isaacson, Daniel; left; new left
Oppenheimer, J. Robert, 51, 85, 88, 251 n. 84
Orwell, George, 190
"Ozzie and Harriet," 96

paternalism, corporate, 44
patriarchy, 235 n. 36
Patterson, Robert, 32
PEN international, 154
Pentagon, march on the, 150, 151
people, role of the, 26–27
perfecting myths. *See* Burke, Kenneth
Perl, William, 89–90
phallic mother, 254 n. 122
Phantom, the: in *Public Burning,* 164, 169, 176, 177, 193. *See also Public Burning*
Plath, Sylvia, xii, 216
pluralism, 13; defined, 230 n. 20
policy advisers, role of, 17
political correctness, 244 n. 84
pop culture, 128
Popular Front, 19, 20, 21, 28
postatomic age: individual obligation in, 196
postmodernism: *Book of Daniel* and, 132–33; breakdown of, 126–27, 138; Kenneth Burke and, 160–64; critiquing cold war and, 220–21; defined, 227 n. 22; *Public Burning* and, 162–64
post-Rosenberg era: the arts in, 125–30; *Book of Daniel* and, 132; characteristics of, 121, 127, 130
poststructuralism: Robert Coover and, 162; criticism and, 128; defined, 225 n. 8; Jacques Lacan and, 233 n. 35; Rosenberg story and, xv
postwar period: changes in, 8–10; struggles of, 26; voices of, 12. *See also* cold war
power: elite, 15; global, 10; meaning equals, 220
projection. *See* splitting
prosecution (Rosenberg): actions of, 78–83, 85, 112; advantages of, 67–68, 82; arguments of, 71–72; Fifth Amendment and, 91–95; government story aids, 98–102; perjury and, 63; witnesses for, 85–86. *See also* Cohn, Roy; Hoover, J. Edgar; Kaufman, Irving; Lane, Myles; McGrath, J. Howard; Saypol, Irving
Public Burning: anality in, 182–87; *Book of Daniel* and, 188; Kenneth Burke and, 161, 162; controversies of, 157–59; Coover comments on, 174; design of, 164–67; ethical challenge of, 192; gender in, 178–81; J. Edgar Hoover in, 171; incongruities in, 167–71; masculist extremes of, 159, 160, 166, 184; Nixon's role in, 167–85; Ethel Rosenberg in, 180–84, 193; Uncle Sam (Sam Slick the Yankee Peddler), 159, 164–66, 168, 169, 171–74, 177–78, 184–87, 191, 193–94; voices of, 165; women in, 159–60. *See also,* Coover, Robert; Nixon, Richard M.

race: class and, 178
racism, 24, 178
Randolph, A. Philip, 24
reader: active, 162, 199; *Book of Daniel* and, 142; "ideal," 246 n. 14; *Public Burning* and, 170–71, 176; Rosler and, 210

Index

Index

Virginia Carmichael, a writer and editor living in Missoula, Montana, received her doctorate in English at Rice University. She has published articles on British and U.S. literature and culture.